Rome
Modernity, Postmodernity and Beyond

LEGENDA

LEGENDA is the Modern Humanities Research Association's book imprint for new research in the Humanities. Founded in 1995 by Malcolm Bowie and others within the University of Oxford, Legenda has always been a collaborative publishing enterprise, directly governed by scholars. The Modern Humanities Research Association (MHRA) joined this collaboration in 1998, became half-owner in 2004, in partnership with Maney Publishing and then Routledge, and has since 2016 been sole owner. Titles range from medieval texts to contemporary cinema and form a widely comparative view of the modern humanities, including works on Arabic, Catalan, English, French, German, Greek, Italian, Portuguese, Russian, Spanish, and Yiddish literature. Editorial boards and committees of more than 60 leading academic specialists work in collaboration with bodies such as the Society for French Studies, the British Comparative Literature Association and the Association of Hispanists of Great Britain & Ireland.

The MHRA encourages and promotes advanced study and research in the field of the modern humanities, especially modern European languages and literature, including English, and also cinema. It aims to break down the barriers between scholars working in different disciplines and to maintain the unity of humanistic scholarship. The Association fulfils this purpose through the publication of journals, bibliographies, monographs, critical editions, and the MHRA Style Guide, and by making grants in support of research. Membership is open to all who work in the Humanities, whether independent or in a University post, and the participation of younger colleagues entering the field is especially welcomed.

ITALIAN PERSPECTIVES

Editorial Committee
Professor Simon Gilson, University of Warwick (General Editor)
Dr Francesca Billiani, University of Manchester
Professor Manuele Gragnolati, Université Paris-Sorbonne
Dr Catherine Keen, University College London
Professor Martin McLaughlin, Magdalen College, Oxford

Founding Editors
Professor Zygmunt Barański and Professor Anna Laura Lepschy

In the light of growing academic interest in Italy and the reorganization of many university courses in Italian along interdisciplinary lines, this book series, founded by Maney Publishing under the imprint of the Northern Universities Press and now continuing under the Legenda imprint, aims to bring together different scholarly perspectives on Italy and its culture. *Italian Perspectives* publishes books and collections of essays on any period of Italian literature, language, history, culture, politics, art, and media, as well as studies which take an interdisciplinary approach and are methodologically innovative.

Managing Editor
Dr Graham Nelson, 41 Wellington Square, Oxford OX1 2JF, UK
www.legendabooks.com

Rome

Modernity, Postmodernity and Beyond

❖

EDITED BY
LESLEY CALDWELL AND FABIO CAMILLETTI

l

LEGENDA

Italian Perspectives 39
Modern Humanities Research Association
2018

Published by Legenda
an imprint of the Modern Humanities Research Association
Salisbury House, Station Road, Cambridge CB1 2LA

ISBN 978-1-78188-717-2 (HB)
ISBN 978-1-78188-718-9 (PB)

First published 2018

Copy-Editor: Dr Nigel Hope

CONTENTS

❖

NOTES ON THE CONTRIBUTORS

❖

Lesley Caldwell is Honorary Senior Research Fellow in the Italian Department at University College London (UCL) and Honorary Professor in the Psychoanalysis Unit, also at UCL. She is a psychoanalyst in private practice. With Helen Taylor Robinson she is Joint General Editor of the *Collected Works of Donald Winnicott* 2016). She was Co-Investigator for the AHRC network *Roman Modernities*.

Fabio Camilletti is Reader at the School of Modern Languages and Cultures, University of Warwick. He worked extensively on Giacomo Leopardi, Alessandro Manzoni, D. G. Rossetti, and Italian culture of the 1950s and 1960s (Carlo Levi, Gothic cinema and 'Occulture'). Among his latest publications is *Italia lunare. Gli anni Sessanta e l'occulto* (2018). He was the Principal Investigator for the AHRC network *Roman Modernities*.

Alessandro Coppola is a research fellow at the Social Science Department of the Gran Sasso Science Institute in L'Aquila, Italy, and a member of the Phd School in Urban Studies and Regional Studies at the same institution. He has taught courses in the areas of urban ethnography, urban sociology and urban planning at Politecnico di Milano, Ca' Foscari di Venezia, Università di Roma III, Accademia di Architettura di Mendrisio, and Kent State University in Florence. His research and publishing has focused on neighbourhoods politics and policy, community organizing and development, urban shrinkage and urban resilience. He recently edited (with Cora Fontana and Valentina Gingardi) *Envisaging L'Aquila: Strategies, Spatialities and Sociability of a Post-disaster City* (2018). Previously he published *Apocalypse Town: cronache dalla fine di una civiltà urbana* (2012).

Carlotta Fioretti is a scholar in urban studies and planning with a PhD in 'Territorial Policies and Local Project' obtained at University of Roma Tre (2011). Her research interests concern urban regeneration, migration and the city, sustainable urban development, EU cohesion policy. She worked as researcher at Architecture and Design Scotland (2007), Censis Foundation (2012–14), Sciences Po (2016) and University of Roma Tre (2008–17). From 2009 to 2017 she contributed to the teaching at Cornell University, Rome programme. She is currently research fellow at the Joint Research Centre (JRC) of the European Commission in Seville, Spain. Her publications include: (with Paola Briata) 'Consumption and Encounter in (Multi)cultural Quarters: Reflecting on London and Rome's Banglatowns', *Urban Research & Practice*, 2018 [epub ahead of print] and 'Inclusione fragile. Migrazioni nei piccoli comuni del Lazio/Fragile Inclusion: Migrations in Small Municipalities of Lazio', *Quaderni — Urbanistica*, 11.4 (2016); (with M. Cremaschi) 'Diversity and Interculturalism, a Critique and a Defence: Going through Multiethnic

Neighbourhoods in Rome', in *The Intercultural City: Migration, Minorities and the Management of Diversity*, ed. by G. Marconi and E. Ostanel (London: I. B. Tauris Publisher, 2016).

Federica Mazzara is a Senior Lecturer in Intercultural Communication at the University of Westminster. The principal area of her research revolves around the interdisciplinary field of migration studies, the arts and contemporary Italy. She has published widely on literature of migration in Italy, theories of intermediality and visual arts a form of political resistance. She has curated art installations on migration in London. Her latest monograph, *Reframe Migration: Lampedusa from the Border Spectacle to the Aesthetics of Subversion*, is forthcoming (Peter Lang).

Kevin McLaughlin is Dean of the Faculty and George Hazard Crooker Professor of English and Comparative Literature, Professor of English, Comparative Literature, and German Studies, Brown University, Providence.

Giorgio Piccinato is Emeritus Professor of Urbanism, Roma Tre University. Past president of the Association of European Schools of Planning, consultant to the United Nations and the European Union. Publications: *La costruzione dell'urbanistica. Germania 1870–1914* (Rome 1974, Wiesbaden 1983 and Barcelona 1993); *Un mondo di città* (Turin 2002 and Caracas 2007); *Atlas de centros históricos do Brasil* (Rio de Janeiro 2007); *Fermoimmagine. Studio sulla felicità urbana* (Macerata 2008); 'Il senso del moderno nella città americana', V. Pravadelli ed., *Modernità nelle Americhe* (Rome: 2016), pp. 47-57; 'Any Place for Urban Conservation in the Post-Modern Metropolis?', *disP — The Planning Review*, 53:2 (2017), 84–85.

Eugene Pooley is Old Master specialist at Christie's.

Filippo Trentin is an Andrew W. Mellon Postdoctoral Teaching Fellow in the Humanities at the University of Pennsylvania. He completed his PhD at the University of Warwick specializing in twentieth-century Italian cinema and literature. He has held academic positions as visiting assistant professor at the Ohio State University (2015–16) and as postdoctoral fellow at the Institute for Cultural Inquiry in Berlin (2013–15). His areas of research include film studies, queer theory and aesthetics, and his publications have appeared in *The Journal of Romance Studies, Modern Language Review* and *Forum Italicum*, among others. He is currently co-editing a special issue of *GLQ: A Journal of Lesbian and Gay Studies*, and he is working on a book entitled *Rome and the Margins of Modernism*.

CHAPTER 1

❖

Introduction

Lesley Caldwell

In December 2015 the Fondazione MAXXI, with the Comune di Roma, presented the exhibition *Roma 20–25 Nuovi cicli di vita della metropoli/New Life Cycles for the Metropolis*, initially conceived by Professor Giovanni Caudo of Roma Tre when he held the post of Assessor for Urban Transformation in the short-lived Marino administration (June 2013–October 2015). The overall project consisted in three different but related initiatives: the *Roma 20–25* research, and a series of planning conferences held in each of Rome's fifteen municipalities which led to the production of a Charter of Values. (These events were run as workshops for inhabitants and local associations to develop specific databases for that area.) The third, *Resilient Rome*, formed part of a wider international project *100 Resilient Cities*, supported by the Rockefeller Foundation.

The exhibition explicitly invoked the *Roma interrotta* event of 1978 and its origins in a revisiting of Nolli's city map of 1748. In that earlier initiative, a Rome of the future was projected onto a Rome of the past. Nolli's map was divided into twelve squares, each of which was entrusted to an established architect. For *Roma 20–25*, the current urban area of Rome (*c.* 50 km^2) was divided into a grid of twenty-five squares, only one of which comprised the city centre, the area encompassed by Nolli's map and the focus of the architects of the 1970s. The contemporary research presented at MAXXI was set up across twenty-five universities, eleven of them Italian; each was invited to work on plans for the future of a section of greater Rome. As Caudo says in his contribution to the catalogue of the exhibition, 'Each studied the trends of the Rome to be in 2025. They read and explored the built up city in search of a trend, of a drift that moves towards the city of the future'.[1] The number of teams involved ensured that no single perspective would dominate, but that the collective activity, taken as a whole, would produce a series of priorities and aspirations for a future city seen as growing from that of the present.

The detailed research by groups of architects, historians, planners, ecologists, landscape experts, and urban theorists focused on specific local areas within an overall framework that emphasised accessibility and public transport, what Caudo calls 'a support network for the quality of life and health'.[2] In the words of one of the catalogue editors, Pippo Ciorra, the idea was also linked to an earlier history of urban workshops dating from Quaroni's *Immagine di Roma*, which 'produced one of the first design-oriented readings of the city's history'.[3] Ciorra sees the contemporary project as 'part of earlier debates about the idea of the city where the city was no longer analysed according to the linear and ideological sequence of episodes typical of historiography, but, rather, as a diachronic mosaic of events and projects'.[4]

Indirectly, the themes of both the 1978 exhibition and these recent initiatives, with their concern with the entire area of greater Rome and its future, draw upon detailed engagement with Rome as both existent and imagined city, even if the impossibility of the task of the 1978 exhibition also made it a distinctly postmodern exercise. The individual projects comprising *Roma 20–25* were dedicated to making Rome a more liveable city by attending to each area's natural resources, in combination with the kinds of infrastructure essential for any enduring local focus. Each team was responsible for a particular land area and the natural features, rivers, sea, and hills that shape it, drawing on the interpenetration of past and present as articulated around various research problems relating to contemporary urban living.

Giovanna Melandri, the president of the MAXXI foundation, began her introduction to the catalogue of the exhibition with a quote from Venturi and Scott-Brown's foundational text *Learning from Las Vegas* (1972). 'Learning from the existing architecture is a way of being revolutionary for an architect [...] creativity is based on observing what is around us.'[5] As a further development of workshop-based research on Rome, Melandri hopes that 'this experience will become a model for collaboration between culture and territory when imagining and planning the city's future'.[6] She applauded the research's internationalism, and its potential for what she calls 'a point of departure': the territory as city, an 'expanded' Rome, a metropolis with boundaries that are not clear cut, where the idea of territory takes on the connotations of civil society. Describing MAXXI itself as 'a cultural institution, an open space that welcomes and at the same time presents and describes the contemporary', she offers it as 'a "porous" space [...] that aims to connect three dimensions, research, territory and internationalism'.[7]

This international investigation represents an extended in-depth encounter with the continuing debates about the history of modern Rome and their results for the city's contemporary projects. On a far more modest scale, the AHRC network from which this book derives also aimed to engage in this history and its consequences through a series of conferences and workshops. In his chapter, originally a keynote address to the opening event at the British School in Rome (BSR), the Benjamin scholar and translator Kevin McLaughlin also alludes to a notion of porosity in approaching Rome through others' accounts. Beginning from a Benjamin who had little or nothing to say of the city, McLaughlin identifies Benjamin's interest in the notion of 'solidity' through which Goethe had insisted upon the continuing interpenetration of classic and modern for any reading of Rome.[8] The idea of porosity of living and the contribution of the architectonic elements in Benjamin and Lacis's account of Naples[9] brings together an imaginative and visual repertory and applies it to Rome, much of whose built environment precisely depends on a porous stone, travertine, for many of its distinctive visual elements. Rome and

Naples are both instances of the way architecture stages and enacts spectacle and drama in set pieces that, despite their grandeur and their public presence, also provide the settings for everyday life.

McLaughlin locates the fascination with ruins as continuingly central for any account of modern Rome, since both Roman classicism and Roman modernity depend on the interpenetration of solidity and porosity, culture and barbarism. Did Rome, he asks, fail to exclude the modernity discovered by Benjamin in Paris, or did Benjamin overlook a modernity in process of formation in his lament for how that past impedes the activities of the modern *flâneur*?

> But in Rome is not dreaming itself drawn along streets that are already too well paved? And isn't the city too full of temples, enclosed squares, and national shrines to be able to enter undivided into the dreams of the passer-by (*Passanten*), along with every paving stone, every shop sign, every flight of stairs, and every gateway?[10]

Benjamin's image of Rome's excess and potential exhaustion is redolent of a key scene in Tarkovsky's *Nostalghia* (1983), which the director chose to shoot on the Campidoglio. The film's cinematographer, Gianni Lanci, insisted that such an iconic landmark would not have been the choice of a Roman director. But when Tarkovsky's sequence is taken in conjunction with the earlier expressed wish of the film's protagonist, Gorcakov, to detach himself from the joys of the west since the Renaissance, 'sono stanco di vedere queste bellezze eccessive', it seems to represent the paradoxical wish of Tarkovsky himself.[11] McLaughlin's Benjamin, if not McLaughlin himself, seems to be caught up in a similar ambivalence about the weight of the past for the mental freedom and creativity of the modern individual on being confronted with Rome's cityscape.

The urban fabric of the city of 1870 and what was saved and what destroyed, together with continuing attempts to encapsulate its fascination, have provided a consistent reference in present-day choices and accounts of the city, a city whose familiar images are awkwardly yet insistently accommodated to its contemporary reality.

Whatever the place of a potential modernity, the town of *c.* 200,000 that became the much-contested capital of a united Italy in 1870 was thought of as 'unmodern'. The notable absence of those infrastructures essential for the functioning of a capital city together with the choices and procedures involved in their introduction contain the roots of its subsequent history and development.[12] The entrenched interests of the Roman aristocracy and the Catholic Church produced strategic choices that set the pattern for Rome's expansion and the kind of city it has become. A form of expansion based on the division of lands and the razing of historical sites within the walls produced an economy based primarily on construction and on cycles of building booms and crises. The demands of what became its major industry, the agreement to block industrial development, and the consistent focus on the development of master plans for the city that aimed to regularise already existing situations and have, in any case, largely been known for their non-implementation, continue to shape the city of today.

Much of the debate has concerned specific areas of the *Centro storico* and its place in successive political and ideological visions of Rome's function. Increasingly for an area in which a very small percentage of Romans actually live, the policy decisions of successive local and national governments have circulated around a potential contradiction between the *vivibilità* of the city for its citizens and the demands of its status as heritage city and its major industry, tourism.

Invocations of amenity and versions of the much earlier proposal (1909) for a central archaeological zone, itself a kind of revisiting and updating of the early proposals of Napoleon's planner, De Tournon, have resurfaced regularly in plans for the city,[13] as has the most recent revival, by the former mayor, Ignazio Marino, of the proposal for the pedestrianisation of Via dei Fori Imperiali, a decision that has divided both those concerned with the care of monuments and those concerned with the livability of the city.

The Renzi government's (2014–16) proposed reorganisation (now postponed) of the regulation of the *Soprintendenze*, the departments responsible for the management of artistic heritage, also produced an extended debate, distinguished by an impassioned exchange on the irresponsibility of the directions of this proposal by the academic, Carlo Ginzburg[14] and the equally impassioned response of the noted Roman archaeologist and urbanist, Daniele Manacorda, who disputed any easy decision about the allocation of responsibility for artistic resources, their past tutelage, or the foundations of any serious commitment to how the Roman (and Italian) patrimony should best be protected and fostered. This debate demonstrated the level of informed public feeling about the care of Rome's patrimony, what is to be prioritised and how this is best undertaken.

But while these are debates of continuing relevance for the contemporary city, concentrating as they do on its most visible aspect in terms of monuments and heritage, they address only one aspect of Rome's development to a city of almost 3 million in a little over a hundred years. Employment and migration, and the provision of basic services, housing, electricity, water and sewage, transport, have all been and continue to be essential to continuing debates about the city and its provision for its citizens.

The contributors to this book are agreed about a Rome whose modernity has not and does not conform to the anticipated cycle of modernisation, but they differ in the emphases assigned to what such modernity connotes historically and in the present. While all accept a model of multiple modernities for the awkward, uneasily accommodated forms of Rome's evolution, the chapters exemplify different approaches to an account whose implications are vital for how the city is to be constituted for its future. It is this emphasis that was established in the extended project referred to earlier.

Eugene Pooley's chapter discusses the development of the discipline of planning in early twentieth-century Rome and its contribution to the creation of a modern capital. Using the creation of the Scuola Superiore di Architettura in 1919 and its role in defending Rome's cultural heritage, he identifies Gustavo Giovannoni's emphasis on an 'art' of urban planning as a critical response to the destruction of whole areas of the Rome of 1870 following the urgent claims for its speedy modernisation as fundamental to its status as capital. The extensive loss of the monuments of the past was deplored by the AACAR, an organisation of leading architects dedicated to the defence of the city's patrimony. They argued for a different mentality in regard to the transformation of the landscape of the city, drawing upon debates about urban planning from abroad and organising a series of meetings with foreign experts. Giovannoni, an architect and architectural historian, and the organisation's president from 1910, advanced an idea of *diradamento*, a less brutal destruction of inner city areas than the *sventramenti* that had distinguished the post-1870 period and which would return under Mussolini. Some of his priorities — the opening up of vistas, the need for space around monuments — were subsequently adopted by Fascist planners and architects. Both the discipline itself and its new professionals were compromised by the Fascist regime's politicisation of city development so that the inevitable aspects of any modernisation programme[15] have been embedded historically in the links between the ideological programmes of fascism and the compromises of post-war liberal democracy. The issue of how to accommodate a modern city with a well-preserved historic past has continued to be a major concern of Roman architects, planners and politicians and embodies a history of competing visions of Rome and its future.

The introduction of *Piani regolatori* (master plans) from 1873 and the limits they have presented and continue to present has been one focus for the priorities for the city; with different emphases, the *Piani regolatori* of 1883, 1909, 1931, 1942, 1962, and 2003 ostensibly project the growth of the city, both in what they address and in what was argued over, but even more importantly, they remain distinctive for what they have consistently omitted. They form the essential background in the chapters of Piccinato, Fioretti, Coppola, and Caldwell, but Trentin, in his interrogation of modernism, also sees them as significant. Challenged by the art historian T. J. Clark's assertion that 'the modernism that mattered most to him was that of film and literature in Italy in 1945',[16] Filippo Trentin approaches both cinematic and literary neorealism as an aesthetic deriving from the ruined landscape of Rome and its forms of post-war reconstruction and modernisation. He begins by linking Clark's remark with Deleuze's account of the time image in cinema and the centrality it accords to neorealist films.[17] Trentin is interested in the idea of an underlying modernism to the neorealist classics and in pursuing it he widens his own approach to describe the debates on writing and the writer in three journals based in Rome, completing this with a reading of *Portonaccio*, Elio Filippo Accrocca's collection of poems.[18] Trentin argues for the representation of space and time across these culturally diverse forms as based on a lowering or lowered gaze in terms of looking and critical attention in the Rome of the period.

Florian Mussgnug explores the representation of Rome's radioactive ruins in Mario Soldati's cold war satire *Lo Smeraldo* (1974). Soldati's vision of a post-catastrophic future Italy, violently split into two unequal parts, offers a reconsideration of notions of scale, power, and territory, which Mussgnug approaches through contemporaneous debates about social and environmental collapse, with reference to Roberto Vacca's *Il medioevo prossimo venturo* (1971) and Superstudio's *Salvataggi di centri storici italiani* (1972). Drawing on recent research in economic geography and queer ecology, he proposes that Soldati offers an experience of space as a relational arrangement that is *intensive* rather than extensive. He highlights how *Lo smeraldo* (1974) subverts a common lived experience of time through oneiric forecast and the disruption of generational and familial ties and locates its most important illustration in the characters' reaction to the ruins of Rome.

Giorgio Piccinato emphasises the extent to which post-war reconstruction and the modernisation that accompanied it made Italy one of the most industrialised countries. Together with the large migratory movements that especially concerned Rome, he argues that this fed into an intense debate around planning issues. Although the master plan of 1942 had proposed a number of innovations, including the extension of master plans to the whole municipal territory, support for regional planning, and a clear distinction between master plan as indicating the lines of future development, and detail plans, intended to provide guidelines for immediate implementation, the 1942 plan never came into official use and, again with the excuse of urgency, rather basic norms enshrined in *Piani di fabbricazione* (building plans) were adopted. They proved totally inadequate in exercising any real control of development and the more far-reaching proposals of the 1942 law were ignored despite strong public interest in urban issues like housing, transport, and building regulations. The protracted debates and difficult design of the new master plan (1962) opened the door to every possible variety of political alliance and deals, but if the building of a range of new structures for the 1960 Olympic Games contributed to the continuing development of the city, they too failed to consolidate a rational planning approach to the city's future.

The final four chapters offer detailed studies of very different areas of Rome from the 1960s to the present. Alessandro Coppola's chapter discusses two neighbouring areas, Morena and Centroni, part of the extended Roman periphery. He focuses on the relation between formal and informal networks and their local development from the 1960s in these two *borgate* in the south-east. His chapter is the only one to address directly the part of Rome that falls beyond the extended city centre, though Pigneto, the subject of Carlotta Fioretti's study, is just outside the walls to the east, famous for its depiction in Pasolini's first film *Accattone* where it appeared as a wilderness of types of housing, unmade roads, and countryside. Fioretti discusses the range of initiatives, public and private, local and national, and mixtures of the two that have been directed at improvements in social inclusion in Pigneto. Beginning from the Area-Based Initiatives (*Contratti di quartiere*) introduced in neighbourhoods affected by multiple deprivation, Fioretti compares the respective outcomes of institutional policies and informal practices in terms of social inclusion, the improvement of the built environment, and the development of the local economy. Both Coppola's and Fioretti's work offers earlier examples of some of the preoccupations that remain key goals in the current regeneration of urban areas (as *Roma 20–25* demonstrates).

Federica Mazzara takes up the recent transformation of the Esquilino, an area associated with the post-1870 planning initiatives which produced the wholesale destruction of famous villas and lands. Its recent regeneration, together with its location near significant transport hubs and major roads (the primary motive for its 1870 identification as crucial to the development of the capital), has made it the contemporary centre of multi-ethnic Rome. Mazzara discusses the extent to which recent immigration into Italy has produced new cultural representations, which assist in understanding the everyday practices that are currently transforming and redefining Italian urban spaces.

In the final chapter, Lesley Caldwell undertakes an initial study of an area just outside the walls, which, she suggests, was developed from the projections of the town plan of 1931. She approaches the area through a discussion of the relation between housing, monuments, tradition, commemorative practices, and the area's contemporary involvement in the problems of Rome's homeless and their future.

The juxtaposition of different pasts is the condition of any modern city but appears acutely in the case of Rome where it forms part of a long history of continuing demolition and reuse of buildings from antiquity on. While Rome shares with other large metropolitan areas many taken-for-granted features which emphasise its commonality rather than its uniqueness, it is different because of the specificity of the city fabric with which its administrators are concerned and because of the close relation of the past as heritage for the economic foundations of the city of today.

Notes to Chapter 1

1. Giovanni Caudo, 'Roma prossima/Future Rome', *Roma 20–25. Nuovi cicli di vita della metropoli* (2015), 18–31.
2. Ibid., p. 29.
3. Pippo Ciorra, 'Citta, musei, architetture/City, Museums, Architectures', in *Roma 20-25*, pp. 32–43.
4. Ibid.; L. Quaroni, *Immagine di Roma* (Rome and Bari: Laterza, 1969).
5. Giovanna Melandri, 'Introduction', in *Roma 20-25*, pp. 10–11 (p. 11).
6. Ibid.; Robert Venturi, Denise Scott Brown and Steven Izenour, *Learning from Las Vegas*, rev. edn (Cambridge, MA: MIT Press, 1977).
7. Melandri. 'Introduction', p. 11.
8. Johann Wolfgang von Goethe, *Poetry and Truth*, cited in Walter Benjamin, 'Goethe's *Elective Affinities*', in *Selected Writings*, I, 297–360 (p. 316); 'Goethes Wahlverwandtschaften', in *Gesammelte Schriften*, ed. by Helia Tiedemann-Bartels, 7 vols (Frankfurt am Main: Suhrkamp, 1972–89), I, 123–201.
9. Walter Benjamin, 'Meine Reise in Italien Pfingsten 1912', in *Gesammelte Schriften*, VI, 252–92 (McLaughlin's translation). Walter Benjamin and Asja Lacis, 'Naples', in Benjamin, *Selected Writings*, I, 414–21 (p. 416).
10. Walter Benjamin, *Gesammelte Schriften*, III, 195; *Selected Writings*, II, 263.
11. Lesley Caldwell, 'The Ultimate Public Space: Filming on the Campidoglio', in *Beyond the Piazza: Public and Private Spaces in Modern Italian Culture*, ed. by Simona Storchi (Oxford and New York: PIE Peter Lang, 2013), pp. 167–80.
12. Italo Insolera, *Roma moderna. Un secolo di storia urbanistica 1870–1970* (Turin: Einaudi, 1992; repr. 2001); Vieri Quilici, *Roma capitale senza centro* (Rome: Officina Edizioni, 2007); Michael Herzfeld, *Evicted from Eternity: The Restructuring of Modern Rome* (Chicago: University of Chicago Press, 2009); Vittorio Vidotto, *Roma contemporanea* (Rome and Bari: Laterza, 2006); John A. Agnew, *Rome* (Chichester and New York: Wiley, 1995).

13. Insolera, *Roma moderna*; Antonio Cederna, *Mirabilia urbis. Cronache romane 1957–1965* (Turin: Einaudi, 1965); Carlo Aymonimo, *Progettare Roma Capitale* (Roma and Bari: Laterza, 1990); Agnew, *Rome*.
14. Carlo Ginzburg, 'Perche dobbiamo salvare le soprintendenze', *La Repubblica*, 29 July 2014. And see the response by Daniele Manacorda, 'Per salvare il nostro patrimonio serve un'alleanza con i cittadini', *La Repubblica*, 1 August 2014 <http://ricerca.repubblica.it/repubblica/archivio/repubblica/2014/08/01/per-salvare-il-nostro-patrimonio-serve-unalleanza-con-i-cittadini36.html>, [accessed 3 August 2014].
15. Leonardo Ciacci, 'The Rome of Mussolini: An Entrenched Stereotype in Film', in *Spaces in European Cinema*, ed. by Myrto Konstantakaros (Exeter: Intellect Books, 2000), pp. 93–100.
16. Timothy James Clark, *Farewell to an Idea: Episodes from a History of Modernism* (New Haven: Yale University Press, 1999), p. 405.
17. Gilles Deleuze, *Cinema 2: The Time-Image*, trans. by Hugh Tomlinson and Roberta Galeta (Minneapolis: University of Minnesota Press, 1997).
18. Elio Filippo Accrocca, *Portonaccio* (Milan: All'insegna del pesce d'oro, 1949).

CHAPTER 2

❖

City and Porosity:
Walter Benjamin's *Passages*

Kevin McLaughlin

> Paris created the figure of the *flâneur*. A wonder that it was not Rome.

This remark appears in Walter Benjamin's 1929 review of Franz Hessel's *Spazieren in Berlin*. This is one of the rare allusions to Rome in Benjamin's work; it comes in the context of a set of reflections under the heading of 'the return of the *flâneur*'. Benjamin writes:

> Paris created the figure of the *flâneur*. A wonder that it was not Rome. But in Rome is not dreaming itself drawn along streets that are already too well paved. And isn't the city too full of temples, enclosed squares, and national shrines to be able to enter undivided into the dreams of the passer-by (*Passanten*), along with every paving stone, every shop sign, every flight of stairs, and every gateway?[1]

The historical way in Rome is, it seems, too clear — the past too memorialised — for the mode of distracted receptivity that Benjamin associates with the *flâneur*. If Rome is preserved through its temples, squares, and shrines as a memorial to the city's history, he goes on to say, Paris spreads out as a 'landscape' in which the past emerges from 'the scent of a single weathered threshold or the touch of a single tile'.[2] Or, as Benjamin specifies, for the Parisian *flâneur* 'the city splits into its dialectical poles. It becomes a landscape that opens up to him and a parlor that encloses him.'[3]

Benjamin does not elaborate here or elsewhere on this image of Rome. Indeed, beyond the sentences I have cited he has almost nothing to say about Rome in his voluminous musings on cities. For Benjamin urban modernity emerges in Paris, not in Rome. For those interested in Benjamin's work the field has been left wide open for scholars of Roman modernity. In Rome Benjamin is nowhere in sight, and this is not necessarily a bad thing (he can get in the way in Paris or simply get there first, which itself can be an annoyance). Evidence, if there is any, that the city of Rome with its history and its myths provides fertile ground for Benjamin's theoretical speculations and historical research on nineteenth-century Paris will have to come from others. Nevertheless, my thesis is that Benjamin's approach to urban modernity has explanatory force with regard to a city about which he said almost nothing, namely, Rome. My focus is on two points where Benjamin's work does touch on Rome *obliquely* in order to suggest how they exemplify an aspect of his theory of modernity that may have some more direct bearing on the study of *Roman* modernity. The first starts with an allusion to Roman ruins in an early autobiographical text (from 1912); the second concerns an allusion to Carthage in a late historical-philosophical essay (from 1940).

In the spring of 1912 at the age of twenty, having just completed his *Abitur* and about to begin his university studies, Benjamin travelled to Italy for what he characterises as 'an educational journey' (*eine Bildungsreise*). As this heavily freighted term suggests, Goethe seems to hover over every aspect of this undertaking. Before going further, let me say a word about Benjamin's complex relationship with Goethe, especially as it is manifested in the great essay titled 'Goethe's Elective Affinities' completed by Benjamin just before he was to undertake his second Italian journey in 1924. I will not be able to develop this but it may help clarify my first example.

Like every German of the last two centuries Benjamin's attitude towards Italy and towards Rome is shaped by Goethe; unlike almost every German of the last two centuries Benjamin discovers in Goethe's writing about his journeys to Italy and to Rome a deeply disturbing element that is utterly alien to the harmonising, immortalising vision of the classical world associated with the *Italian Journeys* — an element that Goethe characterises as 'daemonic' in a remarkable passage cited by Benjamin at a key point in his essay on Goethe. It comes at a moment in *Poetry and Truth* when Goethe looks back in fear at a force breaking through and interrupting the developmental process of *Bildung* that is the guiding thread of the life he has been recounting:

> He [Goethe is referring to himself] believed that he perceived something in nature (whether living or lifeless, animate or inanimate) that manifested itself only in contradictions and therefore could not be expressed in any concept, much less in any word. It was not divine, for it seemed irrational; not diabolical, for it was beneficent; and not angelic, for it often betrayed malice. It was like chance (*Zufall*), for it lacked continuity, and like destiny (*Vorsehung*), for it suggested connectedness (*Zusammenhang*). Everything that limits us seemed penetrable by it, and it appeared to do as it pleased with the elements necessary to our existence, to contract time and expand space. It seemed only to accept the impossible and scornfully to reject the possible. — This being, which appeared to infiltrate all the others, separating and combining them, I called 'daemonic', after the example of the ancients and others who had perceived something similar. I tried to save myself from this fearful thing.[4]

A recognition or, perhaps better, a feeling for this 'daemonic' force in Goethe, I would like to suggest, is already evident in Benjamin's early retracing of his great predecessor's first Italian journey, as we will see. Here is how Benjamin begins the 1912 diary:

> The journey will first emerge in the diary that I want to write. In it I want to let develop the total essence (*Gesamtwesen*), the silent, self-evident synthesis that is required of an educational journey (*Bildungsreise*) and that constitutes its being. This is all the more imperative to me in that throughout no single experience

should authoritatively stamp (*prägten*) the impression of this entire journey. Nature and art should culminate everywhere equally in what Goethe calls 'solidity' (*Solidität*). And no adventure, none of the soul's craving for adventure, should present an effective or alluring background.[5]

The reference to 'solidity' at the end of this passage alludes to Goethe's diary entry for 10 November 1786 in the first *Italian Journey*. In it Goethe describes the effect of Roman ruins as building a kind of 'solidity' in him. At first glance, this solidity seems to exemplify the harmonising, immortalising influence of the classical world commonly associated with Goethe's Italy and, in this case, Rome, but then the disruptive element just mentioned appears on the scene. Here is the passage from Goethe on 'solidity' that Benjamin cites at the beginning of his diary:

When I come back to myself, as one does so happily on these occasions, I discover a feeling, that pleases me endlessly, indeed that I even venture to express. Whoever looks around himself and has eyes with which to see, must become solid (*solid*), he must grasp a concept of solidity (*Solidität*) that is never more alive to him. The spirit is stamped into soundness (*Der Geist wird zur Tüchtigkeit gestempelt*); it attains a seriousness that has no dryness, a composed, joyous existence. To me at least it is as if I had never so correctly estimated the things of this world as here [i.e. in Rome]. I rejoice at the blessed consequences for my entire life. Thus let me take things as they come, order will come of its own. I am not here to enjoy according to my own fashion, I want to work myself with great objects, to learn and to form myself, before I am forty years old.[6]

Although this passage might serve as a model for the kind of classical *Bildung* associated with Goethe — the emphasis on the harmonious agreement of the senses with the intellect that is characteristic of aesthetic education — Benjamin develops this vision in a different direction.[7] The difference starts to become evident right away in Benjamin's diary in the description of Palladio's Basilica in Vicenza in spring 1912 that follows closely on the allusion to 'solidity' in the opening paragraph. To appreciate the divergence from the classical model let me cite first Goethe's account of his visit to Vicenza 130 years earlier.[8] Here is Goethe:

It is impossible to express how Palladio's Basilica stands out next to an old building with uneven windows that resembles a citadel and that the architect must have thought of as being absent [literally: 'to think away' — *weg gedacht hat*]. I can only sum up my feelings in a wonderful manner: unfortunately it is always the same; what I flee and what I seek are right next to each other.[9]

Here is Benjamin's diary entry describing the effect of this same building on him:

Palladio's Basilica stands a few side streets farther. No architectonic impression can be more sublime (*erhabener*) than the two-tiered marble row of arches with the impenetrable darkness of its interior. The impression of the colour of the marble that still glowed through the dirtiness and of the dark recesses of the arches makes a forceful impression and the height and extent of this row of arches take on the image (*Bild*) of Romantic obscurity such that here the sublime must appear in monstrosity and clarity alike. On the other side of the piazza stand old buildings — entirely without beauty, however. One goes through the archway on the other side — one can only enter the building itself with special permission (that is to say, with money) — it is simpler — it stinks in every corner.[10]

Both passages move from an appreciation of the aesthetic effect of the building — the formative, fortifying, or *solidifying* impression of Italian architecture — to the jarring eruption of the formal incoherence, repulsive worldliness, and sheer empirical deterioration from which the basilica seeks in vain to remove itself. Solidity, we might say, does not exclude sordidity. Thus Benjamin's account underlines the way Goethe draws attention to the element that will not stay out of the image of the basilica and in this way expressly brings into the picture precisely the dimension that would be shut out of the aesthetic experience of *Bildung* in the classic sense. The effect of the basilica (and here the history of this architectural form is relevant: originally a Roman structure built for the worldly purposes of transacting business and adjudicating legal matters, the basilica was adopted early by Christians for religious ends: the form oscillates between the profane and the sacred) — the effect of the basilica, which both writers associate with the formation of an image (*ein Bild*), derives from what Goethe describes as an effort to 'think away' of the present — a task that itself never seems to go away from an experience of the building. In this sense Benjamin highlights in Goethe an awareness of an irreducibly contradictory element in the aesthetic image that produces profound ambivalence (as Goethe says, 'what I flee and what I seek are right next to each other'). According to this logic the solidifying effect associated by Goethe with Roman ruins is inseparable from a 'daemonic' element that exposes the subject to self-division and rupture.

The reinterpretation of Goethean 'solidity' at which Benjamin's 1912 diary hints is developed further by the second Italian journey he undertook in the spring of 1924. This period and in particular a six-month stay on Capri where he read Lukács's *History of Class Consciousness* are often understood as a turning point in Benjamin's work from a concern with aesthetics to a politically engaged criticism. Although Benjamin himself at times encouraged this view, I believe that the terms of this change participate in a logic of irreducible tension or oscillation that can be found throughout Benjamin's work and that we have just encountered in the diary of his first Italian journey. A turn to politics for Benjamin can never be a simple turn away from aesthetics. The same holds for the terms classic and modern that seem to inform Benjamin's remarks on Rome and Paris with which I began. Modernity, according to this logic, cannot simply exclude the classical. We might even say that Paris cannot exclude Rome, and indeed this is a lesson Benjamin learned from Marx's historical writings. Our question is the reverse: to what extent does Rome with its well-paved streets to the classical past — streets of 'temples, enclosed squares, and national shrines' — fail to exclude the modernity discovered by Benjamin in nineteenth-century Paris? Following Benjamin's stress on phenomena that resist the concept of modernity itself as a radical break with the classic means remaining open in Rome to the interpenetration of the classical and the modern. This, it seems to me, is the question of Roman modernity that Benjamin allows us to ask, even if he does not ask it himself.

One way to approach this Rome in Benjamin's writing is through Naples, more specifically, through a reading of the essay titled 'Naples' that Benjamin composed with Lacis during his stay on Capri in 1924. The principle of the Neapolitan cityscape, according to Benjamin and Lacis, is 'porosity' (*Porosität*):

> As porous (*porös*) as this stone [of the caves and grottoes along the shoreline of Naples] is the architecture. Building (*Bau*) and action (*Aktion*) interpenetrate (*übergehen*) in the courtyards, arcades, and stairways. In everything is preserved a space (*Spielraum*) with the capacity to become a theater (*Schauplatz*) of new, unforeseen constellations. The definitive and the stamped (*Geprägte*) is avoided. No situation appears precisely as it is, nothing is considered eternal, no figure asserts itself as existing 'thus and not otherwise'.[11]

Instead of standing forth and setting itself apart definitively, Neapolitan architecture provides a stage and bears a 'space' (*Spielraum*) for action. It makes room for the improvised constellations of social life. Incompletion is the principle of this architecture:

> nothing is finished and concluded. Porosity meets, not only with the indolence of the southern artisan, but also, above all, with the passion for improvisation, which demands that space and opportunity be preserved in every case. Buildings are used as a popular stage (*Volksbühne*).[12]

According to this description, what we usually think of as architectural structure (*Bau*) is interpenetrated with action (*Aktion*) to such an extent that it becomes impossible to discern where buildings end and social movement begins. In this context, architecture must be understood as action — as an active building. The aim of this action, moreover, is, not completion, but the preservation of the possibility of endless completion — the point is to save 'space and opportunity' for a kind of building that is indistinguishable from social life. Such life takes place where the architectural structure in the usual sense remains open and where architecture can be endlessly in-completed through collective, as distinct from private, dwelling.[13] 'Courtyards, arcades, and stairways' are prominent examples of such openings in the Neapolitan cityscape, according to Benjamin and Lacis. These may be considered concrete manifestations of what they repeatedly call the city's 'porosity', a word that derives from the Greek root meaning 'passage'. With this etymological connection in mind, we might say that the essay on 'porosity' in Naples is extended by Benjamin in the study of the arcades or passages of Paris on which he would begin to work three years later and which would themselves remain unfinished. In this sense Benjamin's approach to modern Paris can be traced in part to his reflections on the porosity of the ancient caves and grottoes of Naples. More important for the question of Roman modernity, though, is that the porosity of Neapolitan architecture — the way it remains open to social life and refuses the self-enclosure of a classical architectural frame — was already evident to Benjamin in the 'solidity' Goethe discovered in Roman ruins and in the ruination of the Roman *basilica* in Vicenza. Roman modernity thus raises the question of the return of this porosity to the solidity of the city's ruins.

A second point at which Benjamin touches obliquely on Rome comes in an allusion to Carthage in his late historical philosophical theses. Once again this occurs by way of a citation, this time of a letter written by Flaubert to his friend Ernest Feydeau in 1860. 'Few will be able to guess', writes Flaubert, 'how sad one had to be in order to resuscitate Carthage'.[14] Flaubert is referring to his novel-in-progress, *Salammbô*, which would appear in 1862. Here is the entire (itself very often cited) passage from Benjamin:

> To historians who wish to relive an era, Fustel de Coulanges recommends that they blot out everything they know about the later course of history. There is no better way of characterizing the method with which historical materialism has broken. It's a process of empathy whose origin is the indolence of the heart, *acedia*, which despairs of grasping and holding the genuine historical image as it flares up briefly. Among medieval theologians it was regarded as the root cause of sadness. Flaubert, who was familiar with it, wrote: '*Peu de gens devineront combien il a fallu être triste pour resusciter Carthage*' [Few will be able to guess how sad one had to be in order to resuscitate Carthage]. The nature of this sadness stands out more clearly if one asks with whom the adherents of historicism actually empathize. The answer is inevitable: with the victor. [...] Historical materialists know what that means. Whoever has emerged victorious marches in the triumphal procession in which the present rulers step over those who are lying prostrate. According to traditional practice, the spoils are carried along in the procession. They are called cultural treasures, and a historical materialist views them with cautious detachment. For without exception the cultural treasures he surveys have an origin which he cannot contemplate without horror. They owe their existence not only to the efforts of the great minds and talents who have created them, but also to the anonymous toil of their contemporaries. There is no document of civilization which is not at the same time a document of barbarism. And just as such a document is not free of barbarism, barbarism taints also the manner in which it was transmitted from one owner to another. A historical materialist therefore dissociates himself from it as far as possible. He regards it as his task to brush history against the grain.[15]

Benjamin's point here is more complex than it might seem at first. There is the bourgeois historian like Fustel de Coulanges, who believes in progress and who 'empathises' with the victors, on the one hand, and the historical materialist who takes a 'distanced' stance towards a process of cultural accumulation based on exploitation, on the other. This is straightforward. Yet if the bourgeois historian takes part in the 'triumphal procession' of historical progress on the basis of sadness (*Traurigkeit*), the historical materialist's horror at the barbaric parade of history is rooted in hope. As the reference to *acedia* suggests, the logic of this somewhat unconventional picture lies in Benjamin's complex theory of melancholy in his study of the German Baroque mourning play. Rather than entering into the very interesting details of this theory, I would like to focus on Benjamin's remarks about history and culture by pursuing briefly his allusion to Flaubert and to the significance of resuscitating Carthage in this context.

Let me start with the parallel Benjamin seems to suggest between Flaubert and the French historian Fustel de Coulanges. Reference is made here to Fustel de Coulanges's *La Cité antique*, first published in 1864 (two years after the appearance of *Salammbô*). The allusions to Fustel de Coulanges and to Flaubert point to works that emerged during the last years of the Second Empire — and indeed both works may be understood as characteristic of this moment in French history in different senses. *Salammbô* was another best-seller by the author of *Madame Bovary* and *La Cité antique* went through numerous re-editions (not surprisingly, it was selected for distribution as the annual prize given to top students in Lycées across France in 1870). Empathy with the victor — with the Athenian and especially with the Roman — emanates from every page of Fustel de Coulanges's history of the ancient city (indeed Carthage is only mentioned on a couple of occasions and only in passing in the nearly 500 pages of 'the ancient city'). *Salammbô* is a more complex case. This is of course suggested by Flaubert's decision in the first place to make Carthage the focus of the novel. In what sense can Flaubert's elaborate reconstruction of the city life and the cityscape of Carthage be considered empathising with the victor? In one limited sense Carthage is the winner in *Salammbô* — the novel is based on the history of the triumph of the Carthaginians over the barbarian mercenaries in the conflict that took place between the two Punic wars, the so-called Mercenary War.[16] But of course Carthage is far from being the clear victor in the broader historical perspective, for example, of the history of Roman triumph — a triumph also itself qualified by the vengeance of Hannibal that is to come in the Second Punic War.[17] Flaubert's Carthage occupies an intermediate space of tension where victory merges with defeat and where winning now portends losing in the future. By focusing in *Salammbô* on Carthage between the Punic Wars Flaubert might have imagined a parallel to the situation of France after the failure of 1848 and before an as yet unknown calamity that lay ahead (in retrospect we might say between 1848 and the fall of the Commune in 1871). That the selected details from the historical record (from Polybius and others) correspond to the particulars of mid-nineteenth-century France has been demonstrated by the scholarship on the novel. And indeed these correspondences show to what extent Flaubert's approach is at odds with that of Fustel de Coulanges.[18] But to get a more precise sense of the significance of Carthage from Flaubert's point of view on the Second Empire we must look to the crucial element of *Salammbô*'s plot that is not part of the historical record of Carthage, namely, the story of the purely fictional Carthaginian heroine Salammbô and the barbarian mercenary Mâtho. This plot-line, we know, was developed by Flaubert from his intensive study of comparative mythology, in particular the early nineteenth-century work of the German scholar Friedrich Creuzer, which appeared in an annotated four-volume French edition from the 1820s to the 1850s. On the basis of Creuzer, Flaubert constructs the Salammbô–Mâtho connection as a version of the Pasiphaë myth. Pasiphaë, it will be recalled, is the wife of Minos, who lusts after a white bull given to her husband by Poseidon. Because Minos has refused to sacrifice the bull in honour of Poseidon, Pasiphaë is cursed with an erotic attraction to the bull. She copulates with the bull and gives birth to the Minotaur. In this mythic context Salammbô plays Pasiphaë to Mâtho's white bull, a relation that corresponds on another level to the connection between Carthage and the barbarian mercenaries. Simply put, Salammbô is attracted to Mâtho as cultured Carthage is drawn to the barbarian mercenaries. And as they are forced together their places are reversed as Carthage becomes barbarous and the mercenaries become the bearers of culture. This reversal is demonstrated most spectacularly in the ritual slaughter of Mâtho by the Carthaginians before the eyes of Salammbô at the end of Flaubert's novel. In this scene, the very effort ritually to destroy and to expel the barbarian mercenary is presented as barbarous.[19]

In other words, the reversal at the end of *Salammbô* illustrates perfectly Benjamin's historical philosophical thesis about the interpenetration of culture and barbarism. But of course the culture of Carthage was also the barbarism of Rome and so in this sense Benjamin's citation of Flaubert may be understood to allude obliquely to Rome... or, as Flaubert might have understood it, Paris. In other words, to sum up, just as the solidity of Rome does not exclude the porosity of Naples (which is also the porosity of Rome), so the culture of Rome does not rule out the barbarism of Carthage (which is also the barbarism of Rome and by extension, from Flaubert's point of view, the barbarism of the Second French Empire and its capital Paris). Thus, to come quickly to a conclusion, Benjamin's oblique allusions to Rome lead to the following possibility: perhaps it is through the interpenetration of solidity and porosity, culture and barbarism, that we may discover a Roman modernity that breaks with, rather than simply breaking from, the force of the past.

Notes to Chapter 2

1. Walter Benjamin, 'The Return of the *flâneur*', in *Selected Writings*, ed. by Michael W. Jennings with Marcus Bullock, Howard Eiland, and Gary Smith, 4 vols (Cambridge, MA: Harvard University Press, 1996), II, 262–67 (p. 263); 'Die Wiederkehr des Flaneurs', in *Gesammelte Schriften*, ed. by Helia Tiedemann-Bartels, 7 vols (Frankfurt am Main: Suhrkamp, 1972–89), III, 194–99 (p. 195).

2. Benjamin, 'The Return of the *flâneur*', p. 263.

3. Ibid.

4. Johann Wolfgang von Goethe, *Poetry and Truth*, cited in Walter Benjamin, 'Goethe's *Elective Affinities*', in *Selected Writings*, I, 297–360 (p. 316); 'Goethes Wahlverwandtschaften', in *Gesammelte Schriften*, I, 123–201 (pp. 149–50).

5. Walten Benjamin, 'Meine Reise in Italien Pfingsten 1912', in *Gesammelte Schriften*, VI, 252–92 (p. 252) (my translation).

6. Johann Wolfgang von Goethe, *Sämtliche Werke*, ed. by Friedmar Apel, Hendrik Birus, Anne Bohnenkamp, and others, 40 vols (Frankfurt am Main: Deutscher Klassiker Verlag, 1993), XV, 157–58 (my translation).

7. Benjamin's desire that his diary provide a formal coherence to the Italian journey may also be understood as an echo of Goethe. As Nicholas Boyle ('Goethe in Paestum: A Higher-Critical Look at the *Italienische Reise*', *Oxford German Studies*, 20–21 (1991–92), 18–31), observes: 'we must bear in mind that from the beginning of his Italian adventure — and not just when he was composing the *Italienische Reise* — Goethe was exercised by the need to find in that adventure a definite meaning and to give it a definite shape' (p. 22).

8. The importance of Palladio to Goethe is well documented. See David Lowe and Simon Sharp, *Goethe and Palladio: Goethe's Study of the Relationships between Art and Nature, Leading through Architecture to the Discovery of the Metamorphosis of Plants* (Herndon, VA: Lindisfarne Books, 2006).

9. Goethe, *Sämtliche Werke*, XV, 60 (my translation).

10. Benjamin, 'Meine Reise in Italien Pfingsten 1912', p. 276 (my translation).

11. Walter Benjamin and Asja Lacis, 'Naples', in Benjamin, *Selected Writings*, I, 414–21 (p. 416); 'Neapel', in *Gesammelte Schriften*, IV.1, 307–16 (p. 309).

12. Benjamin and Lacis, 'Naples', pp. 416–17; 'Neapel', p. 310.

13. 'Dispersed, porous, and traversed is private life (*Ausgeteilt, porös und durchsetzt ist Privatleben*). What distinguishes Naples from every other large city is what it has in common with the African kraal: each private attitude or act is permeated by streams of communal life. To exist — for the northern European the most private of affairs — is here, as in the kraal, a collective matter.' (Benjamin and Lacis, 'Naples', p. 419; 'Neapel', p. 314) Cf. Ernst Bloch, 'Italien und die Porosität', in *Verfremdungen II. Geographica* (Frankfurt am Main: Suhrkamp, 1964), pp. 155–63.

14. See Gustave Flaubert, *Correspondance (1854–1861)* (Paris: Conard, 1927), p. 348 ('Peu de gens devineront combien il a fallu être triste pour entreprendre de ressusciter Carthage!'). It is noteworthy that Flaubert's letter was to his friend, Ernest Feydeau, the author of a book on Algiers written in 1860 — the year of the annexation of the Place du Maroc as part of Paris's new arrondissements. Feydeau's book focuses on the city of Algiers at the intersection between 'culture' and 'barbarism' that interests Benjamin. See, for instance, the final chapter, which goes from a discussion of urban renewal (the dangers of trying to make Algiers 'une cité européene') to a denunciation of the colonialist sentiment, Feydeau summarises with the phrase 'malheur aux vaincus!' (Ernest Feydeau, *Alger* (Paris: Lévy, 1862), pp. 269–80).

15. Walter Benjamin, 'Theses on the Philosophy of History', in *Illuminations*, trans. by Harry Zohn (New York: Schocken, 2007), pp. 253–64 (pp. 257–58); 'Über den Begriff der Geschichte', in *Gesammelte Schriften*, I.2, 691–704 (pp. 696–97).

16. The Mercenary War (240–238 BC) was between the Carthaginians and the mercenaries employed by Carthage in the first Punic War.

17. The victory to come of Rome in the Second Punic War is also qualified, as is suggested by the aria of Dido in Berlioz's opera *Les Troyens* (first performed in 1863) which closes this work that is precisely contemporary with *Salammbô* by adding to her acknowledgement of the glory of Rome a prophetic appeal of Hannibal:

> Mon souvenir vivra parmi les âges.
> Mon peuple accomplira d'héroïques destins.
> Un jour sur la terre africaine,
> Il naîtra de ma cendre un glorieux vengeur . . .
> J'entends déjà tonner son nom vainqueur.
> Annibal! Annibal! d'orgueil mon âme est pleine!
> Plus de souvenirs amers!
> C'est ainsi qu'il convient de descendre aux enfers!

[My memory will survive across the centuries. My people will fulfil a heroic destiny. One day, on the African land, a glorious revenger will arise from my ashes . . . I already hear the thunder of his triumphal name. Hannibal! Hannibal! My soul is full of pride. No more bitter memories! Thus, must one fall to the underworld!]

18. Here is Fustel de Coulanges's advice to historians:

> Pour connaître la vérité sur ces peuples anciens, il est sage de les étudier sans songer à nous, comme s'ils nous étaient tout à fait étrangers, avec le même désintéressement et l'esprit aussi libre que nous étudierions l'Inde ancienne ou l'Arabie. Ainsi observées, la Grèce et Rome se présentent à nous avec un caractère absolument inimitable. Rien dans les temps modernes ne leur ressemble. Rien dans l'avenir ne pourra leur ressembler. Nous essayerons de montrer par quelles règles ces sociétés étaient régies, et l'on constatera aisément que les mêmes règles ne peuvent plus régir l'humanité. (Numa Denis Fustel de Coulanges, *La Cité antique. Étude sur le culte, le droit, les institutions de la Grèce et de Rome* (Paris: Durand, 1864), p. 2)

19. Let me cite just three brief passages from the final chapter to illustrate this point: 'On aurait voulu un genre de mort où la ville entière participât, et que toutes les mains, toutes les armes, toutes les choses carthaginoises, et jusqu'aux dalles des rues et aux flots du golfe pussent le déchirer, l'écraser, l'anéantir' (Gustave Flaubert, *Salammbô* (Paris: Charpentier, 1881), p. 343); 'Le

corps de cette victime était pour eux une chose particulière et décorée d'une splendeur presque religieuse' (p. 348); as Mâtho begins to expire, 'Ce dernier des Barbares leur représentait tous les Barbares' (p. 349).

CHAPTER 3

❖

Re-visioning Rome:
the AACAR, Gustavo Giovannoni and
the Invention of *Urbanistica* in the 1920s

Eugene Pooley

In an interview published in 1979, Giulio Carlo Argan, the cultural historian and mayor of Rome from 1976 to 1979, pinpointed a key moment of rupture for the city. Locating Rome's historical identity in its anti-programmatic nature, Argan contended that the city had long approached change through invention and imagination rather than calculated economic or sociological planning. But when Rome was made capital of a unified nation in 1870, passing from papal to Italian state control, the city was psychologically and materially recast, no longer an imagined space but the object for programmatic change.[1] This shift in perception identified by Argan was symptomatic of a new mentality in and around Rome that was signalled by the realisation of *Roma capitale*, described by Federico Chabod as

> the *birth* not of a problem with well-defined historical and political contours but the advent of a new *mental* world in which individual problems were seen in a different light, and in which the ruling impulses were not those of the generations of the past.[2]

The change wrought by the creation of *Roma capitale* was palpable, as the city 'opened itself up dramatically to people and ideas',[3] and was positioned at the nexus of new relationships and pressures, that established a set of 'conditions that were unique and different from those of any other capital'[4] and would subject Rome to a process of modernisation with an imperative to shape its material and moral identity as the centre of a nation-state. The new leaders of unified Italy were faced with immediate questions: how can Rome accommodate the apparatus of a new state? How can an ancient city be modernised? What image should *Roma capitale* project to the world? These were the questions that informed the approaches to urban change in Rome from the late nineteenth century, and this chapter discusses how these approaches resulted in a radical shift in the way urban change was perceived in Rome, and subsequently how this gave birth to a new, entirely modern planning culture throughout Italy. As Argan underlined, the ambition of Rome at that time was deceptively simple: 'In the end it is no more than a city seeking to become modern'. But the fulfilment of that ambition was a deeply complex and transformative process.[5]

The birth of the AACAR

On 30 September 1870, only days after the breach of Porta Pia, an initial planning committee was created, tasked with reforming the city ahead of its new role. As a result, a series of town plans, *Piani regolatori*, were drawn up in 1873, 1883, and 1909, the second two of which were officially sanctioned and, in part, implemented.[6] These plans essentially provided for a pattern of basic outward expansion in order to cope with the pressures of an increased population: initially towards the east perimeter of the city walls, around the Esquiline and Caelian hills and Castro Pretorio, then subsequently to the west, in Prati and Testaccio, and eventually south along Via Appia Nuova and north in Flaminio.[7] Amidst continuing debate new arteries were created and extant roads widened and straightened, to facilitate movement in the centre and connect old districts to the new.[8]

By the close of the century, however, the process of urban change had drawn marked criticism. Administratively, it was ruled by chaos, dogged by technical and ideological disputes. The blame for the failure to devise and execute a coherent, long-term plan for the city was laid chiefly at the door of the municipal authority, which was consistently undermined by its lack of strength and stability.[9] Power regularly shifted hands, with the ambition of liberal reformers to renew the city reined in by the regular success of conservative and Catholic candidates who succeeded in gaining representation at local level throughout the 1870s and 1880s. Ultimately, private economic ambition outweighed planning goals, and individual interests ruled public concern.[10]

The result was that a desultory image of the capital had been created and the neglect of Rome's historic character in the first decades of *Roma capitale* had become notorious. Scant attention had been paid to the city's extant physiognomy, to its characteristic shaded roads, gardens and fountains, and numerous villas were demolished, including, most notably, the Villa Ludovisi in 1886.[11] By the 1880s the historic and environmental character of the city was perceived to have been damaged by rampant building speculation, the so-called *febbre edilizia*, which was followed by the bubble's collapse, reaching a nadir at the end of 1888 when half of the 470 construction projects in the capital had been forced to a halt.[12] Though much development occurred outside the Aurelian walls, areas inside suffered too,[13] with the resultant 'destruction' of the city condemned in Italy and abroad.[14] The archaeologist Rodolfo Lanciani evoked the dramatic shift in the city's appearance:

> Rome [...] is no more the Rome of our dreams, of a beautiful brownish hue, surrounded by dense masses of green: it is an immense white dazzling spot [...] Rome is assuming the looks of a modern capital, with all its comforts and disadvantages.[15]

Modernisation then, such as it was, had come at great cost. But it triggered an intellectual resistance in the capital amongst those who sought to counteract this pervasive threat to Rome's heritage, resulting in the creation, in January 1890, of a society with the specific aim of defending the artistic and architectural patrimony of the capital — the Associazione Artistica fra i Cultori di Architettura di Roma, or 'AACAR'. Its founders were the leading architects of post-unification Rome, namely, Gaetano Koch, Giulio Magni, Manfredo Manfredi, Pio Piacentini and Giuseppe Sacconi, with Giovanni Battista Giovenale as president.[16] Over the course of the next thirty years, the group would expand in number and influence, becoming the most important lobby group and architectural forum in the capital. From the start the group was remarkably ambitious and proactive: an early mission statement explained their desire to counteract the development of positivist and scientific thinking that had been fervently promoted in the opening decades of *Roma capitale*, most vocally by Quintino Sella, a development that appeared, in Giovenale's opinion, to have marginalised the liberal arts.[17] From the outset, they sought both cultural and social reform, to engage directly in the capital's development and to disseminate information to the public at large, seeking to effect a change in mentality amongst Romans as much as exert an influence on Rome's landscape.[18] The following sections will examine how the AACAR achieved its goals through organising exhibitions, hosting conferences, devising plans and publishing papers, and through exerting pressure on authorities to take account of Rome's historic character when making urban alterations. It was these activities that would, ultimately, drive the revolution in planning culture in Rome and beyond.

'L'esthétique de Rome'

Arguably the most significant early move of the AACAR was the decision to look beyond the confines of Italy and embrace new ways of perceiving city change and modernisation, in line with Pio Piacentini's description of the group's purpose to 'promote and guide the development of the architectonic art of our city'.[19] It is important to note that Italy had cut a distinctly peripheral figure in the town planning movement that emerged in the United States and Western Europe at the turn of the twentieth century. A slower and more disparate process of industrialisation, together with weak planning legislature, had left Italy marginalised as the idea of urban planning 'swept the world' in the decades either side of 1900.[20]

But soon after, channels had slowly begun to open between Italy and the European planning movement. Texts dealing with modern city growth began to appear in Italian,[21] and the attention of architects in Rome was caught by one of the most significant strands of the early movement, which hypothesised an 'art' of city-building. This was engaged in the creation of both an aesthetically resonant and functional contemporary urban space that sought to modernise cities in a manner sympathetic to architectural, historic and panoramic concerns. Probably the most important and influential theorist of this idea was the Austrian Camillo Sitte, the author of *Der Städte-Bau nach seinen künstlerischen Grundsätzen* in 1889 and the editor of the journal *Der Städtebau*, while its key early exponent was Charles Buls, the mayor of Brussels from 1881 to 1899.[22] Buls had written an influential tract, *L'esthétique des villes*, that drew heavily on Sitte's theories, attempting to synthesise a more holistic approach to the problem of modernising historic cities, which would be highly localised but sensitive to aesthetic, archaeological, technical and public needs. The implementation of these reforms in Brussels drew attention to Buls from outside Belgium, with some of his ideas corresponding to the so-called 'City Beautiful' movement in the United States,[23] and, at the turn of the century, plans for cities worldwide showed the influence of the 'city aesthetic' idea.[24]

In 1902, at the request of the AACAR, Buls was invited to speak in Rome. He delivered a lecture on 14 January, entitled *L'esthétique de Rome*, applying his approach to the 'art' of urban change to the capital itself.[25] Buls was critical of the *Piani regolatori* that had sought to map orthogonal road grids onto the city, sacrificing a nuanced approach for the commercial profit of developing building land. He urged construction to chime with local aesthetics, and to give priority to Rome's grandeur. The dissemination of Buls's ideas in the capital was an important first step in signalling a more cadenced understanding of how an historic city and its monuments were best served by urban planning. The message was clear: modernising Rome meant adopting more integrated planning approaches that responded, rather than dictated, to the city.[26] In the following decade, the group worked to apply such new approaches to urban change: in 1907, it published a plan for the centre of the city, proposing the cutting of an artery from Piazza Barberini down across the Corso, past Piazza Navona and on to the river. And two years later it published its analysis of Sanjust's 1909 *Piano regolatore*, passing critical judgement on the lack of attention accorded to the city's heritage.[27] Sanjust's plan had, in fact, come to the attention of the international planning community and, when Rome hosted the ninth International Congress of Architects in 1911, as part of the World Exhibition, Hermann Josef Stübben, a third key figure in the 'art' of city-building alongside Sitte and Buls,[28] was critical of the aesthetic dimensions of a plan he felt was unworthy of the heritage of Rome. He suggested launching international competitions for specific districts of Rome, following the lead of Berlin and Vienna, to resolve the problem of satisfying modern needs while retaining artistic value, seeking to frame the city through picturesque architecture and achieve an ideal balance of function and beauty, and so reach 'the ideal goal, [...] to build a city that is a true work of art'.[29] By that moment, then, not only had the AACAR firmly established itself as a key voice in the city, but had succeeded in making the modernisation of Rome an issue on the agenda of the world's leading planners.[30]

A Change in Leadership: Gustavo Giovannoni

At this important time in the group's development, the presidency was taken over in 1910 by Gustavo Giovannoni. Roman by birth, Giovannoni was not only an architect of some distinction but also a considerable architectural historian, described by Bruno Zevi as an 'implacable lover of Rome'.[31] His impact was decisive: as head of the most influential cultural collective in the capital he would play a highly significant role not only in popularising architecture and further deepening aesthetic debates, but also in pushing in a new direction, arguing for long-term educative reform in architecture and planning in Rome and beyond.

Giovannoni's initial work elaborated on the 'art' of city-building, and prompted him, together with another key young member of the AACAR, Marcello Piacentini, to write articles in the summer of 1913 that looked afresh at the future of Rome. They sought to incorporate and further develop the key themes of 'city aesthetics' to produce analyses that squared with what Giovannoni termed in a letter to the leading critic Ugo Ojetti, as a 'new school of the "art of city-building" in Rome'.[32] The articles underlined again the haphazard and short-sighted *Piani regolatori*, and proposed fresh ideas that elicited, rather crucially, the tension between the old and the new that lay at the very centre of the modern planning movement. Indeed, it was the conscious and sustained reflection on the negotiation between the past and the future that marked out the 'modernity' of the planning movement; the very act of overtly engaging with the past, and differentiating it from the modern, has been identified as the essence of modernity itself, where modernity is 'complicit' in 'locating and defining tradition'.[33]

This explicit consideration was brought to the fore in Giovannoni's article of 1913, 'Vecchie città ed edilizia nuova', which reflected on the rupture in historic cities such as Rome. Giovannoni sketched a picture of a *fin-de-siècle* breakdown between modernists and conservatives, possessed of two seemingly irreconcilable stand-points, 'between two opposite concepts, between Life and History', fighting over the future of the city. Giovannoni saw, however, in the new planning movement, a rapid evolution in the manner in which the city was considered, giving birth to a 'new science and a new art' capable of synthesising artistic ideals and building practice. Citing Sitte and Buls as the 'heroes' of aesthetic planning, he outlined the shift from seeing the building of the city less as a field of irreconcilable conflict and more as a considered, rationalised 'art'. Rome, however, in Giovannoni's eyes, had not benefited from any such new approach. Rather, since 1870, the city had developed with neither a reasoned consideration of the capital's future growth nor a valued understanding of its past heritage.[34]

To this end, Giovannoni wrote a companion piece that sought to describe a practical solution to the problem of modernising Rome. In order to 'valorise' monuments and accommodate modern life, without compromising either, he proposed the application of a sensitive and limited approach that advocated the 'thinning', rather than the wholesale demolition, of dense and difficult areas.[35] Using the Renaissance district around Via dei Coronari in Rome as a case study, Giovannoni's approach, labelled *diradamento*, marked a breakthrough in the way planners approached city renovation, capable of standing up in place of the more brutal notion of Haussmannian gutting, or *sventramento*, that had dominated the first decades of Rome's existence as capital.[36] This softer approach sought to promote and beautify the city by opening up vistas, framing monuments and stressing the artistic qualities of the urban environment. It was a highly localised approach that took as its starting point the 'individuality of each and every urban society and form', recognising that monuments of different periods and of different styles required tailored approaches and that their value and worth could be accentuated or diminished by their surroundings.[37] Giovannoni noted, for example, how the dominant forms of ancient Roman monuments required more space, and how the attempts of urban developers to erect buildings around such monuments, in the hope of creating a harmonious environment, inevitably ended in failure; they only succeeded in eliciting a 'fictitious stucco monumentality' next to the ancient work.[38] Through such an approach, Giovannoni sought to create, above all, a disciplined and concrete awareness of the ephemeral notion of the city's 'total environment' or *ambiente*. Indeed, he located the city's real artistic spirit less in the idea of single monuments and more in the appreciation of artistic variability and shades of value as constitutive of an urban 'composition'.[39]

In his article of the same year, Piacentini was equally eager for a greater consideration to be made of the city's artistic 'composition', citing the influence of the recent work on the art of city-building of Ugo Monneret de Villard, an archaeologist, epigrapher and historian who taught in Milan and Rome. Piacentini specified concerns over the idea of those institutional planning schemes in Italy that had benefited the material and sanitary improvement of cities at the expense of artistic consideration of urban development. Piacentini lamented the results of this approach to planning, born of short-sighted material and practical concerns, that had left *Roma capitale* with a glut of roads, such as Via Nazionale, Via Cavour and those of the Esquiline, that created an 'insipid tonality'. Piacentini, in similar vein to Giovannoni, urged the striving for a greater artistic harmony, through plays of perspective, use of colour and the linking of small details to a wider picture. This, in turn, he saw as the opportunity to instigate a cultural education in Rome's citizens, understanding planning as an ennobling activity that was both an art of construction and an instrument of diffuse social edification.[40]

Piacentini's concern over the priority given to sanitisation in planning acknowledged the rather dominant role of hygienic engineers in the reconfiguration of Italian cities at the turn of the century.[41] This dominance was evident in the imagery and vocabulary that was created to map urban change too, where planning (such as it was) had become virtually analogous with pathology. Naples had been cast as the 'sick' city, in need of surgical intervention: the aim of the urban plan was the creation of both a healthy physical environment, and, at the same time, the effecting of a form of 'moral' sanitation.[42] The vocabulary of intervention reinforced the notion of the city as a body to be treated, detailing processes of *sventramento* and *risanamento*. Giovannoni and Piacentini, on the other hand, employed a contrasting set of bodily and spatial images as they sought to reform the manner in which the city was imagined. Instead of conceiving of the city as a body on the theatre table under the knife, it was treated as a living organism, embedded in its environment. A softer, more integrated vocabulary considered the city 'organically', with Giovannoni's *diradamento* replacing *sventramento*, and emphasis laid on spatial integration — on *ambiente* — rather than operational excision. Giovannoni saw the weaving together of roads and buildings as the creation of a 'new living organism' out of the capital,[43] reflecting the desire in post-First World War Italy to knit together 'architecture and urban context'.[44] Though the use of bodily imagery to describe the city had a long tradition, dating back to the Renaissance,[45] the contrasting sets of images employed by diverse sets of professionals at the turn of the century underlined the fact that Rome, and the manner in which it was imagined, was very much the object of keen contest, and provided the platform for genuine reform during this process of modernisation.[46]

It is worth noting that the year these articles were published, 1913, also marked the year that the International Federation for Housing and Planning (IFHP), was created, at a conference held in Ghent. Patrick Geddes believed that conference marked a seminal moment of intellectual engagement, beginning an unprecedented interdisciplinary discourse between historians, architects and thinkers on the city and witnessing an awakening in the 'practical man' of a city's past and its future.[47] Perhaps coincidentally, by the end of the same year, and in the wake of the work of Giovannoni and Piacentini, the idea of adopting a more sensitive and attuned artistic mentality with regard to Rome appeared to be gathering more widespread recognition in the city itself. Giuseppe Zucca wrote that he was astonished to hear mention in a political speech of the 'necessity that the artistic tradition of our Rome be defended'. Zucca believed the speech to reveal the political innocence of the young candidate, but nonetheless confided that he felt there was 'an increased warmth of public interest towards the artistic heritage of the capital [...] it is undeniable, slowly, but surely, a new state of mind is taking root'.[48] A 'renewed love' for the city was measured by a greater, and demonstrable, concern for Rome's heritage. Letters flooded in to newspapers marking concerns over destruction wrought by tramlines in Via Condotti, for example. Rather than it being the exclusive territory of cultural commentators, the public at large began to take an engaged, passionate interest in the urban future of Rome.[49]

Creating the planner: the Scuola Superiore and the architetto integrale

But Giovannoni saw this positive change in mentality as only the beginning of even deeper reform in planning culture in the capital. He identified education as of paramount importance, both to sustain cultural interest and to safeguard the city's future. At the time, not only was there was no such professional figure as the 'planner', but the teaching of architecture itself had long been regarded as a secondary discipline, subordinate to engineering and confined purely to fine art schools. Indeed educative reform of the architect had been the subject of a long-running struggle in the capital, intimately linked to the development of the city itself. After decades of sometimes bitter and violent debate, and false dawns, over the education, definition and civic function of the architect, the Scuola Superiore di Architettura was created in Rome in 1919 (law no. 2593, 31 October 1919).[50] The school finally gave the teaching of architecture an autonomous institution at university level.[51] For Giovannoni, it was a personal and lasting triumph, the legacy of his lifelong commitment to the teaching and promotion of Italian architecture.[52]

It was highly significant for two particular reasons. First, the curriculum sought to reflect the ambitious ideal of creating an architectural professional who would be capable of permanently rescuing Italian cities from an administrative and theoretical muddle. Giovannoni provided the lead in determining how this figure would be educated, feeling it needed to reflect a singularly broad range of expertise, with a wide cultural and historical knowledge, backed up by artistic training, technical proficiency and practical experience. This would create the *architetto integrale*, a 'total architect', a complete, rounded figure that would be capable of reforming cities with an acute sense of *ambiente*, astutely adapting the urban environment, whilst enhancing, without compromise, its heritage or artistic sensibility.[53]

Second, it was seen as the opportunity to create an organic new culture and new architectural style for the capital. Not only was the creation of the school vaunted at international conferences,[54] but it provided for the emergence of the so-called *Scuola romana* of architecture, an arguably loose, but frequently used, term to capture the large quantity of talented graduates that emerged in successive years.[55] Giovannoni later reflected on both the significance of the school as a cornerstone for the vast Fascist building programme, the 'point of departure for that which I could call the vast architectonic politics of fascism'.[56] The lead of Rome was followed as other schools were subsequently created in Turin (1925), Naples (1928) and Florence (1930),[57] and the long journey for the recognition of the professional architect, as distinct from the engineer, was finally confirmed through a succession of laws from 1923 to 1927, creating a new 'class' of architects with their own separate union.[58] Above all, though, it succeeded in forming a generation of architects in the capital who were immersed in the culture of Rome and capable of implementing urban change in the manner in which Giovannoni's city aesthetic programme described.[59]

If the AACAR had played a central role in achieving a key professional and administrative breakthrough with the establishment of the Scuola Superiore, then it continued to make it a primary objective for those young students and graduates to encourage and disseminate artistic and architectural culture to a wider public. Together with Accademia di San Luca, the AACAR challenged new architects to produce innovative work through the organisation of regular competitions in Rome in the 1910s.[60] The AACAR pursued its aim of reaching beyond the confines of the architect's studio to draw more public attention to the field, through editorial publications and exhibitions, in an effort to engage the architect with the public and vice versa.[61] And in 1921, the AACAR published the first issue of its new journal, *Architettura e Arti Decorative*, a publication that achieved conspicuous success by distinguishing itself from other reviews in the continent through not focusing exclusively on new architecture but also seeking to provide a broader cultural and historical context.[62]

Towards Grande Roma and urbanistica romana

The unresolved problem of Rome's *Piano regolatore* continued, however, to loom. And the AACAR applied itself to the issue, with Piacentini delivering a key lecture at the headquarters of the organisation in 1916, *Sulla conservazione della bellezza di Roma e sullo sviluppo della città moderna*. This was seen as a real breakthrough moment in planning culture in the capital, articulating a vision of Rome that attempted to deliver a wide-ranging solution to the problems of accommodating modern society in an historic city.[63] In subsequent years, the AACAR set up committees in 1919 and 1920 to examine the historic centre of Rome and the area around the Campidoglio. This eventually led to the formation of a group, created in July 1923, to look more systematically into the future of the capital, with artistic sensibilities determined as the guiding principle for urban reform.[64] With change to the capital high on the agenda, Stübben was invited by the AACAR, of which he would become a member, to give a lecture in Rome on 22 May 1924, only months before the findings of the committee were published in July of the same year.[65] This publication, the *Relazione della Commissione Municipale per lo Studio della Riforma del Piano Regolatore*, acknowledged the approach of Stübben and showed the heavy influence of both Giovannoni and Piacentini.[66]

The plan was the culmination of decades of development and the product of clear progress. In broad terms, the committee recommended minimal intervention in the historic centre, by executing a form of selective and artistically sensitive *diradamento*, favouring the creation of a new hub for the city set out to the east. Commercial growth was envisaged along the Via Appia Antica, with the city served by new transport links, including an underground network and new central station.[67] The possibility of shifting the city's main rail terminal was hypothesised too, an idea that had been elaborated in a 1922 project by Ugolotti and Coppedè, who drew up a five-year plan that would have moved the station from Termini to Porta Maggiore.[68] The committee's proposal sought to address the critical problems of overcrowding and imbalance brought about by poorly regulated development since 1870, which had left streets unsuitable for modern traffic and slow communications.[69] This collaborative plan was termed *Grande Roma* and would go on to provide much of the substantive basis, as well as the title, for Piacentini's study of October 1925, which came to represent the consensus view, at that moment, of the city's leading cultural voices on Rome's future.[70] Finally, Rome had a town plan that was modern, progressive and sensitive to its ancient structure.

Meanwhile, Italy had begun to make further strides in formulating its own planning discipline, progress that was intricately linked to Rome itself. While the theories on the art of city-building still carried weight, the international movement had begun to envisage the act of bringing about urban change as an instrument of social science, conceiving of a discipline of far-reaching influence that was not solely concerned by negotiating pleasing aesthetic outcomes, as the 'art of the city' had prioritised. The notion was established that the urban domain could be considered and controlled in every dimension by the town plan, and that it could be used as a key tool with which to re-write the problems of a community and alter the social structure of society.[71]

Key theorists in Italy, such as Silvio Ardy and Cesare Chiodi, both proposed the creation of a centralised institute in Italy, carving out a new space for planning as a discipline in its own right, as the French had done with the Institut d'Urbanisme, created in Paris in 1924.[72] They shared the view that planning was a social science, founded on the relationship between construction and demography, between the city and its inhabitants, 'l'urbs e la civitas'. These early proposals were, however, met with resistance in Rome and were eventually rejected. The idea of creating a dominant new professional figure, as Ardy's programme proposed, was problematic: Ardy, in line with northern schools of thought, saw the figure as a 'supertechnical' professional with civic and economic responsibility,[73] whereas opinion in Rome favoured the creation of a pre-eminently artistic planner, in line with Giovannoni's *architetto integrale*, an idea promoted through the teaching of the Scuola Superiore.[74]

The contention over the direction of the incipient discipline would catalyse its dynamic growth over the following months and years,[75] during which time the idea of city planning was distinguished by the increasing use of a new term, *urbanistica*. When outlining their proposals, Ardy and Chiodi had used either *urbanismo* or *urbanesimo* to describe the inchoate discipline, but these terms slipped out of use in favour of *urbanistica*, with *urbanesimo* coming to describe instead the process of urbanisation and the phenomenon of urban migration. It does not seem that this was a strategic choice,[76] but it has been proposed that *urbanistica* was a term more commonly employed by architects and artists who were focused on the aesthetic development of cities, an interchangeable term for the 'art of constructing the city'. As such *urbanistica*, as a discipline and an idea, can be seen to reflect its strong roots in the *arte cittadina* movement promoted by Giovannoni and the AACAR.[77] Whether by design or chance, though, the application and diffusion of this new term at once asserted the independence of the discipline and distinguished the specificity of Italian planning from the international movement.[78]

Urbanistica was propelled by the first self-nominated groups of *urbanisti*, who positioned themselves as thinkers and practitioners of the discipline, including the first genuine planning group of the capital, the Gruppo degli Urbanisti di Roma, alternatively called Gruppo Urbanisti Romani (GUR), formed in October 1926.[79] The establishing of the GUR, which included graduates of the Scuola Superiore, represented the interest sparked in the capital by *urbanistica*, with a new generation in Rome whose 'spirit has been won over by the problems of that newly born science, which [...] is called "urbanistica"...'.[80] Much like the AACAR, the GUR aimed to perpetuate a change in approach, with its stated goal to 'formulate [...] a planning mentality'.[81] The need to spread this mentality, or *coscienza urbanistica*, became a mantra in planning circles, with the suffusion of a planning mentality being urged not just amongst the discipline's practitioners but, crucially, amongst the public at large. This could be achieved, Giovannoni suggested, through saturating the public and academic arena with the cultural trappings of *urbanistica*, through planning groups, education programmes, conferences and competitions.[82] Giovannoni called, too, for a more favourable climate in which *urbanisti* could develop, wanting *urbanistica* departments in local governments.[83] The idea of a *coscienza urbanistica* was touched with a sense of the unknown too: emerging in rapid time with few boundaries, *urbanistica*, as Alberto Calza Bini reflected, was a 'mysterious science' in these early years.[84]

The idea of diffusing a *coscienza urbanistica* held particular cachet in Rome. The very notion of urban planning, it was claimed, was rooted in the capital, with commentators underlining the historically important role Rome had played in the mapping of cities. *Urbanistica* was coloured as a discipline of Latin origin,[85] an ancient art that had been revived to meet the demands of a new era.[86] New ways of visualising the ancient city and its planning heritage were introduced too in the 1920s, with three-dimensional models created by Paul Bigot and Henry Lacoste paraded at fairs and appearing in the press, together with works by Giuseppe Gatteschi picturing a 'Rome restored', all offering a new popular, reconstructed image of the town.[87] The modern pursuit, then, of *urbanistica romana* was deemed to be, where Rome was concerned, the continuation of the 'most noble of the arts'.[88]

Mussolini intervenes

By 1925, then, the approach to urban change in Rome had altered beyond recognition; driven on by the AACAR, the distinct discipline of *urbanisitica* had finally emerged and the capital had a carefully considered proposal for its future growth, labelled *Grande Roma*. But by that same year, political circumstances in Rome and Italy had changed decisively. The Fascist regime had firmly established itself, and late in 1925, Mussolini moved to exert more direct control over the development of the capital, by creating a *governatorato* in the city, an administrative body headed by a state-appointed governor. It was on the occasion of the inauguration of the first governor, Filippo Cremonesi, on 31 December 1925, that Mussolini famously chose to outline publicly his wish to create a great metropolis out of Rome. He spoke of a five-year project to create a 'vast, ordered and powerful' city, as during the Augustan Empire, stripped of the 'contamination' of tramlines, where 'the millennial monuments of our history should appear gigantic in necessary isolation', identifying the Theatre of Marcellus, the Mausoleum of Augustus and the Capitoline hill as such monuments, and specifying that the Pantheon be made clearly visible from Piazza Colonna. He envisaged the city as the *Terza Roma*, the third Rome, expanding towards the hills and the sea with new satellite towns managing the increased population, a city replete with modern infrastructure and fit for a Fascist society.[89] The speech prompted great debate in newspaper columns in the subsequent months, and by February 1926 the cultural environment of the capital was awash with intense debate over Rome's future. The steady, rational modernisation conceived by the AACAR was suddenly marginalised, and the new discipline of *urbanistica* was swiftly politicised. Ugo Ojetti instead identified activist cliques that developed in cafés and artistic circles with individuals pushing the cause of one particular architect or another to be given the honour of realising Mussolini's vision.[90] The project of one Roman architect, Armando Brasini, came to the fore. He had outlined plans to reconfigure the area between Piazza Colonna and Montecitorio, which some commentators believed to be the inspiration behind Mussolini's vision. But Brasini came under fire for his impractical and anachronistic plans, which would have required a return to the old ways of *sventramento*. The careful control that the AACAR had cultivated over the capital was under great threat, and the group called for a series of meetings to devise a strategy to counter the situation.[91] And when it became evident that Mussolini had in fact approved Brasini's plan in 1927, Giovannoni led the way in sending a letter of condemnation to the Duce, with the supporting signatures of leading fellow architects.[92] The plan was shelved as a result, but it had become clear that Mussolini's intervention had caused the fulcrum of debate to shift away from the founding concerns of the AACAR: modernising Rome had now become an increasingly political, rather than cultural, concern.

It proved the beginning of the end of the group's remarkable influence, and signalled a fracturing of previously solid relationships. Giovannoni and Piacentini, perhaps the two leading figures on the path of the 're-visionising' of Rome, met with markedly different fates as the regime moved into its second decade in power. To Giovannoni's dismay, both the AACAR and its review were subsumed by the Fascist architectural union, the Sindacato Nazionale Fascista Architetti, in November 1927. Giovannoni himself became increasingly marginalised, while Piacentini usurped him in becoming one of the most prominent architects under Mussolini. Their struggle over the direction of the AACAR's journal was a pivotal point: having initially founded and edited the review together, from 1921 until 1927, Piacentini scored a decisive victory by taking sole control of the journal in January 1932 under the new title *Architettura*. It was an episode that both marked down as one of the most significant of their careers, prompting a fall-out within the architectural fraternity in Rome. For Giovannoni to be 'stripped' of the direction of the journal, and the opportunity to expound his methodology, was a bitter disappointment. He confided to Ojetti: 'You know that this has been one of the unhappiest loves of my life. In small measure I had succeeded in realising [my aim] in "Architettura ed Arti Decorative" until they stripped me of it without ceremony.'[93]

The story of Rome's subsequent urban development during the Fascist regime is well documented, with the 1931 *Piano regolatore* and the construction of the Via dei Fori Imperiali, much vaunted by the regime. And whilst the influence of Giovannoni diminished, and the AACAR essentially ceased to exist after 1927, their roles deserve to be remembered for the considerable change they effected. In a relatively short space of time, they oversaw some great advances and left a significant legacy: a new school of architecture was inaugurated, town planning, or *urbanistica*, came into existence, and the problem of modernising Rome was positioned at the forefront of daily concerns and openly debated. The city was perceived in a new way, as an entity to be valued, privileged and cultivated, through times of significant upheaval.

In memory of Christopher Duggan

Notes to Chapter 3

1. Giulio Carlo Argan, *Un'idea di Roma. Intervista di Mino Monicelli* (Rome: Editori Riuniti Interventi, 1979), pp. 59–60.
2. Federico Chabod, *Italian Foreign Policy: The Statecraft of the Founders*, trans. by William McCuaig (Princeton: Princeton University Press, 1996), p. 150. Francesco Bartolini identifies the advent of a modern, discursive mindset in Rome after 1870, where the city was the stage

for 'experimenting with the politico-symbolic potential of the image of Rome itself, in an institutional and cultural scenario that was entirely new, liberal and positivist': see Francesco Bartolini, *Roma. Dall'unità a oggi* (Rome: Carocci, 2008), p. 12.

3. Fiorella Bartoccini, 'Roma di fine secolo. Realtà e interpretazioni', in *Il Decadentismo di Roma*, ed. by Fiorella Bartoccini (Rome: Istituto di Studi Romani, 1980), pp. 18–22.

4. Filippo Clementi, *Roma accattona?!* (Rome: Enrico Voghera, 1902), p. 5.

5. Argan, *Un'idea di Roma*, p. 10.

6. For an overview of these plans and their genesis, including details of committees, rejected proposals and reports, see Italo Insolera, 'Storia del primo piano regolatore di Roma: 1870–1874', *Urbanistica. Rivista trimestrale dell'Istituto Nazionale di Urbanistica*, 27 (1959), 74–90; Italo Insolera, 'I piani regolatori dal 1880 alla seconda guerra mondiale', *Urbanistica. Rivista trimestrale dell'Istituto Nazionale di Urbanistica*, 28–29 (1959), 6–34, and Carmen Carbone Stella Richter, 'Roma 1870–1883: Una capitale senza piano regolatore', *Rivista di urbanistica* (1993), pp. 123–200, 393–464.

7. Rome's population grew from 226,000 in 1870 to 540,000 in 1911. For details on the growth of the areas to the east of the centre see *L'Esquilino e la Piazza Vittorio. Una struttura urbana dell'ottocento*, ed. by Franco Girardi, Gianfranco Spagnesi and Ferderico Gorio (Rome: Editalia, 1974), and on the specific demand for housing see Taina Syrjämaa, 'Roman Homes: The Housing Question in "Roma Capitale"', in *The Welfare State. Past, Present and Future*, ed. by Henrik Jensen (Pisa: Edizioni Plus-Pisa University Press, 2002), pp. 111–26.

8. The most significant of the new roads were the east–west arteries carrying traffic across the city: Via Nazionale, linking Termini to the centre; Via del Tritone, down from the Quirinal hill; Via Cavour, from the Esquiline; and Corso Vittorio Emanuele, taking traffic west to Ponte Sant'Angelo.

9. 'La vita dei municipi in Italia', *L'Opinione*, 5 July 1872, p. 1, emphasised the need for a 'strong and authoritative municipality' in Rome.

10. Alberto Caracciolo, *Roma capitale. Dal Risorgimento alla crisi dello Stato liberale* (Rome: Editori Riuniti, 1984), p. 104. The triumph of individual concern over public planning was evident in the practice of some councillors who chose to defend property holders whose interests were endangered by the drive for the city to become a capital: cf. Denis Bocquet, *Rome ville technique (1870–1925): une modernisation conflictuelle de l'espace urbain* (Rome: École française de Rome, 2007), p. 350.

11. Diego Angeli, 'I problemi edilizi di Roma', *Nuova antologia. Rivista di lettere, scienze e arti*, 204 (1905), 19–32 (pp. 22–23). Other villas destroyed included Villa Sciarra, Villa Spada (both on the Janiculum) and Villa Barberini (by Via XX Settembre).

12. Clementi, *Roma accattona?!*, p. 54.

13. Insolera, 'I piani regolatori dal 1880', p. 8.

14. Giosuè Carducci famously prayed for the protection of Rome's monuments against the effect of the speculation in 'Dinanzi alle Terme di Caracalla', in the first book of the *Odi Barbare*: 'Febbre, m'ascolta. Gli uomini novelli | quinci respingi e lor picciole cose: | religioso è questo orror: la dea | Roma qui dorme.' Hermann Grimm regretted the loss of Rome's sense of calm in *La distruzione di Roma* (1886), in *Roma communis patria*, ed. by Luigi Salerno (Bologna: Cappelli, 1968), p. 126, and Augustus John Cuthbert Hare lamented the 'destruction of Rome [...] The old charm is gone forever, the whole aspect of the city is changed', in *Walks in Rome* (London: George Allen, 1893), p. 10.

15. Rodolfo Lanciani, 'Notes from Rome', *The Athenaeum*, 3137 (10 December 1887), 790.

16. 'Elenco dei soci promotori', *Associazione Artistica fra i Cultori di Architettura di Roma. Annuario*, 1 (1891), 7.

17. 'Resoconto morale', *Associazione Artistica fra i Cultori di Architettura di Roma. Annuario*, 1 (1891), 19–28 (p. 19).

18. Writing in 1927, Antonio Nezi saw the proactivity of the AACAR as a unique trait of the body; it was 'perhaps the only body that in the midst of all the general sluggishness has always, with impassioned feeling and courageous action, sought to avoid irreversible aesthetic damage', in Antonio Nezi, 'Sistemazioni urbane e questioni edilizie: Padova, il piano regolatore e la zona monumentale', *Emporium*, 387 (1927), 185–94 (p. 185).

19. Pio Piacentini, 'Rendiconto morale', *Associazione Artistica fra i Cultori di Architettura di Roma. Annuario*, 7–11 (1897–1901), 3–5 (p. 5).

20. Anthony Sutcliffe, 'Introduction: The Debate on Nineteenth-Century Planning', in *The Rise of Modern Urban Planning 1800–1904*, ed. by Anthony Sutcliffe (London: Mansell, 1980), pp. 1–10 (p. 6), and Donatella Calabi, 'The Genesis and Special Characteristics of Town-Planning Instruments in Italy, 1880–1914', ibid., pp. 55–70 (pp. 56–57).

21. Donatella Calabi, 'Italian Town Planning and the Idea of the City in the Early Twentieth Century', *Planning Perspectives*, 3.2 (1988), 127–40 (p. 128).

22. For an overview of Sitte's significance to the planning movement, see George R. Collins and Christiane C. Collins, *Camillo Sitte and the Birth of Modern City Planning* (New York: Random House, 1965).

23. A translation of Buls's work appeared in a special volume of *Municipal Affairs* on the City Beautiful movement: see Charles Buls, 'City Aesthetics', *Municipal Affairs*, 3 (1899), 732–41.

24. For a range of plans designed in this manner, see Wolfgang Sonne, '"The Entire City Shall Be Planned as a Work of Art": Städtebau als Kunst im frühen modernen Urbanismus 1890–1920', *Zeitschrift für Kunstgeschichte*, 66. 2 (2003), 207–36.

25. Charles Buls, *L'esthétique de Rome*, extract from *Revue de l'Université de Bruxelles* (March 1903). Buls's visit to Rome was reported by Filippo Galassi, 'La conferenza del Sig. Charles Buls', *Associazione Artistica fra i Cultori di Architettura di Roma. Annuario* (1902), 9–14. The AACAR published the Italian translation of *L'esthétique des villes*, 'L'estetica delle città', in 1903.

26. Galassi, 'La conferenza del Sig. Charles Buls', p. 12. Numerous rectilinear roads had been proposed after 1870 either to improve communications or to provide monumental centrepieces for the new capital. One of the most noteworthy proposals was the Via Massima, proposed by Giovanni Carlo Landi to provide a central axis for the new city running from the Esquiline across to the Vatican, *Relazione sul progetto della Via Massima dell'Ingegnere ed architetto Comm. Gio. Carlo Landi* (Rome: Accademia Romana degli Ingegneri, Architetti ed Agronomi, 1875).

27. 'Il piano regolatore del centro di Roma', *Associazione Artistica fra i Cultori di Architettura di Roma. Annuario* (1906–07), 13–18, and 'Relazione sul piano regolatore di Roma', *Associazione Artistica fra i Cultori di Architettura di Roma. Annuario* (1908–09), 19–35.

28. Stübben's 1890 publication, *Der Städtebau*, arguably demonstrated a greater practical intent than Sitte's work, and Stübben himself was very active in town and city planning. Contributing to the opening of channels to the European planning movement to Italy, a substantive Italian adaptation of *Der Städtebau* was penned by Aristide Caccia in 1915, entitled *Costruzione, trasformazione e ampliamento delle città: compilato sulla traccia dello Städtebau di J. Stübben ad uso degli ingegneri, architetti, uffici tecnici ed amministrazioni municipali*.

29. 'Conferenza del Dott. Ing. J. Stübben di Berlino sull'arte di costruire le città', *Atti del IX Congresso internazionale degli architetti* (Rome, 2–10 October 1911), p. 185.

30. The AACAR was represented at an international planning conference in London in 1910 by one the group's associate members, Thomas Ashby and Gustavo Giovannoni, 'Resoconto morale per l'anno MCMX', *Associazione Artistica fra i Cultori di Architettura di Roma. Annuario* (1910–11), 5–15 (p. 13).

31. Guido Zucconi, '"Dal capitello alla città". Il profilo dell'architetto totale', in Gustavo Giovannoni, *Dal capitello alla città*, ed. by Guido Zucconi (Milan: Jaca Book, 1997), pp. 9–70 (p. 12). Cf. Guglielmo de Angelis D'Ossat, *Gustavo Giovannoni, storico e critico dell'architettura* (Rome: Istituto di Studi Romani, 1949), p. 3: '[Giovannoni] was a determined advocate and a deep lover of the idea and civilization of Rome'.

32. Galleria Nazionale d'Arte Moderna (GNAM), Fondo Ojetti, Gustavo Giovannoni, cass. 36, ins. 12, Giovannoni to Ojetti, 8 August 1913.

33. Nezar AlSayyad, 'The End of Tradition or the Tradition of Endings?', in *The End of Tradition?*, ed. by Nezar AlSayyad (London and New York: Routledge, 2004), pp. 1–29 (p. 12).

34. Gustavo Giovannoni, 'Vecchie città ed edilizia nuova', *Nuova antologia*, 249 (1913), pp. 450–65.

35. Gustavo Giovannoni, 'Il "diradamento" edilizio dei vecchi centri. Il quartiere della rinascenza in Roma', *Nuova antologia*, 250 (1913), 53–76.

36. Dario Barbieri, *Per la grande Roma. Formazione e sviluppo delle grandi città moderne* (Rome: Società

Editrice D'Arte Illustrata, 1927), p. 34, and 'Risanamento e diradamento', *La casa*, 17 (1937), 7–9.

37. Dennis Rodwell, *Conservation and Sustainability in Historic Cities* (Oxford: Blackwell, 2007), p. 46.

38. Giovannoni, 'Il "diradamento" edilizio dei vecchi centri', pp. 56–57.

39. Gustavo Giovannoni, 'Ricostruzione del vecchio centro o decentramento', *Capitolium*, 4 (July 1925), 221–25 (p. 224).

40. Marcello Piacentini, 'Estetica regolatrice nello sviluppo della città', *Rassegna contemporanea*, VI, II, VII (10 April 1913), 31–33. Piacentini refers to Villard's work, *Note sull'arte di costruire le città*, published in 1907.

41. For more on the importance accorded to hygienists in early planning culture in Italy, see Guido Zucconi, 'La cultura igienista nella formazione dell'urbanistica', *Urbanistica. Rivista trimestrale dell'Istituto Nazionale di Urbanistica*, 86 (1987), 35–37.

42. Edoardo Zabban, 'Napoli e l'Esposizione di igiene', *Nuova Antologia*, 87 (1900), 61–85 (p. 84).

43. Gustavo Giovannoni, 'Questioni urbanistiche', *L'Ingegnere*, 1 (1928), 9–10 (p. 9).

44. Calabi, 'Italian Town Planning', p. 137.

45. Rosario Pavia surveys the history of the *città corpo* idea in *Le paure dell'urbanistica. Disagio e incertezza nel progetto della città contemporanea* (Rome: Meltemi, 2005), pp. 14–16. And Carlo Cattaneo's study of the Italian city, published in 1858, saw how 'the city formed an inseparable body with its territory', in *La città considerata come principio ideale delle istorie italiane* (Florence: Vallecchi, 1931), p. 53.

46. Guido Zucconi, *La città contesa. Dagli ingegneri sanitari agli urbanisti (1885–1942)* (Milan: Jaca Book, 1999), pp. 11–13. Zucconi's work considers how the Italian city was the object of competing approaches from the social sciences, arts, and engineering.

47. Patrick Geddes, 'Two Steps in Civics: "Cities and Town Planning Exhibition" and the "International Congress of Cities"', *The Town Planning Review*, 2 (1913), 78–94 (p. 79).

48. Giuseppe Zucca, 'La tutela di Roma e una nuova coscienza della cittadinanza — Illusione o realtà? — Le vecchie quistioni di Via Condotti e della Fontana dell'Esedra: la crisi', *Rassegna contemporanea*, VI, II, 20 (25 October 1913), 311–14 (p. 312).

49. Ibid.

50. Gustavo Giovannoni, 'Discorso Commemorativo', *Annuario della Regia Scuola di Architettura di Roma* (1927–28), 19–34 (p. 29).

51. For the greater background to the story of the 'creation' of the modern architect in Rome, including the specific legislative stages of this process, see the thesis by Barbara Berta, *La formazione della figura professionale dell'architetto. Roma 1890–1925* (PhD Thesis, Università degli Studi di Roma Tre, 2008).

52. Giovannoni told Ojetti: 'You know how I have dedicated my whole life to the teaching of architecture, to the raising of the profile of Italian architecture', GNAM, Fondo Ojetti, Gustavo Giovannoni, cass. 36, ins. 12, 27 June, no year.

53. Gustavo Giovannoni, 'Gli architetti e gli studi dell'architettura in Italia', *Rivista d'Italia. Lettere, scienze ed arte*, 19.1 (1916), 169–76.

54. Gustavo Giovannoni, 'Per le scuole superiori d'architettura', *Architettura e Arti Decorative*, 3 (November 1924), 137–43 (p. 143).

55. Zucconi, '"Dal capitello alla città"', p. 14.

56. Gustavo Giovannoni, 'Relazione sull'anno accademico 1931–32', *Annuario della Regia Scuola di Architettura di Roma* (1932–33), p. 20. For more on the school, its origins and development, see *La facoltà di architettura dell'Università "La Sapienza" dalle origini al duemila. Discipline, docenti, studenti*, ed. by Vittorio Franchetti Pardo (Rome: Gangemi, 2001).

57. Giovannoni, 'Relazione sull'anno accademico 1931–32', p. 22.

58. Laws on 24 June 1923, no. 1395, 23 October 1925, no. 2537 and 27 October 1927, no. 2145 regulated the separation of the two professions, in Alberto Calza Bini, 'Tutela e inquadramento statale degli artisti', *Rapporti dell'architettura con le arti figurative*, Convegno di Arti (Rome: Reale Accademia d'Italia, 1936), 258–64 (p. 260).

59. 'We have seen [...] groups of young men come out of the Association amazingly prepared [...]

who have understood the character of Rome and have set about designing new buildings, new layouts, and new decoration with passion' (Edgardo Negri, 'La scuola romana degli architetti e l'opera della associazione artistica fra i cultori di architettura in Roma', *Atti del I° Congresso Nazionale di Studi Romani*, Istituto di Studi Romani, Rome, II (1929), p. 85).

60. Berta, *La formazione della figura professionale dell'architetto*, pp. 100–10 and 154–65. For details of the competitions of the Accademia di San Luca, see *I disegni di architettura dell'Archivio storico dell'Accademia di San Luca*, ed. by Paolo Marconi, Angela Cipriani and Enrico Valeriani (Rome: De Luca, 1974).

61. The AACAR wished for 'the architect to mingle with city life' and aimed to 'effectively, and in an Italian manner, bring art closer to the lives of our population', in 'Per un'associazione italiana di cultori d'architettura', in Gustavo Giovannoni, *Questioni di architettura nella storia e nella vita. Edilizia, estetica architettonica, restauri, ambiente dei monumenti* (Rome: Società Editrice d'arte illustrata, 1925), pp. 204–05.

62. Negri, 'La scuola romana degli architetti', p. 10.

63. Barbieri, *Per la grande Roma*, p. 34.

64. The committee was 'guided step by step by artistic thought', in Gustavo Giovannoni, 'Sistemazioni edilizie della vecchia Roma', *Annuario. Associazione artistica fra i cultori di architettura di Roma* (1916–1924), 5–19 (p. 13).

65. Stübben's lecture was reported in 'Notiziario', *Roma. Rivista di studi e di vita romana*, II (1924), p. 242.

66. *Relazione della Commissione Municipale per lo Studio della Riforma del Piano Regolatore*, July 1924, p. 12.

67. Ibid., pp. 13–25.

68. Barbieri, *Per la grande Roma*, p. 145. Designs for the Ugolotti Coppedè station are held at the Archivio Storico Capitolino.

69. Dario Barbieri, 'The Urban Problem of Modern Rome', *The Town Planning Review*, 10.3 (1923), 145–70 (p. 146).

70. Barbieri, *Per la grande Roma*, p. 25.

71. Paolo Sica, *Storia dell'urbanistica. III. Il Novecento* (Bari: Laterza, 1980), pp. 5–6.

72. Silvio Ardy, *Proposta di creazione di un Istituto Italiano di Urbanesimo e di alti Studi Municipali*, Congresso Internazionale di Urbanesimo, Turin, 28 May 1926, and Cesare Chiodi, 'Per la istituzione di una scuola d'urbanismo', in *Scritti sulla città e il territorio 1913–1969*, ed. by Renzo Riboldazzi (Milan: Unicopli, 2006), pp. 136–39 (pp. 136–38). For an overview of Cesare Chiodi's work and writing, see Renzo Riboldazzi, '"Armonia e calcolo, necessità e bellezza". Città e progetto urbanistico negli scritti di Cesare Chiodi', ibid., pp. 9–111.

73. Paolo Nicoloso, 'Competenze e conflittualità nelle prime proposte sulla figura del tecnico urbanista', *Urbanistica. Rivista trimestrale dell'Istituto Nazionale di Urbanistica*, 86 (1987), 38–41 (p. 39).

74. Giuseppe Caffarelli, 'Urbanistica Romana', *Atti del I° Congresso Nazionale di Studi Romani*, II (1929), p. 14. The importance of Giovannoni's *architetto integrale* concept in the evolution of the *urbanista* is acknowledged by Giorgio Ciucci in two articles, in 'L'urbanista negli anni '30: un tecnico per l'organizzazione del consenso', in *Il razionalismo e l'architettura in Italia durante il fascismo*, ed. by Silvia Danesi and Luciano Patetta (Venice: La Biennale di Venezia, 1976), pp. 28–30, and in 'Il dibattito sull'architettura e le città fasciste', in *Storia dell'arte italiana. Parte seconda. Dal Medioevo al Novecento*, ed. by Federico Zeri, 15 vols (Turin: Einaudi, 1982), III, 266–78, and again in his book Giorgio Ciucci, *Gli architetti e il fascismo. Architettura e città 1922–1944* (Turin: Einaudi, 1989).

75. 'The idea of *urbanistica* has progressed, and competitions, debates and conflicts have promoted its cause', in Luigi Piccinato, 'Cammino dell'urbanistica italiana', *La Tribuna*, 24 April 1937, p. 6. Donatella Calabi emphasises the characterisation of *urbanistica* as a dynamic, flexible discipline in its early stages, in *Storia dell'urbanistica europea. Questioni, strumenti, casi esemplari* (Milan: Mondadori, 2004), p. xvii.

76. I thank Donatella Calabi for sharing her thoughts on this point.

77. Zucconi, *La città contesa*, pp. 13–14.

78. Giulio Ernesti, 'La formazione dell'urbanistica in Italia (1900–1950): intersezioni di discipline, conflitti. Fra utopia e realtà', in *La costruzione dell'utopia. Architetti e urbanisti nell'Italia fascista*,

ed. by Giulio Ernesti (Rome: Edizioni Lavoro, 1988), pp. 163–73 (p. 165). It was characteristic of the international planning movement that each nation created its own terminology for the discipline, sustaining the notion that, despite its global reach, planning was an intrinsically localised undertaking.

79. 'Notizie varie. Gli urbanisti di Roma', *Architettura e Arti Decorative*, VI, 2 (October 1926), unpaged and 'Notiziario', *Roma. Rivista di studi e di vita romana*, IV (1926), p. 432. The makeup of the GUR shifted but counted Luigi Piccinato and Gaetano Minnucci among its founding and most prominent members. The latter's early involvement with the planning movement was evident in his report on the July 1924 planning conference in Amsterdam, Gaetano Minnucci, 'Edilizia cittadina e piani regolatori', *Architettura e Arti Decorative*, 4.2 (1924), 62–90.

80. Domenico Delli Santi, 'L'Opera del Governo Fascista per Roma', *Capitolium*, 12 (March 1928), pp. 637–56 (p. 642).

81. 'Notizie varie. Gli urbanisti di Roma', *Architettura e Arti Decorative*, 6.2 (1926), unpaged and 'Notiziario', *Roma. Rivista di studi e di vita romana*, 4 (1926), p. 432.

82. Gustavo Giovannoni, 'Questioni urbanistiche', *L'Ingegnere*, 2.1 (1928), 6–10 (p. 6).

83. Ibid., p. 10.

84. 'Discorso dell'On. Prof. Arch. Alberto Calza Bini. L'architetto nella vita moderna', *Annuario della R. Scuola Superiore di Architettura di Firenze* (1932–33), 16–33 (p. 28).

85. Giuseppe Caffarelli, 'Urbanistica Romana', *Atti del I° Congresso Nazionale di Studi Romani*, 2 (1929), p. 18.

86. '*Urbanistica* can be defined as the art of creating cities or organising their development. If the word is new, the art is ancient' in 'Per una scienza dell'urbanistica', *L'Impero*, 3 March 1926, p. 4.

87. See Manuel Royo, 'Le temps de l'éternité, Paul Bigot et la representation de Rome antique', *Mélanges de l'école française de Rome*, 104.2 (1992), 585–610. Giuseppe Gatteschi had worked on imagined restorations of Rome from the early part of the century, publishing several works that depicted restorations of the ancient city. In his *Restauri della Roma Imperiale*, published in 1924, contemporaneous photographs were placed alongside visions of a restored cityscape, a confrontation between the height of empire and the current capital (Giuseppe Gatteschi, *Restauri della Roma Imperiale nel 310 d.C.*, 6 vols (Rome: Comitato di Azione Patriottica fra il personale postale-telegrafico-telefonico, 1924). The work was reissued, indeed, in 1931, the decision to do so explicitly linked in the work's introduction to the capital's renewal under fascism, and the publication dedicated to Mussolini rather than the king, as had been the case in 1924.

88. Caffarelli, 'Urbanistica Romana', p. 20.

89. Benito Mussolini, *Opera omnia*, ed. by Edoardo Susmel and Duilio Susmel, 35 vols (Florence: La Fenice, 1964), XXII, 47–48.

90. Ugo Ojetti, 'Il rinnovamento edilizio di Roma. Pro e contro il centro a Piazza Colonna', *Corriere della Sera*, 7 February 1926, p. 5.

91. The AACAR met to discuss the plan on 3 February, 12 February and 15 May 1926: cf. Alberto Calza Bini, 'Resoconto del Biennio', *Associazione artistica fra i cultori di architettura di Roma. Annuario* (1925–28), 67–71 (p. 69).

92. Archivio Centrale dello Stato, PCM, 1931–33, 7.2. n. 4982, Direttori dei Sindacati Romani degli Ingegneri, degli Architetti e degli Artisti to Mussolini, 23 April 1928.

93. GNAM, Fondo Ojetti, Gustavo Giovannoni, cass. 36, ins. 12, Giovannoni to Ojetti, 18 January, no year, probably after 1937.

CHAPTER 4

❖

Rome in Ruins Revisited:
Mario Soldati's *The Emerald* and
Catastrophic Futurism

Florian Mussgnug

Rome, Italy, is an example of what happens when the buildings in
a city last too long.

ANDY WARHOL[1]

Rome is unthinkable without its ruins. Their cultural influence — their ability
to trigger contemplation, meaning, affective engagement — reaches powerfully
into our present, *pace* Warhol. To bring this overdetermined, complex code to
bear on the contemporary (or a vision of the future) means to raise particular
challenges to the social, visual and discursive fields associated with the Eternal City
and, more generally, the city as such. In this chapter, I will examine catastrophic
tales of the collapse of the modern metropolis and assess their specific importance
to Italian culture in the 1970s. My discussion focuses on Mario Soldati's post-
apocalyptic novel *Lo smeraldo* (1974) [*The Emerald*], which imagines Rome as an
abandoned, radioactive wasteland.[2] Written at the height of the Cold War, *The
Emerald* captures the predicament of a deeply pessimistic age: any hope for a better
future, Soldati insinuates, is merely a passing delusion. In a world that sees itself
on the brink of destruction, there is no space for grand dreams of progress or
growth-driven consumption. Instead, Soldati's fictional future takes the shape of
a bleak, impoverished post-catastrophic world that is clearly recognisable as the
nightmarish, protracted aftermath of our own short-lived hopes. Reflecting on
the novel's immediate political and cultural context, I suggest that *The Emerald*
is best understood as an anxious contemplation of the vast transnational pressures
that shape and transform the local in an age of accelerating globalisation: political,
military and economic interests that operate on a planetary scale; weapons of
mass destruction; industrialisation; irreparable environmental degradation; human
population growth; forced mass migration; genocidal wars. Oscillating between
now (New York in the early 1970s) and then (Italy after the nuclear war), *The
Emerald* also highlights the specific temporal scale of planetary devastation: what

Rob Nixon has appositely called 'the temporal topography of fear'.[3] Catastrophe, in Soldati's novel, unfolds slowly — over time, but across space as well — and erodes a rich, historically textured landscape shaped by the interaction between communities, across generations, and between humans and non-humans within their specific, shared environment.[4]

Soldati's harrowing vision of Rome in ruins reflects contemporaneous fears about the decline of the modern city. The twentieth-century metropolis, for Soldati and for his contemporaries, is no longer a space filled with immeasurable promise, but a harbinger of doom that epitomises the fatal interconnectedness of major risks. In the first part of my chapter, I will map this new perception of the city through a close reading of Roberto Vacca's *Il medioevo prossimo venturo: la degradazione dei grandi sistemi* (1971) [*The Coming Dark Age*].[5] Vacca's prediction of the collapse of the city, I argue, is echoed, in more recent years, by environmental philosophers, ecocritics and risk analysists. Attention to shifting geographies of power is also prominent in the social sciences, where scholars have moved away from the idea that authority radiates from a stable centre — a political capital, the headquarters of a business corporation, a financial centre or an entire 'global city' — and is exercised outwards and downwardly, within the limits of a clearly circumscribed territory.[6] As geographer John Allen notes, the modern era was largely defined by the experience of blunt forms of coercion and constraint, associated with unprecedented levels of state violence, whereas more recent decades have seen the emergence of less palpable and strident but similarly pervasive registers of power: *intensive* power relations that shape our lives less overtly but no less radically than the *extensive* ties that link us topographically to traditional centres of authority.[7]

My discussion of *The Coming Dark Age* and *The Emerald* suggests that such shifts occurred long before the beginning of the twenty-first century and especially, as we will see, during the Cold War era. My chapter thus presents a cultural-historical perspective on the 'death of the city', as it was experienced and recorded by artists and cultural commentators in the 1970s. As literary theorist Roland Végsö has argued, atomic holocaust fiction of the period evokes two simultaneous and conflicting images: the globe as a terrain of infinite political possibilities ('mass utopia') and the planet as an intrinsically threatened totality (the notorious view of Earth from space, as a fragile *Blue Marble*).[8] Between them, these two diverging notions of 'the world' contributed to erode the cultural significance of earlier symbols of sovereignty, especially at the national level. Soldati's novel, as I will show, captures this vertiginous transformation of symbolic space through the eyes of a temporally displaced narrator-protagonist, who belongs simultaneously to the author's present and to an unspecified, post-catastrophic (and post-national) future. In this context, the vanishing significance of traditional, geographic centres of power *over time* is specifically evoked by Soldati's disturbing vision of the 'eternal city' in ruins.

The final part of my chapter focuses on Soldati's description of Rome and on the ruin as a marker of epistemological uncertainty, thus echoing Walter Benjamin's famous assertion that 'Allegorien sind im Reiche der Gedanken was Ruinen im

Reiche der Dinge' [allegories are, in the realm of thoughts, what ruins are in the realm of things].[9] The figure of the ruin, I suggest, acts as a powerful marker of paradoxical temporality: it affirms the importance of linear time — catastrophe as 'the end of history' — but also draws attention to a natural cycle, dominated by disaster, death and decay. *The Emerald* thus evokes the contrast between what Benjamin calls 'homogenous empty time' — the featureless, calendrical time across which progressive history supposedly marches forward — and the intimate, interlocking temporalities of the emotions: nostalgia, regret, forecast, desire.[10]

Writing from the perspective of comparative literature, I argue that such juxtapositions of different temporalities are necessarily culture-specific and linked to particular geographic, historical and linguistic contexts. Interestingly, this focus on cultural specificity and different temporalities has not featured prominently in recent debates about power and space. Allen's study, for example, privileges global perspectives and foregrounds the growing importance of supranational networks and planetary threats ranging from forced mass migration to climate change, but pays little attention to alternative voices and to the experience of those whose lives are arguably less affected by new technologies. My specific focus on Italy — a self-perceived 'periphery' in Cold War political geography — thus serves to decentre supposedly 'global' approaches that are primarily defined through North American and Northern European experience and that privilege broadly 'Western' perspectives on other regions. In this respect, my article builds on recent, important research in Cold War studies which aspires, in Andrew Hammond's words, to 'compare literary output in various regions, teasing out an overarching set of concerns and aesthetic values, while at all times remaining aware of local faiths, practices and histories'.[11] As cultural historians of the Cold War have argued, some of the most interesting and fertile perspectives on mid-twentieth-century politics and society emerged far from the presumed centres of political, cultural and military power and were overtly critical of the paradigmatic idea of a single, global conflict and of the expansive, abstract geographies associated with a seemingly bipolar world.[12] Once again, Soldati's novel is particularly relevant here, since it explicitly addresses Italy's geopolitical status and the devastating effects of Cold War globalisation.

Waiting for the Coming Dark Age

First published by Arnoldo Mondadori in 1974, Mario Soldati's *The Emerald* is one of the earliest works of post-apocalyptic fiction in Italian, written at a time when novels with a future setting were still uncommon in Italy, especially outside the specific context of genre literature in translation.[13] Despite Elsa Morante's famous appeal to the novelist, in 1965, to resist the species' 'occulta tentazione di disintegrarsi' [obscure longing for self-annihilation] and to become 'un uomo a cui sta a cuore tutto quanto accade fuorché la letteratura' [a person who cares about everything that happens except literature], explicit and extensive literary treatments of nuclear Armageddon did not appear until the early 1970s, when doomsday fiction acquired a sudden, unprecedented popularity in Italy.[14] During the decade that followed, descriptions of global nuclear war and its aftermath featured in over a dozen novels in Italian, including Paolo Volponi's *Corporale* [*Corporal*, 1974] and *Il pianeta irritabile* [*The Irritable Planet*, 1978], Salvatore Satta's *Il giorno del giudizio* [*Judgement Day*, 1977], Antonio Porta's *Il re del magazzino* [*King of the Warehouse*, 1978], Carlo Cassola's so-called 'atomic trilogy' (1978–82) and Elsa Morante's *Aracoeli* (1982). Many of these stories, as Bruno Pischedda has shown, captured a specifically Italian mood of pessimism, which spread through the nation in the 1970s and which, according to Pischedda, had its most immediate causes in the aberrations of uncontrolled urban growth, environmental degradation and the excesses of property speculation.[15] Fears about political tensions and right-wing and left-wing terrorism also played a major role, but not all worries about the future originated at the national level.[16] The stock market crash of 1973 and the subsequent oil crisis, for instance, had profound effects on the daily lives of Italians, who were forced to come to terms with unprecedented austerity measures including traffic restrictions and the dimming of street lights. Meanwhile, the risk of global atomic war remained a source of great concern. The presence of American nuclear weapons in Western Europe had prompted political controversy since the mid-1950s, when missiles with nuclear warheads were first installed in Northern Italy, but debates grew more heated during the 1970s, in response to American plans to deploy enhanced radiation weapons, better known as 'the neutron bomb'.[17] While Italian pacifists and left-wing politicians raged against 'the inhuman bomb', India's first successful nuclear bomb test in May 1974 shattered many people's hopes about the long-term efficiency of the global Non-Proliferation Treaty that had entered into force only four years earlier.

Apocalyptic fears dominated everyday life, not only in literature, as shown by the extraordinary success of Roberto Vacca's bleak, popular-scientific bestseller *Il medioevo prossimo venturo* [*The Coming Dark Age*, 1971], which shares some interesting similarities with Soldati's post-apocalyptic novel. Vacca, a Roman electrical engineer and expert in industrial control systems, began his career as a science-fiction writer in the mid-1960s with the novel *Il robot e il minotauro* [*The Robot and the Minotaur*, 1963], but achieved national and international fame only in the early 1970s when he prophesied a complete breakdown of communication, traffic and utility networks across the Western world. Despite his technical expertise and life-long, passionate defence of scientific research, Vacca's popularity thus reflected a characteristically Italian scepticism about technological progress which Pierpaolo Antonello, drawing from Paolo Rossi, has associated with the figure of the 'teorico dell'apocalisse' [apocalyptic theorist].[18] The 'coming dark age' of Vacca's proverbial title is in fact imagined as a combined result of rapid population growth, urbanisation and unmonitored technological progress, which eventually lead to widespread system failure and a collapse of all essential infrastructures. The end of the modern world, Vacca claims, will not be the result of military action or climate change — which he surprisingly dismisses as a relatively minor risk — but will be brought about by the brittle and overburdened 'large systems' of advanced capitalist societies.[19] Drawing his examples from contemporaneous events — including the infamous north-east blackout of 1965 — Vacca draws attention to a variety of risk factors: urban sprawl will paralyse traffic networks (67–84); increasing global demand for water and electricity will lead to dramatic shortages (57–66); military defence systems are not adequately controlled (127–32); international telecommunication networks depend on outdated technologies (85–98); automated production systems are supervised by incompetent managers (142–51); and so on. Vacca's seemingly endless list of grievances foments a generally pessimistic view of Western industrialised society. Local system failure, for Vacca, is not a worst-case scenario but an immanent condition of the present, and global catastrophe must be imagined as a set of intersecting and mutually reinforcing calamities: a chain reaction triggered by a seemingly minor mishap that culminates in widespread chaos, violence, disease and death.

More than forty years after its first publication, Vacca's melodramatic vision of a post-apocalyptic, 'neo-medieval' society plunged into poverty, political anarchy and religious superstition may seem fanciful. His demand that scientists form quasi-monastic orders appears, with hindsight, like a timely homage to the imaginative traditions of Cold War speculative fiction.[20] *The Coming Dark Age* is rife with reactionary and xenophobic overtones that appear obviously problematic today. The Chinese, for example, are imagined as the new 'Goths, Pannonian Avars or Huns' (21), but South East Asia is also seen as the site of a potential second Renaissance (125). Environmentalists are dismissed as squeamish and unrealistic, while the student protests of 1968 are viewed as futile, naïve and involuntarily complicit with authoritarian regimes (133–35). Conjectures like these, and Vacca's recklessly specific forecast that the new dark age will begin 'between 1985 and 1995' (158), make his book obviously dated. Nevertheless, Vacca's attention to the potentially catastrophic interconnection of technologies, exchanges and movements continues to speak powerfully to our own cultural present, and resonates in interesting, uncanny ways with the reflections of contemporary environmental thinkers. The Belgian philosopher of science Isabelle Stengers, for instance, has repeatedly warned that the future may herald the rise of a new 'barbaric age' of genocidal wars fought over diminishing resources.[21] In a different, but closely related context, Vacca's preoccupation with 'large systems' now recalls Timothy Morton's definition of the *hyperobject*, and is echoed by Jean-Luc Nancy's more recent reflections on 'the equivalence of catastrophes' and 'the spread or proliferation of repercussions from every kind of disaster'.[22] Analysts of global risk have similarly warned against the specific dangers associated with interconnection. The *Global Risks Report*, for instance — published annually by the World Economic Forum — features an 'interconnections map' that now details thirty major risks. At least two — 'failure of urban planning' and 'breakdown of critical information infrastructure' — will look frighteningly familiar to Vacca's readers.[23]

The continued relevance of Vacca's approach is particularly evident in a brief central chapter — 'La congiura dei sistemi urbani' [The conspiracy of urban systems] (118–26) — which imagines, in surprisingly prosaic terms, the unfolding of a major catastrophe from an unfortunate coincidence of seemingly minor calamities. A railway accident in New York causes large, paralysing traffic jams; streets are blocked by abandoned vehicles; air traffic controllers cannot be relieved; their fatigue results in a mid-air collision; planes fall on a network of power lines; without electricity, people freeze (it is January) and whole buildings are destroyed when improvised fires get out of hand. Violence escalates as the city remains isolated for days; disease breaks out and spreads to other parts of the country, where the local population lacks the expertise of the metropolitan elites and struggles to respond adequately to the unfolding emergency. The collapse of the modern metropolis thus triggers a wider crisis, in which people lose faith in the supposedly demiurgic powers of modern technology and global connectedness. The survivors of the first cataclysm are painfully aware of the enormous rift between humanity's cosmopolitical aspirations and its tragic helplessness in a situation of real, collective emergency. For the generation that follows, psychological and political space has become, once again, coextensive with the archaic confines of the clan or the city state. 'Ovviamente, il supersistema — nel quale configuriamo oggi la società — non sarà fra i superstiti', writes Vacca, 'ma si frazionerà in molti piccoli sistemi scarsamente comunicanti fra loro, autarchici e dotati di una certa stabilità' (124) [Of course, the super-system, which we now evoke to define society, will not survive, but will break up into many small poorly interconnected systems, autarchic and endowed with some stability].

Vacca's imaginary North American catastrophe is presented as a *forecast* — the author leaves no doubt that these events *will happen* and that their occurrence is only a matter of time — but is perhaps better understood as a *scenario*: a plausible fiction about a possible, but not inevitable, near future. As the German critic Eva Horn has argued in her recent, important study of modern and contemporary attitudes towards the future, the scenario is arguably *the* most distinctive cultural form to emerge from the early Cold War period, where it is exemplified, for instance, by Herman Kahn's *On Thermonuclear War* (1960) and *Thinking about the Unthinkable* (1962).[24] Unlike earlier forms of prophetic writing, the scenario does not claim to represent a known future, but embraces the uncertainty of the modern age and its increasing attention to quantitative methods. Kahn's oeuvre, for example, contains a variety of different *possible* futures, which are *narrated* in horrifying detail but nevertheless presented as hypotheses: the potential consequences of difficult, impending military-strategic decisions.[25] The new genre of the scenario thus combines the conventions of the philosophical thought experiment and the imaginative traditions of speculative writing.[26] It evokes complex fictional worlds, which are supposed to trigger empathy and concern, and thereby serve to prompt urgent political action. According to Horn, the scenario does not only mark a shift in generic conventions, it also creates a new popular audience, with a specific interest in future catastrophe, and thus gives literature a new, unprecedented social relevance. If we accept this argument, it should not come as a surprise that many contemporary novelists have explored possible futures that closely resemble Vacca's vision of metropolitan catastrophe. Nathaniel Rich's *Odds against Tomorrow* (2014), for example, takes place among the flooded ruins of a New York that has recently been hit by a major hurricane. Similarly — but closer, perhaps, to Vacca's original intent — Amitav Ghosh's long essay *The Great Derangement* (2016) offers a frighteningly detailed description of how Mumbai's nearly 12 million inhabitants would be affected by a Category 4 or 5 cyclone.[27]

The Exploding City

Unlike Vacca's monograph, *The Emerald* appears entirely at ease with the new epistemological and narrative conventions of Cold War futurology. Where the author of *The Coming Dark Age* dons the uncomfortable vests of a modern-day Cassandra, warning against the inevitable, Mario Soldati presents his post-apocalyptic novel as a vertiginous play with past experiences, imagined catastrophes and desired futures, or as Pier Paolo Pasolini put it, '[un] gioco [...] tra i più belli inventati nella letteratura italiana di questi anni' [one of the most beautiful games invented by an Italian writer in recent years].[28] *The Emerald*, in the words of its author, 'poteva anche essere un libro di fantascienza' [might have been a science-fiction novel] but ended up taking the shape of a 'sogno del sogno' [dream within a dream], bursting with hidden and explicit references to Soldati's most intimate, existential concerns: 'il problema dei figli, l'amore-dominazione, l'omosessualità' [worries about the children, love as domination, homosexuality].[29]

Soldati, as Stefano Ghidinelli has shown, originally conceived of *The Emerald* as a work of regular futuristic fiction in the tradition of Jack London's *The Scarlet Plague* (1912) but subsequently opted for a Cold War satire, embedded in a complex, often self-contradictory oneiric narrative.[30] Only the book's two opening chapters are set in the author's present; the rest of the novel consists of a long dream vision, in which Soldati's alter ego finds himself embodied in the twenty-first-century painter Andrea Tellarini ('Un po' ero Tellarini e un po' non lo ero' (126) [Partly I was Tellarini and partly I wasn't] (135)). As this future self soon discovers, Northern Italy, where he lives, has become part of an international military dictatorship, dominated by Russia and the United States. Decades earlier, during a brief but devastating thermonuclear war, atomic weapons were used to create 'the Line': a radioactive no man's land, some 250 miles wide, which spans the globe and separates the technologically advanced North from a much poorer South. Tellarini also discovers that he has inherited an emerald of enormous value, which he cannot sell in the North, where trade has been abolished. His only hope is to reach Southern Italy, which after the war has become part of a decadent feudal empire, controlled by corrupt, ferocious princes and sheiks. Together with his son Dédé, the elderly painter decides to cross the Line by bicycle, hoping that the radioactivity has now reached a level that bears no immediate threat to human beings.

Soldati's reluctance to describe *The Emerald* as a work of science fiction implies a narrow understanding of the genre, which is confirmed by his claim, in 1974, that 'La fantascienza ha basi razionali, direi quasi scientifiche' [science fiction has a rational, almost scientific basis].[31] Dismissive attitudes towards science fiction were surprisingly widespread among early Italian authors of post-apocalyptic literature, but Soldati's extensive experience as television and film director — ranging from award-winning collaborations with Giorgio Bassani, Pier Paolo Pasolini and Ennio Flaiano to numerous adventure and comedy action films — suggests that he was less prejudiced against mass entertainment than many of his peers.[32] Soldati's fascination with dream narrative must hence be understood, above all, as a critique of normative futurology and as the expression of an anti-deterministic, open attitude towards the future. What matters, for the author of *The Emerald*, is not the future as a reliable horizon, but our ability to conjure fears and desires that reveal our most profound affective ties in the present: our relation with our loved ones — including, importantly, our children — and with the rich natural and cultural world we inhabit.

Written in less than a year, *The Emerald* evokes Soldati's mostly negative impressions of the United States during a visit to Berkeley in 1973, which left the writer, as he put it, 'angosciato pensando ai miei figli' [distressed when I think about my children].[33] The novel opens with a description of contemporary New York that bears a striking resemblance to the apocalyptic city described in *The Coming Dark Age*. Like Vacca, Soldati sees the United States in a phase of social decline, which forebodes trouble for the rest of the word, and especially for Western Europe. During a stroll on Fifth Avenue, Soldati's protagonist accidentally meets a mysterious, elderly gentleman, Count Cagliani, who invites him to his home for dinner. When he decides to accept the invitation, the narrator finds himself trapped in a nightmarish, nocturnal metropolis, which is entirely unlike the familiar, cinematic visions of contemporary New York — Soldati cites William Friedkin's *The French Connection* (1971) — but rather resembles the terrifying setting of Richard Fleischer's neo-Malthusian science fiction thriller *Soylent Green* (1973):

> Oggi il subway di New York è un luogo di angoscia e di orrore. Non *French Connection*, mi viene in mente intanto che mi addentro e calo sempre più nel labirinto dei sudici, consunti ipogei incastrati l'uno sotto l'altro, intanto che avanzo tra una folla scarmigliata, affannata, vociante: mi viene in mente *2000, i sopravvissuti*, recente film che descrive un atroce futuro per gli States. (14–15)

> [The New York subway today is a place of horror and anguish. It isn't *The French Connection* I'm reminded of, as I go inside and sink deeper and deeper into the maze of filthy, worn catacombs, set one below the other, as I advance through a dishevelled, breathless, noisy crowd: I am reminded of *Soylent Green*, a film that describes a ghastly future for the States.] (16)

Endless traffic jams, overcrowded, mouldering subway stations and scruffy, hostile strangers, who are seemingly unable to communicate in English: Soldati's fictional New York foments contemporaneous fears about uncontrolled human population growth, famines and forced mass migration, which are also associated with a tragic breakdown of cultural traditions.[34] Obscene graffiti on the walls and trains of the New York subway appear to Soldati's narrator like funereal arabesques from 'un futuro post-apocalittico' [a post-apocalyptic future] (16/15) or contemporary versions of Michelangelo's *Last Judgement*. The oppressive sense of an imminent catastrophe is also emphasised by Soldati's decision to refer to Fleischer's dystopian thriller by its more graphic and alarmist Italian title: *2000: i sopravvissuti* (literally: '2000: the survivors').

Like *Soylent Green* — and like Harry Harrison's novel *Make Room! Make Room!* (1966) which inspired the film — *The Emerald* imagines a global catastrophe brought about by overpopulation. Yet where Fleischer and Harrison play with fears about uncontrolled human population growth, Soldati speculates about the consequences of a brutal crackdown. In *Soylent Green*, the New York of 2020 appears like a decaying megalopolis inhabited by more than 40 million people, who are forced to feed on each other's carcasses. Soldati, by contrast, describes population growth — from the perspective of the novel's hypothetical future — as a problem of the past. , reading from an alleged twentieth-century text, Soldati's fictional twenty-first-century Russian notary Griniev recites: 'The human wave striking our planet has assumed frightening proportions. Every day more than three hundred and fifty thousand new babies appear on earth (130–31/141) ['L'ondata di uomini che sta investendo il nostro pianeta ha raggiunto paurose proporzioni: ogni giorno compaiono sulla terra oltre 350.000 nuovi bimbi']. The fictional dystopia of *The Emerald* imagines the state's brutal response to this real emergence: a desolate and impoverished world controlled — in the industrialised North — by a global dictatorship, which controls population growth through mass sterilisations, allows no contact between children and their biological parents, keeps people segregated in derelict, rural areas, and has outlawed freedom of movement. Moreover, the radioactive wasteland ('The Line') has been created specifically to prevent mass migrations from the South, where — as Tellarini is told — central government was not powerful enough to control exponential population growth.

The Empty City

In the fictional world of *The Emerald*, sovereign power is absolute, not only for those living under the Northern military dictatorship, but also in the feudal tyrannies of the South. 'The Line', which violently cuts the globe (and Italy) into two unequal parts, serves as a stark reminder of what we may call, in Carl Schmitt's terms, the *nomos*: the form in which the political and social order becomes spatially visible, and the ultimate expression of the state's right to order to their death the very citizens in whose name it rules.[35] Tellarini first grasps the geopolitical order of Soldati's bipolar, post-apocalyptic earth when he looks at a world map in Griniev's study, yet when he finally manages, after a long journey, to approach 'the Line', his perception of the symbolic boundary between North and South is subtly transformed. Roaming the woods near Grosseto, he encounters grumpy peasants and an eccentric aristocrat, for whom 'the Line' is not an abstract demarcation but a bewildering and terrifying habitat: a 'wild zone' threatened by the lethal, invisible scourge of radioactivity, in which humans and non-human animals live in freedom, but survive only by chance.[36]

On stolen bicycles, father and son escape the control of the American military headquarters in Siena and flee the bureaucratic, militarised society of the North:

a seemingly endless sequence of barracks, oppressively functionalistic urban con-
glomerates and near-identical army guesthouses (the 'PI 14' in Pisa, the 'SI 5' in
Siena, and so on). Near Viterbo — where levels of radioactivity, as it turns out, are
no longer fatal — 'the zone' features a very different kind of scenery: rolling hills
and abandoned hamlets that look peaceful and even picturesque.

> La disgregazione delle case in mattoni non ha un aspetto così atroce [...]. La
> pietra, infine, la pietra delle vecchie case e delle chiese rivestite di edera, può
> anche avvincere la fantasia: come se prima o poi avesse dovuto incontrare quel
> destino, assumere quella vaghezza sepolcrale e quella malinconia piranesiana.
> (175).

> [The disintegration of brick houses does not look so atrocious [...]. Stone,
> finally, the ivy-covered stone of the old houses and churches, can actually
> bewitch the imagination: as if sooner or later, it was destined to undergo that
> fate, to assume that sepulchral charm and that Piranesi melancholy.] (190)

Northern Lazio is a world without humans, but any sense of loss is fully sublimated
in Soldati's text. Tellarini's laconic description of the small ghost town of Acqua-
pendente makes no mention of suffering and barely acknowledges the bodies of
the dead ('i rimasugli dei poveri cadaveri della terza guerra mondiale parevano
misteriosamente scomparsi' [the poor remains of the Third World War corpses
seemed mysteriously to have disappeared] (176/190)). Ancient ruins are not a marker
of apocalyptic violence, but evoke the deep aesthetic and affective ties associated
with what Rob Nixon calls 'vernacular landscapes': 'historically textured maps that
communities have devised over generations, maps replete with names and routes,
maps alive to significant ecological and surface geological features'.[37] Frozen in
time, the historical villages of central Italy, to Tellarini's delight, have been saved
by catastrophe from the aberrations of modernity — the 'official landscape' of
industrialisation, uncontrolled urban planning and Cold War politics. 'Il passaggio
dei satelliti non sembrava avesse mutato l'aspetto grandioso, barocco e romantico
di questi luoghi: forse lo aveva esaltato e portato alla sua perfezione' [The satellites'
passage seemed not to have changed the grandiose, baroque, and romantic aspect
of these places: perhaps it had exalted that appearance, brought it to its perfection]
(182/197).

The collapsed shapes of modern buildings, by contrast, defy every sense of
proportion and harmony. Iron and concrete bear the traces of thermonuclear
violence, which for Soldati is emblematic of the devastating powers of globalisation.
When Tellarini and his son arrive at the first modern town in 'the zone', the painter
feels dwarfed by powers greater than himself: the rhythm of his remarks turns into
an anxious, rushed *staccato*; his perception is fragmentary; he flees, without even the
small consolation of 'taking a last look' and giving a meaning, however transient,
to the sites of destruction.[38]

> Il ferro e il cemento, forse perché più resistenti, sembravano esplosi dall'interno:
> putrelle, profilati, tondini si levavano aguzzi, arrugginiti, contorti fino al cielo;
> e i blocchi biancastri di calce, qua sbocconcellati o polverizzati, là interi ma
> corrosi e spugnosi come una lebbra, erano ammonticchiati nelle più varie forme,

nelle più bizzarre combinazioni, in una scenografia involontaria dell'angoscia, in uno spasimo della catastrofe, durato pochi istanti e immobilizzato per sempre (175).

[Iron and cement, perhaps because they are stronger, seemed to have exploded from within: girders, iron, sections, rods, sharp, rusting, twisted, jutted into the sky; and the white blocks of cement, chipped or pulverised, or whole but corroded and porous as if with some leprosy, were piled in the most various shapes, in the most bizarre combinations, in an accidental, anguished stage-set, the spasm of a catastrophe that had lasted a few moments and was frozen forever.] (189)

Soldati's opulent, baroque style and his gloomy theme harmonise to perfection. Yet, unexpectedly, even this haunting description of terminal violence reveals traces of self-conscious theatricality, in the manner of an extended 'dream within a dream'. Tellarini — a former filmmaker, like the author of The Emerald — looks at the terrifying ruins of World War Three and is reminded of a *scenografia*: a stage set (as William Weaver translates it) or, perhaps more appropriately, a film set. Seen through the (imaginary) eye of the camera, the remnants of catastrophe do not evoke fear, but present themselves to the reader in the shape of what Susan Stewart famously describes as 'the miniature': a fictional world, clearly limited in space and time, and reassuringly distant — either in the style of Giovanni Battista Piranesi's *Vedute di Roma* or in the manner of a modern disaster film.[39]

As the travellers get closer to Rome, Soldati's narrator is increasingly reminded of 'his' years in the Italian capital, 'senza accorgermi di istituire in quel momento un'illusoria retrospettiva continuità tra Tellarini e me stesso' [without realising I was setting up at that moment an illusory, retrospective continuity between Tellarini and myself] (184/200). Places and objects now trigger rich personal memories, which were largely absent from the first half of the novel, and which are welcomed by the narrator with a mixture of surprise, excitement and regret about the passing of time. The coherence of Soldati's dream-vision begins to evaporate, as Tellarini's thoughts are drawn back to events that are clearly marked as belonging to the author of The Emerald. In Galleria, for example, the elderly painter proudly points out that he visited the archaeological site, many years earlier, to direct a Napoleonic costume film: a thinly veiled allusion to one of Soldati's more commercially successful projects, *Donne e briganti* [Of Love and Bandits, 1950]. Instead of foregrounding the linearity imposed by the post-apocalyptic storyline — nuclear war as the necessary and inevitable destiny of contemporary society — The Emerald thus examines the intimate links between spaces, memories and emotions, and between past, present and future: 'affective histories', as Dipesh Chakrabarty puts it, which can be explored in multiple directions and 'evoke a loving grasp of detail in search of an understanding of the diversity of life'.[40]

Soldati's description of Rome, in the eighth chapter of the novel, relies strongly on the interlocking and conflicting temporalities of nostalgic recollection and apocalyptic forecast. Under the full moon, father and son ride their bicycles through a seemingly unearthly landscape, an endless expanse of white rubble, glowing in mysterious light. The chapter title, 'Le Rane' [The Frogs], is an evident allusion to Aristophanes, and the mood and tone of Soldati's prose mark this section as an otherworldly journey: the adventures of a twenty-first-century Dionysus and his youthful Xanthias on their way to Hades. Tellarini is exhausted, feels lost and has given up all hope. But just as he complains that they will never find their way back to the coast, he suddenly spots, among the ruins, an unmistakable landmark:

> L'Isola Tiberina con le rovine dell'Ospedale Fatebenefratelli e della chiesa di San Bartolomeo, l'Isola Tiberina, lunga e ventruta come la carcassa di un gigantesco alligatore rimasta in mezzo al fiume. [...] Fissavo adesso, al di là del fiume, qualcosa che era ancora più inconfondibile e decisivo dell'Isola Tiberina: l'argentea cupola a padiglione della Sinagoga, l'unico edificio, in quella immensità di macerie, non distrutto. [...] Brillava isolata tra le rovine confuse, intatta nel suo splendore appannato, tranquilla come la luna che la illuminava. (191)

> [Isola Tiberina, with the ruins of the Fatebenefratelli hospital and the Church of San Bartolomeo; Isola Tiberina, long and potbellied like the carcass of a gigantic alligator left in the middle of the river [...]. Now I was staring at something beyond the river, something even more unmistakable than the Isola Tiberina: the silvery dome of the synagogue, the only building not destroyed in that immensity of ruins. [...] It shone, isolated among the confused ruins, intact in its opaque splendor, calm as the moon that illuminated it.] (205–08)

The Great Synagogue of Rome is the only surviving construction in an empty city that has otherwise been reduced to a featureless wasteland. Its unexpected appearance in one of the novel's most dramatic scenes creates, for the discerning reader, a sense of place and perspective: she may even recall historical photographs of the inauguration of the synagogue in 1904, which show the impressive new building amidst the ruins of the demolished Roman ghetto.[41] Soldati's narrator, by contrast, is disoriented and overwhelmed by the sudden realisation that this vast tableau of death marks his own destiny: the insignificance and pointlessness of his entire life. Staring at the desolation that stretches all the way to the horizon, the time-travelling dreamer experiences a sense of vertigo, in which the overlapping temporalities of national history, personal memory and post-apocalyptic future come to collide. The ruins of Rome are not only portents of catastrophe; they also remind Tellarini that death and loss are always inevitably part of the human predicament. Once again, the narrator's thoughts drift back to the places of his youth — the bookstall at the corner of Tor de' Specchi; the little flower shop in Piazzetta Cairoli; and so on — but this time, such memories of past happiness offer no consolation: 'Anni e anni perduti in sciocchezze, in desideri volgari, in illusioni di facili guadagni e di piaceri facilissimi [...]', laments Soldati: 'Sì, avevo gettato la mia giovinezza credendo di salvarla' [Years and years wasted on nonsense, vulgar desires, illusions of easy money and easy pleasure, [...] I had thrown away my youth thinking to save it] (191–92/208). By superimposing the fears, remorse and regret of at least two individuals — the elderly painter, the unnamed first-person narrator and, arguably, the author himself — Soldati exacerbates the sense of a tragic, obsessive fascination with the past, which fails to protect against the certainty of death and the terrible apprehension of a catastrophic future.

The day after, when Tellarini contemplates Rome again from the top of the Quirinal Hill, he can no longer make out any familiar landmarks:

> Cercavo invano i fastigi di Palazzo Colonna e dei Santi Apostoli, che avrei dovuto vedere vicinissimi, le cupole e il campanile di San Carlo al Corso, Montecitorio, Palazzo Venezia, Palazzo della Giustizia, Castel Sant'Angelo, il Colosseo: niente, niente, neanche del cupolone di San Pietro scorgevo la minima riconoscibile traccia [...]: un oceano pietrificato, di stalagmiti, di pinnacoli, di creste, di guglie informi, di contorni slabbrati, sdentati, disordinati, convulsi, neri contro il fuoco radioso del tramonto, o appena orlati di rosa. (218)

> [I sought in vain for the copings of Piazza Colonna and the Church of the Santi Apostoli, which I should have been able to see very near, the domes and spire of San Carlo al Corso, Montecitorio, Palazzo Venezia, the Palace of Justice, Castel Sant'Angelo, the Colosseum: nothing, nothing at all. I couldn't discern the slightest trace even of the great dome of St. Peter's [...]: a petrified ocean of stalagmites, pinnacles, peaks, misshapen spires, jagged edges, cracked, disordered, convulsed, black against the radiant fire of the sunset, or barely outlined in pink.] (235–36)

Tellarini's last view of the eternal city, in plain daylight, captures an experience of terrible magnitude: the encounter with a raw force that exceeds our powers of rational comprehension, triggering a complex mix of terror and awe. And yet, Soldati's image of an immense, featureless ocean of stone is also oddly reassuring. It evokes a timeless, panoptic awareness of catastrophe: a simultaneous and comprehensive vision that beholds the causes of violent devastation, its manifestations and its effects. Significantly, the scene contains no trace of existential anxiety, remorse or dread: apocalypse has become an object of aesthetic contemplation. The wasteland that spreads out before Tellarini is real, but the painter — poised like an archetypal 'last man' at the edge of a cliff — can safely enjoy the sublime spectacle, from a physical and emotional distance.[42]

This is not the end of Soldati's novel. Tellarini succeeds in crossing 'the zone', reaches Naples, enters an ambivalent homosexual relationship with a younger man from Malta, falls under the spell of the *femme fatale* Mariolina, and becomes the victim of a complicated intrigue, which takes him back to the ruins of Rome. Finally, he hopes to be reunited with his son, but when he reaches the empty city, he discovers to his horror that young Dédé has been killed, his mutilated body left in plain sight among the ruins. 'Avevo visto quello che non avrei mai voluto vedere' [I had seen what I would never have wanted to see] (313/343), declares Tellarini, and yet he cannot avert his eyes from the gory scene and from the monstrously impassive ruins that surround it. The lifeless shape at the centre of the silent square is the one figure who, during the whole course of the novel, had come to embody the narrator's hope for a better future, beyond his own death. Dédé is the very image of the vital and optimistic youth, whose simple presence seemed enough to dispel forebodings about war, catastrophic population growth and social collapse.[43] The tragic ending of *The Emerald* thus captures and makes manifest a profound anxiety, which — as we have seen — played a constitutive role in the conception of the novel: the fear that our children may not survive us.[44] But Soldati's conclusion also highlights, once again, the traumatic force of absolute power, which is epitomised by 'the Line'. Violence, as Soldati reminds us, is constitutive of every community, culture and subjectivity: it is coextensive with youth, and with life itself. Soldati's brief Latin epilogue, 'In senectute salus | in juventute jugum' (317/346) must therefore be read as bitterly ironic. Youth is a yoke, but the alleged safety of old age is only frailty, the fading of life. In this sense, then, a complete negation of violence can only be imagined, in Soldati's novel, as a melancholy, post-apocalyptic, empty city: a lifeless and timeless monument to atrocity. Rome in ruins, for the brief duration of Tellarini's sojourn, appears like such a place of tragic closure: a dead world, in which the forward move of time has come to a halt. But Soldati's abrupt and tragic ending takes us beyond the idea of a definitive 'end of history'. With every new generation — with every human life — violence returns with renewed, terrible force, leaving Soldati's ageing protagonists literally speechless. Tellarini is shocked into silence, and the first-person narrator wakes up from his long dream, screaming. The ruins of Rome, however, which appeared like a definitive marker of terminal catastrophe, may now come alive again, overflowing once more with brutal, outrageous vitality.

Notes to Chapter 4

1. Andy Warhol, *The Philosophy of Andy Warhol: From A to B and Back Again* (London and New York: Penguin, 2007), p. 156.
2. All page references in the text will be to the following editions: Mario Soldati, *Lo smeraldo*, intr. by Valerio Evangelisti, notes by Stefano Ghidinelli (Milan: Mondadori, 2008); *The Emerald*, trans. by William Weaver (New York and London: Harcourt, 1977).
3. Rob Nixon, *Slow Violence and the Environmentalism of the Poor* (Cambridge, MA, and London: Harvard University Press, 2011), p. 46.
4. In the Italian context, this approach to human habitat resonates with Franco Arminio's 'paesologia'. Cf. especially Franco Arminio, *Terracarne: Viaggio nei paesi invisibili e nei paesi giganti del Sud Italia* (Milan: Mondadori, 2011). For a more general overview of the recent Italian interest in landscape, environment and heritage, see Serenella Iovino, *Ecocriticism and Italy: Ecology, Resistance and Liberation* (London: Bloomsbury, 2016).
5. Roberto Vacca, *Il medioevo prossimo venturo: la degradazione dei grandi sistemi* (Milan: Mondadori, 1971); *The Coming Dark Age*, trans. by J. S. Whale (Garden City, NY: Doubleday, 1973).
6. See especially Neil Brenner, *New State Spaces: Urban Governance and the Rescaling of Statehood* (Oxford: Oxford University Press, 2004); Saskia Sassen, *Territory, Authority, Rights: From Medieval to Global Assemblages* (Princeton and Oxford: Princeton University Press, 2006); Bob Jessop, *State Power* (Cambridge: Polity, 2007); Stuart Elden, *Terror and Territory: The Spatial Extent of Sovereignty* (Minneapolis: University of Minnesota Press, 2009).
7. See John Allen, *Topologies of Power: Beyond Territory and Networks* (New York: Routledge, 2016).
8. Roland Végső, *The Naked Communist: Cold War Modernism and the Politics of Popular Culture* (New York: Fordham University Press, 2013), pp. 111–17. See also Susan Buck-Morss, *Dreamworld and Catastrophe: The Passing of Mass Utopia in East and West* (Cambridge, MA, and London: MIT Press, 2000); Kelly Oliver, *Earth and World: Philosophy after the Apollo Missions* (New York: Columbia University Press, 2015).
9. Walter Benjamin, *Ursprung des Deutschen Trauerspiels* [1928], (Berlin: Hofenberg, 2016), p. 156; English translation by John Osborne: *The Origin of German Tragic Drama* (London: Verso, 1977), p. 178. For an overview of the rich cultural debate about ruins, see *Ruins of Modernity*, ed. by Julia Hell and Andreas Schönle (Durham, NC and London: Duke University Press, 2010).

10. Walter Benjamin, 'Theses on the Philosophy of History' [1940], in Benjamin, *Illuminations*, ed. by Hannah Arendt, trans. by Harry Zohn (New York: Schocken, 1968), pp. 253–64 (p. 261); annotated German edition: 'Über den Begriff der Geschichte', in *Gesammelte Schriften*, vol. 1.2, 691–704. For an extensive discussion of this contrast, see Elizabeth Freeman, *Time Binds: Queer Temporalities, Queer Histories* (Durham, NC and London: Duke University Press, 2010).

11. *Cold War Literature: Writing the Global Conflict*, ed. by Andrew Hammond (London and New York: Routledge, 2006), p. 5.

12. See, for example, Dubravka Juraga and M. Keith Booker (eds), *Socialist Cultures East and West: A Post-Cold War Reassessment* (Westport, CT, and London: Praeger, 2002); David Forgacs and Stephen Gundle, *Mass Culture and Italian Society from Fascism to the Cold War* (Bloomington: Indiana University Press, 2007).

13. Two early examples of Italian post-apocalyptic fiction, with little direct influence on the subsequent development of the genre, are Giorgio Scerbanenco, *Il cavallo venduto* (Milan: Rizzoli, 1963) and Emilio De' Rossignoli, *H come Milano* (Milan: Longanesi, 1965). For an excellent cultural history of Italian SF, see Giulia Ianuzzi, *Fantascienza italiana: Riviste, autori, dibattiti dagli anni Cinquanta agli anni Settanta* (Milan: Mimesis, 2014) and *Distopie, viaggi spaziali, allucinazioni. Fantascienza italiana contemporanea* (Milan: Mimesis, 2015). Diana Bianchi's ongoing doctoral research concerns the specific role of translators in the early dissemination of SF in Italy.

14. Elsa Morante, *Pro o contro la bomba atomica e altri scritti* (Milano: Adelphi, 1987), pp. 97–99, my translation.

15. Bruno Pischedda, *La grande sera del mondo. Romanzi apocalittici dell'Italia del benessere* (Turin: Nino Aragno, 2004), pp. 10–12.

16. See, for example, Pierpaolo Antonello and Alan O'Leary (eds), *Imagining Terrorism: The Rhetoric and Representation of Political Violence in Italy, 1969–2006* (London: Legenda, 2009); Ruth Glynn, *Women, Terrorism, and Trauma in Italian Culture* (London: Palgrave Macmillan, 2013).

17. See Cesare Merlini, 'A Concise History of Nuclear Italy', *The International Spectator*, 23.3 (1988), 135–52.

18. See Pierpaolo Antonello, *Contro il materialismo: Le 'due culture' in Italia* (Turin: Aragno, 2012). Antonello's lucid discussion of technophobia acknowledges the influence of Paolo Rossi, *Immagini della scienza* (Rome: Editori Riuniti, 1977).

19. Vacca, *Il medioevo*, p. 123. All subsequent page references in the text will be to the Italian edition.

20. Vacca's envisaged neo-medieval future is strongly reminiscent of the fictional universe imagined in Walter M. Miller's famous post-apocalyptic SF novel *A Canticle for Leibowitz* (1960).

21. Isabelle Stengers, *In Catastrophic Times: Resisting the Coming Barbarism*, trans. by Andrew Goffey (Lüneburg: Open Humanities Press/Meson Press, 2015). For an interesting discussion of Stengers's work, see Déborah Danowski and Eduardo Viveiros De Castro, *The Ends of the World*, trans. by Rodrigo Nunes (Cambridge: Polity, 2017).

22. Jean-Luc Nancy, *After Fukushima: The Equivalence of Catastrophes*, trans. by Charlotte Mandell (New York: Fordham University Press, 2015), p. 3; Timothy Morton, *Hyperobjects: Philosophy and Ecology after the End of the World* (Minneapolis: University of Minnesota Press, 2013).

23. http://reports.weforum.org/global-risks-2017/global-risks-landscape-2017/

24. Cf. Eva Horn, *Zukunft als Katastrophe* (Frankfurt am Main: Fischer, 2014), pp. 38–41.

25. Ibid., pp. 91–95.

26. On thought experiments, see Roy A. Sorensen, *Thought Experiments* (Oxford: Oxford University Press, 1992).

27. Amitav Ghosh, *The Great Derangement: Climate Change and the Unthinkable* (Chicago and London: University of Chicago Press, 2016), pp. 37–52.

28. Pier Paolo Pasolini, 'È un gioco diabolico *Lo smeraldo* di Soldati', *Il Tempo*, 29 November 1974, now in *Descrizioni di descrizioni* (Turin: Einaudi, 1979), pp. 417–21.

29. Gianni Mura, 'Il cronista del futuro', interview with Mario Soldati, *Epoca*, 19 October 1974. For an engaging discussion of homosexuality in *The Emerald*, see Nicola Gardini, 'Das Homosexuelle in Soldati', *Studi novecenteschi*, 35.73 (2007), 195–208.

30. Cf. Stefano Ghidinelli, 'Nota al testo', in Soldati, *Lo smeraldo*, pp. xxxv–xli.

31. Cf. Mura, 'Il cronista'.

32. I have written elsewhere about Umberto Eco's ambivalence and about Guido Morselli's and Paolo Volponi's apparent contempt for science fiction. Cf. Florian Mussgnug, 'Finire il mondo: per un'analisi del romanzo apocalittico italiano degli anni Settanta', *Contemporanea*, 1 (2003), 19–32; idem, 'No New Earth: Apocalyptic Rhetoric in Italian Nuclear-War Literature', in *Beyond Catholicism: Heresy, Mysticism, and Apocalypse in Italian Culture*, ed. by Simon Gilson and Fabrizio De Donno (Basingstoke: Palgrave Macmillan: 2013), pp. 195–216. On Soldati's career as a director, see Emiliano Morreale, *Mario Soldati: Le carriere di un libertino* (Recco and Bologna: Le Mani, 2006).

33. Cf. Mura, 'Il cronista'.

34. Soldati was probably familiar with Paul and Anne Ehrlich's alarmist Neo-Malthusian bestseller, *The Population Bomb* (1968), which predicted mass starvation of humans in the 1970s and 1980s, followed by societal upheavals on an unprecedented scale. For a history of the debate, see Matthew Connelly, *Fatal Misconception: The Struggle to Control World Population* (Cambridge, MA, and London: Harvard University Press, 2009).

35. See Carl Schmitt, *Der Nomos der Erde im Völkerrecht des Jus Publicum Europaeum* [1950] (Berlin: Duncker & Humblot, 1997); English translation by G. L. Ulmen, *The Nomos of the Earth in the International Law of Jus Publicum Europaeum* (New York: Telos Press, 2006).

36. 'Modern sovereignties', writes Susan Buck-Morss, 'harbor a blind spot, a zone in which power is above the law and thus, at least potentially, a terrain of terror. This wild zone of power [is] by its very structure impossible to domesticate' (Buck-Morss, *Dreamworld*, p. 3).

37. Nixon, *Slow Violence*, p. 17.

38. On the aesthetics of closure, see Helen Vendler, *Last Looks, Last Books: Stevens, Plath, Lowell, Bishop* (Princeton: Princeton University Press, 2010).

39. See Susan Stewart, *On Longing: Narratives of the Miniature, the Gigantic, the Souvenir, the Collection* (Durham, NC and London: Duke University Press, 1993).

40. Dipesh Chakrabarty, *Provincializing Europe: Postcolonial Thought and Historical Difference* (Princeton: Princeton University Press, 2000), p. 18.

41. See https://www.romasparita.eu/foto-roma-sparita/tag/sinagoga. I am grateful to Scott Lerner for drawing my attention to the architectural history of the Great Synagogue.

42. On the Romantic figure of the Last Man, see especially Fiona J. Stafford, *The Last of the Race: The Growth of a Myth from Milton to Darwin* (Oxford: Clarendon Press, 1994). See also Judith Schossböck, *Letzte Menschen: Postapokalyptische Narrative und Identitäten in der neueren Literatur nach 1945* (Bochum: Projektverlag, 2012).

43. On the pervasive figure of the child in futuristic fiction, see especially Lee Edelman, *No Future: Queer Theory and the Death Drive* (Durham, NC and London: Duke University Press, 2004). See also Rebekah Sheldon, *The Child to Come: Life after the Human Catastrophe* (Minneapolis: University of Minnesota Press, 2016).

44. *The Emerald* contains an explicit reference to Soldati's five surviving sons and daughters — 'Tre in Italia, e due qui in America, dalla mia prima moglie' (47/43) [three in Italy, and two here in America, by my first wife] and to potential grandchildren, which the protagonist claims he would be 'contento di non averne' (46/43) [glad not to have]. Soldati's second son, Ralph, who died in a car accident in 1953, is not mentioned.

CHAPTER 5

❖

Aesthetics of Contingency: Clark, Deleuze and Rome's Post-war Modernism

Filippo Trentin

T. J. Clark's monumental work on artistic modernism, entitled *Farewell to an Idea: Episodes from a History of Modernism*, terminates with an intriguing statement. After more than 400 pages of analysis of modernist paintings — from David's *The Death of Marat* to Cézanne's *The Large Bathers*, and from Picasso's cubist canvases to Pollock's body art — Clark finally confesses that 'the modernism that mattered most to me [...] was that of film and literature in Italy after 1945'.[1] Clark's statement inaugurates the first paragraph of the book's conclusion, which begins with an appraisal of neorealist film directors and writers including Roberto Rossellini, Luchino Visconti, Michelangelo Antonioni and Italo Calvino, and ends with a montage of quotations from Pier Paolo Pasolini's *Le ceneri di Gramsci*, Primo Levi's *Se questo è un uomo* and Samuel Beckett's *Waiting for Godot*. As Clark immediately makes clear, this apparently random assemblage is connected by the fact that 'in their works the present, however vicious and drivelling — and modernism has made it its endless business to show what those two adjectives mean — is only incompletely ripped from its historical frame'.[2] This statement reveals how, for Clark, modernist aesthetics are characterised by an unresolved temporal tension between past and present, and that such a feature is also a crucial characteristic of Italian neorealism.

Clark's decision to conclude his monument to modernist aesthetics with an appraisal of neorealism might well be the most unexpected turn in the scholarly history of modernism. Not only does Clark read neorealism — against the grain — as a modernist aesthetics, but he also interprets it as the peak of a constellation of artistic movements including impressionism, cubism and abstract expressionism, in which contingent reality is not simply 'represented', but rather 'enters' and 'invades' what he calls 'the process of picturing'.[3] In his view, Italian neorealism testifies to 'modernism's changes of face'. In other words, Clark believes that neorealism constitutes the culmination of an aesthetic impulse triggered by the rise of Western modernity and characterised by the attempt to liberate art from representationalist constraints. Unfortunately, Clark does not elaborate on this argument, which occupies only the four concluding pages of the book, leaving the reader with the difficult task of making sense of an observation that openly contradicts traditional readings and chronologies of both neorealism and modernism.[4]

This essay seeks to elaborate on Clark's thesis of a 'modernist ethos' of neorealism. Its aim is twofold: on the one hand, to develop an approach to neorealism as an aesthetics rooted in the material conditions of post-war Italy, and specifically Rome; and on the other hand, to shed light on the non-chronological trajectory of Western modernisms. While canonical studies of European and Italian modernism tend to situate modernism within the period extending from the late nineteenth century to the end of the 1930s, this essay emphasises its deviant and transnational trajectory, which, following Clark's insight, would re-emerge in Italy in the late 1940s. Drawing on this observation, instead of reading modernism as a *poetics* based on a set of stylistic features shared by a corpus of early twentieth-century literary and visual works — the stream of consciousness, the objective correlative, the subjective shot, the dialectical montage, etc. — I instead interpret it as an *aesthetics* that adheres to a different regime of distribution of the sensible.[5] Drawing on Jacques Rancière's definition of aesthetics not as 'a theory of sensibility, taste and pleasure for art amateurs', but as 'the specific mode of being of whatever falls within the domain of art, to the mode of being of the objects of art', I read the modernised cityscape of post-war Rome as the spatial incubator of a contingent and vernacular form of modernism.[6] In this post-Kantian understanding of aesthetics, artistic phenomena appear not as representations of reality, but as forms that adhere to a different sensible configuration of the empirical, of what is 'out there' — in this specific case, the material and urban reality of Rome during and soon after the end of the Second World War. In my analysis, the sensible and thus the modernist ethos of neorealism stems from Rome's post-war modernization process.

To develop this argument, I will first elaborate on Gilles Deleuze's *time-image* as a notion that allows us to foreground Clark's intuition about the re-emergence of modernism in post-war Italy. I will look at the time-image not only as a signature of cinematic neorealism, as Deleuze does, but also, more broadly, as a feature of post-war Italian aesthetics. In the second part of the essay, I will ground my re-elaboration of Deleuze's argument through an analysis of literary debates about the role of the writer in the historical transition from fascism to the post-war democracy as discussed in the Rome-based journals *Rinascita*, *Presente* and *La strada*, and through a reading of Elio Filippo Accrocca's poetry collection *Portonaccio* (1949). My aim is to foreground the existence of what I call an 'aesthetics of contingency' — parallel and, at the same time, intertwined with neorealism — that finds its point of emergence in the surfaces, the concreteness and the squalid materiality of post-war Rome. In my reading, the modernist essence of this contingent aesthetics deeply depends on a process of lowering the artistic gaze from the holistic and vertical perspective of fascist aesthetics such as rationalism to the horizontal and fragmentary observational axis rooted in the dusty, shattered margins of the post-war city.

The Emergence of the Time-Image in Post-war Rome

In his second volume on cinema, published in 1985, Deleuze theorises a paradigm shift of the cinematic image, from what he calls the 'movement-image' to the 'time-image'. For Deleuze, the shift between these types of aesthetics is rooted in a different conception of temporality: while the movement-image institutes a linear and empirical notion of time in which 'the past is a former present, and the future is a present to come', the time-image captures a temporal dynamic in which 'time is out of joint and presents itself in the pure state'.[7]

Here, Deleuze asks us to think about two different visual regimes, one of which — that of the movement image — is based on representation, while the other — that of the time-image — relies on a self-producing matter that marks the cinematic as an autonomous form. With this distinction, Deleuze aims to capture an indexical mutation of cinema from its classical pre-war tradition (in which subject and object are two separate entities and the narration progresses through the sequential development of the action) to its post-war form (in which the emergence of sensorial and optical situations provoke a collapse of the distinction between subject and object and the undoing of sequential narratives). He writes:

> So-called classical narration derives directly from the organic composition of movement-images [*montage*], or from their specification as perception-images, affection-images and action-images, according to the laws of a sensory-motor schema. We shall see that the modern forms of narration derive from the compositions and types of the time-image: even 'readability'. Narration is never an evident [*apparent*] given of images, or the effect of a structure which underlines them; it is a consequence of the visible [*apparent*] images themselves, of the perceptible images in themselves, as they are initially defined for themselves.[8]

Deleuze's distinction between a 'classical' and 'modern' form of narration in cinema should not be confused with the distinction between classical Hollywood versus avant-garde cinema; instead, it corresponds to his differentiation between a form of cinema that operates through the paradigm of movement and a form of cinema that operates through the paradigm of time.[9] Deleuze's argument is particularly interesting in that he identifies the cinematic movement that first captured the potentialities of the time-image as Italian neorealism. According to Deleuze, directors such as Rossellini, De Sica, Antonioni and Fellini developed a new aesthetic form based on a conception of space and time 'said to be dispersive, elliptical, errant or wavering, working in blocs, with deliberately weak connections and floating events'.[10] The moving image produced by these authors is thus characterised by the creation of a 'de-subjectivised' cinematic form, relying on an alternative concept of time characterised by the constant interference of *déjà vu* — something which recalls the modernist attempt to break linear narrative through mnemonic interferences. This dynamic, which materialises, for example, in the abandonment of sensory-motor schemata, as in the directionless wandering of Antonio in *Ladri di biciclette*, also reflects the disruption of linear and measurable time in the name of an internal, anti-chronological temporality. In Deleuze's words, time-images 'break with indirect representation, but also shatter the empirical continuation of time, the chronological succession, the separation of the before and of the after'.[11]

It is at this point that Deleuze delves into sociology, linking the indexical mutation of the cinematic image to the specific socio-historical situation of post-war Italy. This discussion occurs at the end of his first book on cinema, when he asks, 'Why Italy first, before France and Germany?'[12] He then answers that the reasons are to be found in the different ways these countries dealt with their recent fascist pasts. Deleuze highlights how, while France attempted to minimize its complicity with Nazi Vichy and while Germany was occupied with its national sense of guilt, Italy's context allowed it more freedom to develop a new aesthetic language. In Deleuze's words, Italy

> could certainly not claim the rank of the victor; but, in contrast to Germany, on the one hand it had at its disposal a cinematographic institution which had escaped fascism relatively successfully; on the other it could point to a resistance and a popular life underlying oppression, although one without illusions.[13]

Deleuze's historical analysis is succinct, and, while its lack of empirical evidence leaves the reader with a sense of dissatisfaction, it reveals Deleuze's intuitive effort to root aesthetic changes (the Marxist superstructure) within the specific historical and political structure of post-war Italy. Thus, if the time-image is characterised by 'the weakness of the motor-linkages' and by 'weak connections that are capable of releasing huge forces of disintegration',[14] these changes respond to a specific mutation of the socio-historical conditions triggered by the tension between Europe's — and more specifically Italy's — (fascist) past and (democratic) present. In this respect, the time-image emerges as a theory of the image that emphasises an open disposition of the cinematic gaze towards those contingent elements that the realm of aesthetics had overlooked and repressed during the fascist period — those marginal elements stemming immanently from the bottom. As he writes:

> The visual image [...] now reveals the any-space-whatevers, empty or disconnected spaces characteristic of modern cinema. It is as if, speech having withdrawn from the image to become founding act, the image, for its part, raised the foundations of space, the 'strata', those silent powers of before or after speech, before or after man. The visual image becomes archaeological, stratigraphic, tectonic. Not that we are taken back to prehistory (there is an archeology of the present), but to the deserted layers which we juxtaposed according to variable orientations or connections.[15]

Deleuze's analysis of the time-image emphasises the archaeological and tectonic strata of the present, which are related to the deserted and deranged spaces of post-war Europe. This analysis suggests the coming-into-being of a different cinematic form, marked by a lowering of the artist's gaze towards the random and contingent reality of the post-war city. While the movement-image is characterised by a vertical spatial organisation, the time-image expands horizontally in the space of the city.[16]

Here, it is worth noting the proximity between Deleuze's notion of the time-image and Clark's insight into a modernist 'essence' of neorealism. Specifically,

Deleuze's conceptualisation of neorealism in terms of an indexical de-structuring of the image towards the materiality of the post-war landscape can be read as the theoretical basis of Clark's claim about the modernist quality of Italian neorealism.[17] What I am suggesting is that Deleuze's time-image and Clark's analysis of neorealism are both rooted in the disassembled and modernised spatiality of the post-war Italian landscape, and that read together these analyses can help us to foreground the emergence of a modernist aesthetics from the deranged spatiality of post-war Italy. In Deleuze's words, 'In the city which is being demolished or rebuilt, neo-realism makes any-space-whatevers proliferate — urban cancer, undifferentiated fabrics, pieces of waste-ground — which are opposed to the determined spaces of the old realism'.[18]

It is precisely this 'locationist' aspect of the analysis that I would like to stretch further. For Deleuze, Rossellini's *Roma città aperta* and *Paisà* record 'a dispersive and lacunary reality';[19] in *Ladri di biciclette*, 'there is no longer a vector or line of the universe which extends and links up the events';[20] *Umberto D.* is marked by an attraction for contingent and fleeting elements; and Fellini's *Lo sceicco bianco* and *Agenzia matrimoniale* record a proliferating and fabricated reality in which 'the everyday [...] continuously organises itself into a travelling spectacle'.[21] As these examples strikingly suggest, Deleuze's analysis does not simply point to a vague space but quite specifically references Rome's post-war cityscape. In other words, the time-image, this modernist mutation of the moving image, appears as a form deeply entrenched in the material conditions of the post-war city. While the prose of early modernist authors like Virginia Woolf and James Joyce depends on the changing face of metropolises such as London and Dublin, the opening gesture of Italian neorealism — Rossellini's *Roma città aperta* — may be said to be indexically embedded in the shattered cityscape of post-war Rome.

In Deleuze's description of the time-image, we can indeed recognize, by analogy, traces of Rome's post-war topography, characterised by a dispersive urban space in which the ruins of the ancient city are interspersed with the debris of the war city and with the incomplete urban blocks of the fascist city. In this regard, the decisive shift of Rome's post-war cityscape can be traced back to the master plan approved by the fascist government in 1931, which established the ground for the construction of new, hyper-populated residential areas between the Salaria and Appia roads, and of detached and semi-detached houses for the upper classes between the Cassia and Portuense roads. This plan, which promoted a topographical division between a bourgeois Western Rome and a more popular Eastern Rome, aimed to accommodate a doubling of the population, which was expected to reach 2 million within the following twenty-five years.[22] Furthermore, in 1935, Mussolini's urban planners decided to build an entirely new 'modern Rome' completely detached from the body of the old city, the E42 (then renamed EUR), which was originally planned for the 1942 Universal Exhibition[23] and was supposed to become the economic and financial centre of the modern city.

Thus, when Italy entered the war in 1940, Rome was an enormous construction site, and, once the war ended in 1945, the incomplete renovations, together with the debris left by the passage of the war, produced a semi-destroyed cityscape marked by huge voids between the various parts of the city that had not yet been completed.[24] As the urban historian Giuseppe Cassetti wrote, between the 1920s and the 1940s, 'si crea [...] una città nuova, basata su tessuti residenziali diversi — a trama frantumata e a tracciato irregolare, oppure densi e sviluppati in altezza — differenziati a seconda del ceto sociale' [a new city is built, centred on different residential areas — with a fragmented and irregular structure, differentiated by class].[25]

This evocative cityscape, in which ancient ruins had been integrated with new war ruins, was captured by a series of post-war movies. Films such as Rossellini's *Roma città aperta* (1945) and *Paisà* (1946) or De Sica's *Sciuscià* (1946) and *Ladri di biciclette* (1948) captured the striking desolation of a city in historical transition, providing a documentary testimony of the exceptional state of Rome's city space.[26] Deleuze's reading of these films suggests that the point of convergence between neorealism and modernism can be found in these directors' attempts not to represent Rome's post-war cityscape but to incorporate it as an aesthetic residue. In other terms, the point of emergence of the time-image can also be described as an indexical absorption of Rome's urbanscape, marked by ruins, voids and debris. It is precisely this indexical capacity to incorporate a complex spatio-temporal entity that triggers the undoing of mimetic and representational aesthetics. Expanding on this insight, in the next section I aim to show that this aesthetic process is not only a theoretical issue for philosophers and art historians such as Deleuze and Clark, but was also a primary concern for critics and writers operating in Rome in the immediate post-war period.

The Lowering of the Gaze

In the cultural geography of post-war Italy, Rome's intellectual circles represented a sort of compromise between the conservatism of Florence — influenced by the intellectual legacy of two great masters, Eugenio Montale and Carlo Emilio Gadda — and the technical avant-gardism of Turin and Milan, as expressed by Elio Vittorini's *Il Politecnico*, which advocated a strong break with the culture of the *ventennio*. While the Florentine group defended the 'sprovincializzazione' of Italian culture exercised by *Solaria* during the 1920s and 1930s, Northern-based intellectuals such as Vittorini and Francesco Flora proclaimed Milan the spiritual guide for the country, after the city had become the centre of coordination for the Resistance during the last two years of the war. Unlike Florence, Rome could not claim the highbrow experience of *Solaria*, nor could it take the Milanese role of anti-fascist spiritual guide.[27] Nevertheless, Rome was a place of animated cultural debate, as demonstrated by the great number of journals and newspapers published in the city.[28]

The idea of an aesthetics that moved away from an abstract and elitist approach circulated widely amongst artists of the post-war period, particularly in those left-wing circles that soon absorbed the lessons of Gramsci's *Quaderni del carcere*. In Roman literary circles, this discussion focused primarily on the need to break with the poetics of hermeticism, which was condemned as a hyper-intellectualist aesthetic, unable to record the fleeting and transient character of everyday life.[29] Numerous Rome-based magazines published in the post-war period, including *Rinascita*, *Il Presente* and *La strada*, supported this position.

In *Il Presente*,[30] a poetry journal published in Rome during the 1950s, the scholar Mario Petrucciani stated the need for a serious analysis of hermeticism, capable of distinguishing between those elements that had to be erased and others that should be kept, thus establishing a new, more democratic way to look at and represent reality. He wrote:

> Il problema della poesia italiana, oggi, s'incentra nell'interpretazione 'attiva' di tutto il primo novecento e, in particolare, del cosiddetto ermetismo, e nella ricerca di un *ubi consistam*, vale a dire di una consistenza che potremmo definire l'originale sintesi lirica in cui l'uomo si realizzi con tutta l'urgenza delle sue odierne istanze etico-esistenziali, prima che 'letterarie' [...]. Abbiamo condannato come degenerazione solipsistica tutto quell'atteggiamento espressivo astruso e 'prezioso', intellettualisticamente artefatto, nel quale la parola stessa viene svuotata d'ogni realtà di vita e di dolore, per essere proiettata nel meccanismo di un 'gioco' puramente arbitrario e perciò carico di falsificazioni.[31]

> [Italian poetry nowadays focuses on an 'active' interpretation of the literary ethos that characterised the first half of the twentieth century, in particular hermeticism. It moreover focuses on the identification of an *ubi consistam*, which means a consistency that we could define as the original lyrical synthesis in which humanity could fulfil itself through the urgency of its ethical and existential questions rather than its literary ones. We condemned as solipsistic degeneration that abstruse, intellectualistic and 'precious' attitude, in which words are emptied of life and sorrow in order to be projected in the mechanism of a game that is purely arbitrary and thus marked by falsifications.]

Although Petrucciani's argument focused explicitly on poetry, we can interpret it more broadly as a discussion of the role of the writer immediately after the end of the war and following twenty years of fascism. Petrucciani is trying to answer the question 'Which perspective does the author have to assume with respect to the rapidly changing reality of the post-war period?' Fascist censorship had forced writers to abandon references to specific facts or events that portrayed a negative image of the Italian situation, pushing them to adopt a highly controlled language, full of vague allusions.[32] In reaction, post-war intellectuals such as Petrucciani considered hermeticism to be marked by an inward tendency and a detached attitude towards the concrete aspects of lived life. Nonetheless, rather than promoting a definite break with the past, Petrucciani sought to create some sort of continuity between the few 'authentic' voices of the previous period, such as those of Giuseppe Ungaretti and the authors who emerged in the post-war years. Important features for the construction of the new aesthetic were essentiality, clarity and concreteness.

Petrucciani's article represented a sort of final statement on a discourse — based on the necessity of a link between past and present cultural experiences — that filled the pages of many other Roman journals in the immediate post-war period. A similar demand can be seen in Mario Mafai's article 'Possibilità per un'arte nuova'

[Possibilities for a New Art], published in *Rinascita* in March 1945, in which the artist of the 'Scuola Romana' advocates finding an aesthetic language that could capture the new forms of life emerging after the fall of fascism. After underlining that 'La vecchia cultura si sgretola giorno per giorno, cade pezzo per pezzo, si sveste di quegli apparati superficiali, delle verniciature demagogiche' [Old culture crumbles day after day, it falls piece after piece, it strips itself of those superficial structures and demagogic veneer], Mafai argues for the need to give 'una nuova fisionomia a noi stessi e alla società' [a new physiognomy for ourselves and society] through the adoption of a new aesthetic ideal.[33] His words indicate the post-war artist's awareness of the need for a radical appraisal of the previous social structure, which had been characterised by a rigid detachment from everyday situations, elements and forms. The new artist should instead be able to express the ferment of the post-war period by channelling all the vitality and energy of the new historical condition:

> Ripensando a quei vent'anni e più di letargo, dove le cose e gli uomini sembravano verniciati di una patina opaca d'ipocrisia su uno scenario di cartone dorato, farebbe piacere sperare un'arte più serena che s'ispirasse a un nuovo ideale di bellezza dove l'artista ritrovi e sciolga il canto alla vita e all'avvenire.[34]

> [Thinking again about those twenty years and more of lethargy, where things and people seemed painted with an opaque patina of hypocrisy in a scenery made of golden cardboard, we should now advocate for an art that is inspired by a new ideal of beauty, in which the artist can find and dissolve his chant to life and the future.]

Mafai's hope for the establishment of a 'new idea of beauty' is here clearly opposed to the aesthetic ideals that governed the arts during the fascist period. However, Mafai aims to go beyond a simplistic reading of the debate as a quarrel between hermeticists and anti-hermeticists, proposing instead a more complex view of the artistic production of the fascist period. In order to do so, he compares the art of the fascist period with the art of the Renaissance, a time in which both Raphael — 'il più alto rappresentante di quella società' [the most important representative of that society] — and Michelangelo — 'che agita i corpi e annunzia un nuovo dramma che sarà poi la Controriforma' [who agitates the bodies and announces a new dramatic period which will later become the Counter-Reformation] — were active.[35] According to Mafai, Raphael embodies the highest expression of the conformist artist, he who seeks to give form and expression to society's conventional spirit. On the other hand, Michelangelo, by questioning the conventionality of the society in which he lived, appears to foresee the deficiencies of his own time and paves the way for new forms of disruption and renewal.

Mafai's contrasting of Raphael and Michelangelo reflects an ideological dichotomy between conformist or normative art and anti-conformist art, in which the first typology directly emerges from the dominant ideology, while the second, by assuming an external perspective, can dissect and question the most basic assumptions of the artist's time. According to Mafai, it is from this heretical approach to art that post-war artists should draw inspiration in order to establish a new aesthetic.

A more obvious attention to 'low' and marginal elements distinguishes the poetry journal *La strada*, which was edited by the scholar Antonio Russi and published in three issues between 1946 and 1947. The journal, printed by a Roman union of independent publishers called Nuovi Editori Riuniti, promoted a new poetic language, far from the narrowness of hermeticism and tending towards a documentary and 'impure' view of reality.[36] *La strada* consciously sought to capture a change of perspective from 'above' to 'below', and represented an essential contribution to the definition of a new literary language, parallel to that of cinematic neorealism, which would leave important legacies in the literary production of the following years. The title of the journal is itself revealing, as it proposes a shift of the authorial gaze from the 'ivory tower' to the 'lived space' of the street.

The leading article of the first issue, authored by Russi himself, both passes judgment on the state of art during the fascist dictatorship and calls for a break with that past. Russi judges very critically the paradigm of 'poesia pura' that had characterised the poetic production of the previous period, stating: 'tutta questa letteratura manca di tempo preciso, perché manca di impegno' [all this literature is devoid of a precise temporality because it lacks commitment].[37] Far from mediating with the past aesthetic experience of hermeticism or symbolism, Russi calls for a Copernican revolution of the artistic gaze. He believes the post-war artist should move his gaze from the hyper-intellectualistic experiences of hermeticism and the 'prosa d'arte' to the vernacular materiality of the street, in order to incorporate its wasted and impure elements:

> *La Strada* non è dunque una rivista di poesia pura e tanto meno di poesia ermetica. È anzi proprio il contrario di tutto questo.[38]

> [*The Street* is thus not a journal about pure poetry, and least of all is it one of hermetic poetry. It is actually the opposite of all this.]

Russi's claim for a poetry of the impure and his regard for a 'documentary' aesthetic that moved away from the abstract, vertical aesthetic promoted by hermeticism emblematically captures a shift of the artist's gaze from 'above' to 'below'. The discourses characterising the literary debate were not destined to remain in the realm of the intellectual discussion, but were rather the signature of an aesthetic change that marked poetic and narrative aesthetics beyond neorealism.

Russi re-emphasises this position in *Poesia e realtà*,[39] in which he focuses his attention on the years between the outbreak of the First World War and the end of the Second World War. He detects the literary symptoms of this crisis in the purified and obscure language of the 'prosa d'arte' [artistic prose] and hermeticist poetry, a literary language that he labelled 'poesia dell'indifferenza' [poetry of indifference] and that reflected a detachment from the concreteness of life.[40] In Russi's reading, symbolism and the *fin de siècle* aestheticist call for *l'art pour l'art* had soon degenerated into a dry language, leading to the departure of concrete objects from the artist's observation point:

> C'è nell'ultima poesia, una oscurità apparente che è un prodotto dell'indifferenza, dell'incapacità di scelta, del rifiuto degli oggetti. [...] In questo caso estremo,

> non si può più parlare di simbolismo, né di poetica delle 'corrispondenze'. [...]
> L'oscurità dell'ultima poesia coincide col suo distacco dalla vita.[41]

> [Contemporary poetry seems characterised by an apparent obscurity that is a
> product of indifference, of the incapacity of choosing, of the refusal of objects.
> [...] In this extreme case, we cannot talk either of symbolism or of poetics of
> 'correspondence'. [...] The obscurity of contemporary poetry coincides with its
> detachment from life.]

For Russi, the literary paradigm of the 'poetry of indifference' — which dominated
Italian literary writing for decades following the lessons of Giosuè Carducci and
Gabriele d'Annunzio, ultimately leading to the formation of 'artistic prose' — had
to be overcome by a new, more vivid and committed paradigm based on a direct
observation of life in all its forms. Russi saw early symptoms of this perspective
change in Gramsci's *Quaderni del carcere* (1948), Ignazio Silone's novel *Fontamara*
(1933), and the first books of Alberto Moravia, Elio Vittorini and Carlo Levi.[42] He
detected a common thread between these writers in the return of topography in
many of their works — a move for which Russi coined the expression 'fare pace
con la geografia' [make peace with geography] — as shown by their willingness to
name places and locations.

Russi therefore calls for a break with the past in terms of attitude and perspective.
He criticises hermeticist poetry for its intrinsic use of refined and abstract words
that reveal a detached attitude towards the pulsating reality of the post-war period.
Precisely for this reason, Russi claims, the post-war writer should readjust the lens,
turning it towards reality, in the name of a more direct participation with society,
and in order to bear witness to the traumatised humanity that had just emerged
from the war. Downward gazes; top-down movements; time-images; low, impure,
or peripheral elements; the attention to the everyday; the collapse of the high into
a multidirectional and flat horizontality — all these elements characterize the
emergence of a contingent aesthetic from the environment of post-war Rome.

The Aesthetic Inscription of Rome's Margins: Elio Filippo Accrocca's *Portonaccio*

Elio Filippo Accrocca's *Portonaccio*, published in 1949, perfectly captures the horizontal tension towards the contingent that marks both the post-war literary debates
and Deleuze's notion of the time-image. The book is a poetic chronicle of Rome
during the war and the immediate post-war period, and is composed of fifteen
untitled poems. Their chronology proceeds from 29 December 1942 to 22 March
1946, a period corresponding with the fall of fascism (8 September 1943), the Nazi
occupation of Rome (from September 1943 to 4 June 1944), the bombings of Rome
(1943–44), the city's liberation by the Allied troops (4 June 1944), and the beginning
of the post-war reconstruction. *Portonaccio* portrays an anti-monumental image of
Rome constructed of debris and margins, and offers a paradigmatic example of the
ruinous space that, for Deleuze, characterises the post-war Italian landscape.

This shift is already encapsulated within the book's title, whose epigraph explains:
'Portonaccio è un ponte sulla ferrovia, è un quartiere di povera gente. Gli uomini

da vivi lo ignorano, da morti lo abitano' [Portonaccio is a bridge above the railway track; it is an area of poor people. Those who are living ignore it; those who are dead inhabit it].[43] Portonaccio is an area within the Pietralata neighbourhood along the Via Tiburtina, which after the Second World War became a gathering ground for a group of artists and poets that included Accrocca, Renzo Vespignani and Armando Buratti. This group, which formed the so-called 'Scuola di Portonaccio', aimed to record and collect signs and traces left by the war, and advocated a poetics of the marginal rooted in the city's debris. At the same time, *Portonaccio* captures a fleeting, peripheral image of Rome, divested of its official and monumental apparatuses. The area, which had suffered many dramatic bombings during the war, acquired a highly symbolic value in the immediate post-war period, as these artists considered it an allegory of Rome's most atrocious sufferings.

Giuseppe Ungaretti highlighted this allegorical aspect in his introduction to Accrocca's book, describing the language and aesthetic of the Scuola di Portonaccio as characterised by the conviction that 'la verità è nella tragica pietà delle cose' [truth lies in the tragic piety of things].[44] After mentioning, alongside Accrocca, the painters Vespignani and Buratti, Ungaretti writes:

> Già si dice che è una scuola, la scuola del Portonaccio, dal nome di quel rione che essi abitano in case colpite dalla guerra, tra una stazione ferroviaria, un ponte, il cimitero, gli Ospedali, la città degli Studi. [...] È certo che la poesia di Accrocca è la più refrattaria a farsi attanagliare in regole che non siano quelle reclamate dalla propria ispirazione. È, la sua, una voce d'estrema tenerezza davanti alla terribilità degli eventi, voce d'una tenerezza quasi silenziosa per la sua intensità di commozione davanti a inermi povere cose, a poveri esseri travolti.[45]

> [People already say that it's a school, Portonaccio's school, from the name of that neighborhood in which people live in houses hit by the war bombings, between a train station, a bridge, a cemetery, the hospitals, the University. [...] Surely, Accrocca's poetry is the hardest one to describe with rules that are not those of its own inspiration. His voice is one of extreme tenderness in confronting the horror of events; it is the voice of an almost silent tenderness for the intensity and commotion in front of defenceless poor things and crushed human beings.]

As Ungaretti notes, Accrocca gives shape and voice to an alternative image of the Italian capital by lingering on its most degraded areas. For the young poet, post-war Rome is a city in which the vision of the present is interrupted by the sudden emergence of traumatic memories. Around the Portonaccio area, the 'quartiere è sinistrato' [the neighbourhood is destroyed][46] and dead men are 'stesi sotto i marciapiedi' [lying down underneath the sidewalks].[47] At the same time, the neighbourhood is also a visionary and metamorphosing place, in which streetlamps resemble votive candles and people's houses look like graves:

> Si rinnova
> la strada nel quartiere sinistrato.
> La clinica Sant' Elena fa lume
> alla memoria. Il tredici di Marzo

i morti stesi sotto i marciapiedi
i due cavalli aperti dalle schegge
all'angolo di viale Alfredo Rocco.
Fantasmi colorati dalla luce
di questa sera. I tortili lampioni
son lampade votive per le tombe
della mia strada.[48]

[Streets are renovated
in the destroyed neighbourhood.
Sant' Elena clinic is a light
to memory. The 13th of March,
the dead people are lying underneath the pavements,
the two horses revealed by the splinters
at the corner of Alfredo Rocco road.
Ghosts coloured by this evening's light,
The twisted streetlamps
Are votive lights for the graveyards
Of my road.]

In Accrocca's poem, precise geographical and historical references accompany the war's most traumatic memories. For the poet, the time of reconstruction is a time of recollection, in which walking alongside Viale Alfredo Rocco (now Viale Ippocrate), around the Sapienza University area, causes flashbacks to the war. The sight of blue lights reminds the poet of wartime winters, when he was in hiding, and the refurbishment of these same streets recalls images of the dead bodies that once covered the pavement.

This area of Rome, which includes popular neighbourhoods such as Tiburtino, San Lorenzo and, beyond the Verano cemetery, the peripheral area of Portonaccio, was intensively hit by Allied bombings during 1943 and subsequently became the most symbolic location of the Roman Resistance. During the infamous bombing on 19 July 1943, Accrocca's family home was destroyed. The poet captures this traumatic experience in another poem in *Portonaccio*:

Ho dormito l'ultima notte
nella casa di mio padre
al quartiere proletario.
La guerra aborto d'uomini
dementi, è passata sulla
mia casa di San Lorenzo.
Il cuore ha le sue distruzioni
come le macerie di spettri
eppure il cuore ancora grida,
geme, dispera, ma vive
come la Madonna di Raffaello
salvata tra i sassi della mia casa
e un paio di calzoni grigioverdi.[49]

[I slept for the last night
at my father's place
in the proletarian neighbourhood.

War, abortion of foolish
men, has passed over
my house in San Lorenzo.
The heart is destroyed
like debris of spectres
and yet the heart is still screaming.
It cries and despairs, but it lives
like Raphael's *Madonna*,
which was saved from my house's debris
and a pair of green-grey trousers.]

The condensing of these dramatic experiences triggers a topographical change, which moves the from the city's centre to its peripheral margins. Witnessing the process of post-war reconstruction of Portonaccio allowed Accrocca to construct an alternative aesthetic imagery to that of fascism, which was expressed by symbolic landmarks of fascist architecture like Piazza Augusto Imperatore or the E42.

Stylistically, the poem is composed of thirteen verses divided into four tercets followed by a coda. This 'awkward', truncated version of a *sonetto* can be read as a failed attempt to adhere to the most traditional form of Italian poetry, but it also reveals the poet's desire to keep alive a structure that is able to contain a dramatic experience that would otherwise risk overflowing any formal structure. The tercets appear as four poetic blocs that synthetically capture four distinct poetic images: the poet's last night in his father's house; the subsequent bombing of the house; the destruction of the poet's house and of his own inner feelings; and the emergence of Raphael's painting and a pair of trousers from the building's debris. The paratactic transition between the four blocs mirrors the lack of logical connection in such tragic occurrences. However, the sense of desperation that stems from the bombing is followed by a feeling of hope, symbolised by the emergence of the *Madonna* painting and the pair of trousers. This juxtaposition of these two items, belonging to the opposite realms of Renaissance art and everyday life, not only provides us with a time-image of the post-war city, but also constitutes a poetic statement. Together, Raphael's *Madonna* and the green-grey trousers form an allegory of the aesthetic ideal based on a conciliatory act between high art and contingent life.

Unlike figurative artists of the Scuola di Portonaccio, such as Armando Buratti and Renzo Vespignani, Accrocca did not encounter the favour of the critics and soon fell into oblivion. The difficulty of critically positioning Accrocca's work is illustrated in Giuseppe Ungaretti's introduction to the first edition of *Portonaccio*, in which Ungaretti frames Accrocca within a specific style of contemporary Italian poetry characterised by a baroque ideal of form. He writes: 'La poesia moderna italiana toccò un punto del suo rinnovamento alcuni anni fa, e fu proprio qui in Roma, e fu per opera di qualche anziano che si era accorto del significato decisivo in quel momento del Barocco' [Modern Italian poetry reached its peak a few years ago here in Rome, thanks to an old poet who became aware of the decisive importance of the baroque for that historical moment].

By linking Accrocca's poetry to baroque Rome, Ungaretti astutely establishes himself as the initiator of such a tradition. The 'old poet' who previously recognised the importance of the baroque is, of course, Ungaretti himself, who wrote his poetry book *Sentimento del tempo*, 'osservando il paesaggio, osservando Roma sotto il mutamento delle stagioni' [observing the landscape of Rome during those times of change].[50] For Ungaretti, the super-imposition of different architectural eras typical of Rome's baroque form becomes the basis for theorising the emergence of a poetics based on the idea that 'qualche cosa che è saltato in aria, che s'è sbriciolato in mille briciole: è una cosa nuova, rifatta con quelle briciole' [something blew up and crumbled in thousands of small pieces: it is something new, which should be made with those pieces].[51]

Ungaretti's reading of *Portonaccio* suggests a continuity between his own modernism and that of post-war writers such as Accrocca. What is particularly interesting in his argument is the conflation between baroque Rome and the undoing of literary form, recalling as it does Deleuze's description of the time-image as proliferating and de-structured. A Bergsonian theory of time informs indeed both Deleuze's and Ungaretti's attempts to capture a pure notion of time, devoid of sequential progression. Ungaretti, a fervent student of Bergson at the Collège de France in Paris, directly links the emergence of modernist aesthetics such as cubism to Bergson's notions of time and memory:

> Bergson allude di quando in quando a una sensazione purgata d'ogni torbido affettivo. Quella sensazione, sgorgando in una pura forma, e rinnovandosi, e sempre tornando a fiorire, e germinando ancora, in una perfetta continuità, non attuerebbe il tempo bergsoniano? Si videro i cubisti. E si udirono poesie nelle quali le parole si dilatavano, acquistando in intensità musicale, evocativa, in flessuosità ciò che avevan perso in rigor di logica.[52]

> [Sometimes Bergson talks about a sensation stripped of any sentimental feeling. Wouldn't that sensation — springing in a pure form, and constantly renewing, blooming, and germinating in a perfect becoming — actualize Bergsonian time? And then the cubists came. And we started to read poems marked by dilating words, acquiring a musical intensity, evocative and fluid rather than rigid and logical.]

At this point, we can attempt a synthesis of the discussion so far: Clark's argument for an anti-representational invasion of the contingent in post-war Italian film and literature; Deleuze's rooting of the time-image in the lacunary reality of the post-war Italian cityscape; the critical attempt to move beyond hermeticism; and the anti-monumental ethos that characterises Accrocca's poetry. The signature linking these notions is a lowering of the artistic gaze towards Rome's streets, an 'aesthetics of contingency' rooted in the elements of Rome's cityscape that were marginalised and suppressed by the aesthetics of the fascist *ventennio*. The examples above illustrate that this aesthetic shift strictly relates to Rome's experience of twentieth-century modernity. Accrocca's *Portonaccio* could thus be interpreted as the beginning of a de-composition of Rome's image, from the monumentality of the 'eternal city' to the ephemerality of a city of margins, which marks the more well-known representations of post-war Rome, such as Carlo Levi's *L'orologio*, Fellini's *La dolce vita*, Pasolini's *Accattone*, and Antonioni's *L'eclisse*.

Notes to Chapter 5

1. Timothy James Clark, *Farewell to an Idea: Episodes from a History of Modernism* (New Haven: Yale University Press, 1999), p. 405.

2. Ibid., p. 407.

3. Ibid., p. 18. Such an interpretation finds no confirmation in traditional chronologies of European modernism or in studies of Italian modernism. Moreover, it bypasses the canonical dichotomy of modernism and realism proposed by Lukács in *The Meaning of Contemporary Realism*.

4. See *Italian Modernism: Italian Culture between Decadentism and Avant-Garde*, ed. by Mario Moroni and Luca Somigli (Toronto, Buffalo and London: University of Toronto Press, 2004), and Raffaele Donnarumma, 'Tracciato del modernismo italiano', in *Sul modernismo italiano*, ed. by Romano Luperini and Massimiliano Tortora (Naples: Liguori, 2012), pp. 13–38. Moroni and Somigli argue that Italian modernism goes 'from D'Annunzio to the Crepuscolari to the Futurists to Montale and Ungaretti and the Hermetics', while Raffaele Donnarumma talks about a 'modernismo storico', which goes from Pirandello's *Il fu Mattia Pascal* (1904) to Ungaretti's poetry collection *Allegria di naufragi* (1919), and a second phase of modernism, which goes from 1925 to 1939 and includes Montale's *Ossi di seppia* and works by Savinio, Landolfi, Gadda, Moravia and Vittorini.

5. For this definition of aesthetics, see Jacques Rancière, *The Politics of the Aesthetics*, trans. and intr. by Gabriel Rockhill (London: Bloomsbury, 2006), p. 18.

6. See ibid. For an analysis of 'vernacular modernism', see Miriam Hansen, 'The Mass Production of the Senses: Classical Cinema as Vernacular Modernism', *Modernism/modernity*, 6.2 (1999), 59–77.

7. Gilles Deleuze, *Cinema 2. The Time-Image*, trans. by Hugh Tomlinson and Robert Galeta (Minneapolis: University of Minnesota Press, 1997), p. 271.

8. Ibid., p. 26.

9. The authors whom Deleuze includes within the category of the 'movement-image' include the surrealist Luis Buñuel; Soviet authors such as Dziga Vertov, Sergej Eisenstein and Vsevold Pudovkin; and American filmmakers like Howard Hawks and D. W. Griffith. The authors operating according to the regime of the 'time-image' were involved in movements such as Italian neorealism, the French New Wave and the New German Cinema of the 1960s.

10. Deleuze, *Cinema 2*, p. 1.

11. Ibid., p. 155.

12. Ibid., p. 211.

13. Ibid.

14. Ibid., p. 19.

15. Ibid., pp. 243–44.

16. See ibid., p. 265: 'The organization of space here loses its privileged directions, and first of all the privilege of the vertical which the position of the screen still displays, in favour of an omni-directional space which constantly varies its angles and coordinates, to exchange the vertical and the horizontal.'

17. For an analysis of the spatial and modernist implications of neorealism, see Noa Steimatsky's, *Italian Location: Reinhabiting the Past in Postwar Italian Cinema* (Minneapolis: Minnesota University Press, 2008), in which she argues that 'the "neo" prefix betrays here the need to consider realism itself through a modernist lens' (p. xx). Though Steimatsky does not develop her modernist reading of neorealism within the framework of the time-image, she emphasises the contingent and anti-linear elements that characterize the neorealist aesthetic in a way that recalls Deleuze's analysis. She writes: 'Neorealism's destabilizing of the classical cinematic edifice, its episodic, digressive mode by which narrative recedes into the setting to expose rifts and ellipses, may itself be understood, in the strongest work, to mimic and then remake a landscape marked by loss.' (ibid., p. 46) Like Deleuze and Clark, Steimatsky is interested in connecting the emergence of neorealism to the dispersive, deranged and disordered spatiality of post-war Italy.

18. Gilles Deleuze, *Cinema 1: The Movement-Image*, trans. by Hugh Tomlinson and Robert Galeta (Minneapolis: University of Minnesota Press, 2003), p. 212.

19. Ibid., p. 207.

20. Ibid., p. 212.

21. Deleuze, *Cinema 2*, p. 5.

22. See Vittorio Vidotto, *Roma contemporanea* (Bari and Rome: Laterza, 2006), pp. 296–304.

23. However, the 1942 Universal Exposition never took place because of the outbreak of the war in 1939.

24. For a detailed historical account of Rome's twentieth-century urbanisation, see Italo Insolera, *Roma moderna. Un secolo di storia urbanistica 1870–1970* (Turin: Einaudi, 1992; repr. 2001); Leonardo Benevolo, *Roma dal 1870 al 1990* (Bari and Rome: Laterza, 1992); Vidotto, *Roma contemporanea*; Roberto Cassetti and Gianfranco Spagnesi (eds), *Roma contemporanea, storia e progetto* (Rome: Gangemi, 2006).

25. Roberto Cassetti, 'Il ruolo delle "funzioni centrali" nella costruzione di un nuovo ordine urbano della città contemporanea', in Cassetti and Spagnesi (eds.), *Roma contemporanea, storia e progetto*, p. 68.

26. For a study of the intrinsic relationship between post-war cinema and the Italian urbanscape, see Steimatsky, *Italian Location*.

27. For an introduction to the cultural environment of post-war Rome, see Nicola Merola, 'La cultura romana del dopoguerra', *Studi romani*, 25.3 (1977), 387–97. In an important passage of the article, the author talks about the *linea romana* as 'non concepita come cittadella arroccata in un suo orgoglio egemonico, esclusivo, ma intesa in accezione aperta e problematica, e quindi una scuola priva di santuari, refrattaria a liturgie trionfalistiche, senza maestri carismatici [...] dopo le livide stagioni della tragedia dell'Europa una cultura in movimento, inquieta delle attese e dei problemi del nuovo ciclo storico che faticosamente si va snodando per l'uomo d'occidente' [not conceived as a close-minded group sheltered in its own hegemonic and exclusive pride, but moved by an open and complex attitude, and therefore devoid of schools, immune of triumphal liturgies and without charismatic leaders] (p. 388). Merola's description of the move from the 'cittadella arroccata' of the fascist period to a more open and animated situation in the post-war period symptomatically reveals the markers of a top-down movement.

28. See Merola, p. 394: 'il numero delle riviste che si pubblicarono a Roma nel periodo immediatamente successivo alla fine della guerra e fino al 1950 sfiora almeno la quarantina, un livello particolarmente elevato e tanto più se si considerano le difficoltà oggettive particolarmente nei primi tempi.' [the number of journals which were published in Rome from the immediate post-war period to 1950 almost touches the number 40. A particularly high number, especially if one considers the objective difficulties of those times.]

29. This literary style, theorised by Francesco Flora and Carlo Bo in the mid-1930s, advocated a language purged of impurities and detached from a direct representation of reality. The critic Francesco Flora maintained that the difficulty and abstractness of his style had close analogies with the poetic trend of 1930s Italy. See Francesco Flora, *La poesia ermetica* (Bari: Laterza, 1936), and Carlo Bo, *Letteratura come vita* (Milan: Rizzoli, 1994), pp. 3–16 (first published in *Frontespizio* in 1938).

30. The journal *Il presente, poesia e critica* was published in Rome between 1952 and 1958. It was directed by Mario Petrucciani, Romano Romani, Mario Vitti, Cesare Cochetti and Ornella Sobrero.

31. Mario Petrucciani, 'Premesse di una ricerca', *Il presente, poesia e critica*, 4–5 (1952), 1–3 (p. 3).

32. See Guido Bonsaver, *Censorship and Literature in Fascist Italy* (Toronto: University of Toronto Press, 2007).

33. Mario Mafai, 'Possibilità per un'arte nuova', *Rinascita*, 2 (3 March 1945), 89–91 (p. 91).

34. Ibid.

35. Ibid., p. 90.

36. For an historical contextualisation of the poetry periodicals published in the second post-war period, see Sergio Pautasso, 'Le riviste di poesia del dopoguerra', *Aut aut*, 61–62 (1961), 143–61.

37. Antonio Russi, 'Introduzione', *La strada*, 1 (1946), 3–17 (p. 3).

38. Ibid., p. 11.

39. Antonio Russi, *Poesia e realtà* (Florence: La Nuova Italia, 1962). See also idem, *Gli anni dell'antialienazione: 1943–1949. Dall'ermetismo al neorealismo* (Milan: Mursia, 1966).

40. Russi, *Poesia e realtà*, p. 349: 'Di qui si spiega come la poesia dell'indifferenza non riesca ad affermare una realtà. Essa non lavora tanto sugli oggetti, quanto sulla loro ombra' [Here you can understand how the poetry of indifference is not able to affirm reality, as it does not refer to objects, but to their shadow].

41. Russi, *Poesia e realtà*, p. 354.

42. Russi refers to works such as Moravia's *Gli indifferenti* (1929) and *La mascherata* (1941), Vittorini's *Conversazione in Sicilia* (1941), and Levi's *Cristo si è fermato ad Eboli* (1945).

43. Filippo Accrocca, *Portonaccio* (Milan: All'insegna del pesce d'oro, 1949), p. 1.

44. Giuseppe Ungaretti, 'Introduzione', ibid., pp. 1–9 (p. 7).

45. Ibid., p. 8.

46. Accrocca, *Portonaccio*, p. 19.

47. Ibid.

48. Ibid.

49. Ibid., p. 14.

50. Giuseppe Ungaretti, *Vita d'un uomo. Tutte le poesie* (Milan: Mondadori, 2003), p. 764.

51. Ibid.

52. Ibid., p. 85.

❖

CHAPTER 6

Rome in the 1950s:
Plans, Politics and the Olympics

Giorgio Piccinato

Introduction

In this essay I will first list a number of simultaneous developments that occurred in Rome during the 1950s and 1960s, before going on to discuss them in more detail. The first was the extraordinarily passionate public involvement in urban issues like housing, transport and building regulations. The second, which especially relates to the timing of the former, was the lengthy and difficult design of the new master plan (1962), which opened the door to every possible set of political alliances and deals. The third element was the Olympic Games, which offered the occasion for the building of a range of new structures that had a significant impact on the continuing development of the city. These factors combined in the formation of a tense but lively atmosphere in Roman public debate to which I draw particular attention since it is a dimension often missing from the accounts of that era.

The National Background

A somewhat limited view of the 1950s has characterised them as an era of unlimited Americanisation, witnessed in the diffusion of cars, hamburgers and blue jeans, which was accompanied by a sharp division between classes to be seen in continuing clashes between workers and employers. It was also understood as a period of social and sexual constraints supported by Catholic control of private and public behaviour. Now, however, when the strain of old conflicts has somewhat faded and new arenas of contestation have emerged, there is considerable interest in a reconsideration of that period, taking into account the variety of contributing elements, and especially attending to those not fully taken into account previously. While the term 'regeneration' has only recently been used in Italy, it could certainly be adopted for many aspects of the process of reconstruction that characterised the country after the Second World War. The approach to reconstruction was related to or embedded in a number of political choices that changed the previous economic strategy of self-reliance and self-sufficiency into one very open to the world beyond. It included an alignment with the western powers and the United States, and membership of both NATO and the European Common Market. Within this new context and, importantly, with its dependence on cheap labour, manufacturing industry developed rapidly and Italy moved from a basically agricultural country to one increasingly identified by industrial and service sectors.[1] During the 1950s and the early part of the 1960s the central government became more and more involved in many fields including banking, insurance and mixed public–private ventures that established a strong presence in the basic industrial sectors of chemistry, steel and petroleum. This happened in the context of a political framework divided in two, where one group, the left, because of the centrality of the Italian Communist Party (PCI) with its external alliances with the socialist block, was regarded by Italy's allies as unfit for national government. But the left was heavily involved politically at the local administrative level, where it governed many cities and towns, in cultural life, in the universities, in publishing, and in the cinema, in all of which the cultural market was strongly influenced, if not controlled, by the left.[2]

On the other side of the political spectrum, the Christian Democratic Party led the country for almost three decades, heavily shaping the processes of modernisation. Despite a strong state presence in the economy, Italy never became any kind of social-democratic regime, like Scandinavia or Great Britain.[3] The government put most effort into dealing with monetary policy (and obtaining relevant results) rather than developing any real planning strategies so that the private sector had very little to fear, at least until 1962, when the socialist party, having cut its old ties with the communists, came to power on the basis of supporting some limited reforms: the extension of compulsory education to the age of fifteen, and the nationalisation of the electricity companies.

Within such a framework of economic, political and social change, new strategies were developed in land development and construction. The war had left the country with a huge deficit in terms of infrastructure and housing: 3.2 million homes were destroyed together with 40 per cent of schools and 20 per cent of hospitals, plus bridges, viaducts, roads.[4] Throughout the 1950s, investment in the building sector was higher than in industrial plants and machinery. This investment went together with a close alliance with real estate developers that could be explained by the increased demand for housing and its accompanying infrastructure, which were both linked to extensive internal migratory movements. People moved in their millions from the country to the city, from the south to the north, from the mountains to the coasts aiming to escape from the most underdeveloped areas. In this scenario it is little wonder that new policies were adopted for the renewal of the building stock, new actors came into prominence because of the development of the economy, and new social dynamics radically changed the country's fundamentals, including the ambitions and the lifestyles of many.

Parallel to the development of private initiatives in real estate, there was significant public intervention. To the overstretched existing social housing organisations 'INA Casa', a somewhat idiosyncratic public programme, was added which had a double objective: to increase employment and to build new housing for workers. Although these double goals led to some confusion about its operating procedures, some 355,000 homes were constructed, in the course of its two seven-year mandates, from 1949 to 1963. This represents the best result in public housing history.[5] Funds were provided by a compulsory 0.6 per cent taken from workers' salaries together with what the government provided through the National Insurance Institute (INA), which was responsible for managing the programme.

These developments were not the result of explicit public planning; rather they reflected the outcome of the conflict between old and new actors in the field of modernisation. The role of the government itself was much weaker than it had been during the preceding fascist regime, which partly explains why the private sector gained a definite, although politically contested, advantage. This was particularly true in the sphere of urban policies. A new urban planning act promulgated in 1942, during the war, had proposed a number of interesting innovations, which included the extension of master plans to the whole municipal territory, support for regional planning and a clear distinction between master plan — indicating the lines of future development — and detail plans, intended to provide guidelines for immediate implementation. But this plan never came into official use and with the resort to emergency procedures, some rather basic norms were adopted and enshrined in *piani di fabbricazione* (construction plans). They proved totally incapable of providing any real control of development, and at the same time the more far-reaching proposals of the 1942 law were ignored.

The number of reasons for this included the growing demand for housing and services following the war, widespread financial difficulty for the municipalities, which were unable to levy the taxes necessary to provide the infrastructure for the new developments, and the availability of cheap unskilled labour deriving from internal migrations. This was felt particularly in the main centres of the 'industrial triangle' — Milan, Turin, Genoa — which accounted for the greatest influx, but most Italian cities were affected by the abandonment of poor rural areas and the movement to the cities.

Roman Local Politics

Rome was geographically and politically at the centre of these epochal moves. After the war it grew at a pace much faster than the previous regime had anticipated. The city had been a showcase for fascism, which tried to use its archaeological past in order to stress continuity between the new era and the glorious Roman Empire. But the speedily built and quickly inaugurated housing built in the far periphery for inhabitants expelled from the newly excavated areas in the centre alongside the Roman forums had already become slums within a few years.[6] Since most of these settlements lacked any kind of basic service provision, including efficient transport to the city, schools, health services, and in some cases running water, deterioration and decay was inevitable.

After 1945 Rome became an asylum for refugees and migrants from a countryside ravaged by the war, at the crossroad of the great migrations of the country, from south to north, from the country to the city, from the small cities to the large ones. Statistics are unreliable, because of the large number of unregistered people, but shortly after the end of the war inhabitants amounted to 500,000 units more, that is an increase of 50 per cent from 1940, when the population was less than a million, while by 1960 those registered approached 2,000,000.[7] All this happened in the framework of the so-called 'Italian miracle', which saw dramatic changes in the economic and social structure of the country, and the increased role of Rome as economic centre due to the development of public involvement in the industrial and banking sectors.

There was a plan, but it seems meaningless to describe a city and its fate through plans that were forecast rather than actualised. The 1931 master plan (which had been anticipated to be in use for twenty-five years, until 1956) consisted in a general scheme that was to be implemented through a series of more specific detailed plans. This already constituted a more modern approach when compared with the previous master plans where everything had been detailed on a single map. The original number of the projected detail plans for the 1931 overall master plan was 118, but the end of the 1950s had added some 167 more, along with 250 minor variations. Such procedures, harshly disputed by the opposition in the city council, aimed at leaving ample space for ad hoc changes, following the interests of the real estate sector more closely than those of the city, and allowing for every possible dubious alliance in the political arena.

Planning and the Housing Question

As indicated above there was an extraordinarily passionate public involvement in urban issues like housing, transport or building regulations at the time. Planning issues became the main field of confrontation in local politics, primarily because of the objective difficulties that the city was encountering in responding to the almost limitless demand for more and more affordable housing and to the increasing lack of adequate services. But ways of responding to that demand were linked to the interests of a few large landowners rather than to the city as a whole and this had also contributed to the steep reduction in the rental market which had almost disappeared, trapped as it was between periodically renewed rent controls and soaring free market prices. The national commitment to a policy of home ownership, part of the social programme of Christian Democracy, exaggerated the situation, effectively supporting overcrowding in the peripheral areas of the eastern and southern quadrants. The 1950s were a time of unbridled development of private initiatives in the real estate sector. Not only did house prices increase enormously but so did the cost of the building land, which became one major element of the final price. The continuous demand for new housing saw the construction industry accepting the unskilled labour provided by immigrants arriving from the South and the impoverished countryside.

Building densities reached at that time — from 800 to 1,200 inhabitants per hectare[8] — remain the highest in the history of modern Rome, while the housing stock itself kept increasing until the early 1960s. More condominiums were built and they were more and more distant from the centre, built mainly along the consular roads — Tuscolana, Casilina, Appia, Prenestina — as part of the hunt for lower land prices. In order to get a basic public infrastructure established, the developer sometimes donated either the terrain for a school or some comparable basic structure to the municipality so that the undeveloped land in the middle, then equipped with the necessary infrastructure, immediately increased its value. Land speculation became a major element in the city's economy and it was accompanied by widespread corruption of public and political personnel.[9] In those years Rome grew by adopting the stereotypes of modern architecture — high-rise apartment buildings, flat roofs — ignoring public space and endorsing private cars as the main form of mobility.

At the beginning of the 1950s, 22 per cent of the population was still living in shared housing throughout the city, and peripheral conditions were very harsh, with lack of services adding to overcrowding.[10] With housing the main issue — what was later called illegal self-help 'by necessity' — had become a structural element of the Roman building stock. Estimates suggest that in 1962 there were some 400,000 people living in some kind of illegal housing, most of whom were recent immigrants working in the building sector, and building their own homes in areas not suitable, for a variety of reasons, for the legal market.[11] This constituted a heavy burden for many years which was, over time, solved through various forms (or escamotages) of legalisation, and through forcing the municipality to bring basic infrastructure to areas not included in the existing plans. INA Casa promoted and realised a number of neighbourhoods in Rome.[12] Many young architects were involved and the programme provided a focus for new urban proposals. Italian cultural life was and would be dominated by the left for many years to come, and most young architects were communists or on the left. The committed debate within the PCI on how to express the national popular (in Gramsci's terms) roots of our identity was translated in architecture into a refusal of the traditions of the Modern Movement and substituted by an interest in research on the traditional or so-called 'spontaneous' way of designing building and public space. Three or four story building types, sloping roofs, traditional shutters, balconies, twisted streets characterise some of the most significant examples. Such an approach was also consistent with the Catholic-popular view, which was always critical of the modern-capitalist approach. This is why most neighbourhoods realised under the INA Casa programme, although generally well-structured and designed, have a look that distinguishes them from the modernist image current at the time. Some, notably the Roman Tiburtino development, were described as 'neo-realist' alluding to the new movement within the cinema.[13]

Poor public transport, in tune with national policies heavily linked to the kind of infrastructural growth based on roads and the oil industry, favoured the development of private transport — cars or scooters — which made public transport even less efficient. Generally, the main feature of that time was the inability of public administration, traditionally in debt, to cope with the demand coming from such unprecedented growth. The management of the existing 1931 master plan was clearly inadequate, and the legalisation of all possible 'variants', mainly directed to increasing previous building densities, did not reinforce public confidence in the strength of the law, because of the possibility of land speculation. Governed continuously by the moderate Christian Democratic Party from 1947 to 1976, the city experienced the formation of enterprises with direct links to that party and to the Catholic Church, traditionally a large owner of land. Landed property was actually in the hands of a small group of people, sometimes members of old aristocratic families connected with the Church. This was the case for the Società Generale Immobiliare, which was directly controlled by the Vatican.[14] The high cost of housing was largely due to the cost of land rather than to that of construction. At first it was Enzo Storoni, a liberal city councillor, who attacked the dangerous undercover links between the private sector and the public administration. Then it was the radical Leone Cattani and the left who denounced the prevailing interests of the Catholic Church in the real estate market. A slogan introduced in 1955 by *L'Espresso*, the influential leftist magazine: 'capitale corrotta = nazione infetta' [corrupt capital city = infected nation] accusing the mayor (who, after two trials, was acquitted by the Court) of misconduct became extremely popular.[15] Issues like the conservation of the historic centre, the provision of housing and increased land prices all became hot political fields where people looked at the party's interests more than at the actual problems. This was also true for the academic literature produced at the time and also regarding that time, which makes it difficult even today to get away from a simplistic picture of a struggle between good and evil.[16] One distinctive feature of the time, however, was the refusal of all that seemed to be linked to the fascist regime, including strategies, images and specific proposals for the city.

Struggling for a New Master Plan

With the impending (1956) date limit of the master plan of 1931, which was to last twenty-five years, a major aspect of the post-war period consisted in the long and difficult design of a new master plan whose elaboration took ten years because technical problems that specifically regarded planning were regularly subsumed by political pressures. The history of the master plan, which was eventually approved in 1962, is possibly the clearest example of how political life developed in the capital city: here social conflicts shifted to cultural representations, where disciplinary contrasts, whether it was about densities, open space standards or building types, took the form of a struggle between 'good' and 'evil' and every move from any actor was automatically considered as fraudulent by another. While this may sometimes have been true, much of the 'good' was revealed in the long run as naive or inadequate. The elaboration of the new master plan showed the harshness of the conflicts characterising the city and its politics in those years. The idea of a plan based on simple technical expertise was discarded from the beginning, when the project team put together planners who had the seal of approval of a political party.

Throughout its ten-year preparation (1953–62), the plan saw first the prominence of one side, then of the other. While there was agreement on some general principles, everything became unclear and controversial when precise indications had to be conveyed. For example, the left wanted the city to expand eastward, where more flat land (some of it in public hands) was available and where most low-income people were already settled; the right insisted on privileging development toward the west, where the land was largely within the hands of big landowners (including the Catholic Church) and to the south, where the land acquired for the 1942 Universal Exhibition was already being developed. The left opposed developing the south-east, yet most development took place there in the following years. Accepting all such indications together would have driven the city towards increased congestion of the centre, given free way to land speculation, and turned the traffic system into a nightmare. The compromise result was a little of everything, with all parties claiming victory, but with the result that the city would be on the verge of being out of control for decades to come.

One major area of agreement for the new master plan was the need to save the historic centre from the pressure of redevelopment and, consequently, avoid what was called an 'oil-slick' development, since when development expands in all directions (like an oil spot) all interests will remain focused on the centre, with implications for both traffic congestion and building values. One-directional growth, as suggested by most European planners from the nineteenth century on, would have avoided such disruptive consequences. The city council recommended that protection of the historic centre had to involve progressive decentralisation, the growth of new industrial areas, a balanced development between high- and low-density building, provision of green areas, adequate public transport and traffic regulation.

The solution envisaged by the 1962 plan provided for a kind of business district along a main infrastructural axis east of the historic core which would house most government and business headquarters, in an area developed through a comprehensive design on public land.[17] The challenge was extraordinary, and quite beyond local administrative traditions as the ministries did not really wish to move, private developers did not trust such a huge undertaking and the political parties were not ready to support such a programme, because each was suspicious of the other's possible advantage. So the new directional centre was never realised. The historic core remained physically safe, but it was transformed by private and public offices and most residents had to leave. Other offices, the headquarters of national and international big companies or small high tech firms, spread around the territory with no visible logic.

While the city council was furiously debating between the expansion east or west, and already symbolically expressing the struggle between progress and reaction, one area was being developed with great professional care, and this resulted in the best neighbourhood of the new Rome. It was developed on the public land initially assigned to the 1942 Universal Exhibition, but it became a directional centre and a medium-to-high-class residential settlement, which acquired new housing and new offices, offered a high standard of public amenities and the first underground line towards the centre and the central railway station. Thanks to an autonomous charter and the ownership of the land, EUR enjoyed much more funding than the municipality itself: selling building land to the investors, it enjoyed capital availability that ensured administrative efficiency. Unlike the municipality of Rome, EUR was therefore able to control its development and services provisions, including its aesthetic appearance, for many years. Many ministries, public and private corporations, new hotels and upper-middle-class housing were located there, encouraged by the EUR's excellent maintenance of public space.[18] The left, suspicious of the fascist origins of the district, tried to diminish its role in the overall city master plan, but the area of EUR finally succeeded. Although showing marks of decline, since the municipality of Rome took it back into its hands in the year 2000, it is now enjoying a new popularity with the reassessment of its fascist-inspired architecture. The main buildings, designed, but only initiated, in the last years of fascism, were actually completed in the 1950s and constitute a coherent architectural complex that the most recent master plan, that of 2008, puts under the historic conservation rule. Later additions of offices have maintained a rather high profile.

The 1960 Olympics

The Olympic Games offered a further aspect of urban debate in the 1950s, since the construction of new structures was not without an impact on the development of the city. The Games came to emphasise the full recovery of the country and its establishment in the modern world. They opened on 25 July with eighty-three participating nations. Archaeological sites such as the Appian Way, used for the marathon, which ended under the Arch of Constantine, the Basilica of Maxentius, which hosted the wrestling, and the Baths of Caracalla where the gymnastics were held, all offered sumptuous backgrounds. Sporting facilities and terrain were added, mainly in the north, around the Foro Italico (previously Foro Mussolini) and in the south, near the facilities already existing in EUR.

Architects and engineers, with all their creativity, were at the forefront of these projects. They represented a professional elite that was rather indifferent to the intellectual debate that was so intense in the academy and in political circles. Pier Luigi Nervi, an internationally known innovative engineer, designed two sport halls, a main Sports Palace with Marcello Piacentini, where the basketball and boxing took place, and a smaller one that was used for weightlifting; he also designed an elevated highway over the Olympic Village. The brilliant velodrome by Cesare Lugini (recently demolished in the unsuccessful attempt to turn the place into an 'aquatic park') was built near the EUR following a national competition (an exception in the series of Olympic projects). The Olympic stadium itself, which had been completed in 1953 with 65,000 seats by Annibale Vitellozzi, hosted the main ceremonies and track and field events. Some structures already in place from the fascist era were also brought into use: the Stadio dei Marmi [Stadium of the

Marbles], an example of classic architecture by Luigi Del Debbio for field hockey, and the swimming stadium (Stadio del Nuoto) by Del Debbio and Vitellozzi for aquatic sports. The Palazzo dei Congressi [Congress Hall] at EUR by Adalberto Libera, possibly the best building in that neighbourhood, was used for fencing. Other sports facilities and services were realised at the Acqua Acetosa site in the north and at Tre Fontane [Three Fountains] near the EUR.

Luigi Moretti, Adalberto Libera and others were responsible for the design of the Olympic Village, which became an excellent example of public housing: 1,348 apartments in two- or three-storey buildings on 'pilotis' that left open the ground floor, 16 hectares of green space and 12 hectares for squares and streets over a total of 35 hectares.[19] To link the various Olympic locations, new roads and underpasses were built, all involving primarily the northern and western sides of the city. The Via Olimpica [Olympic Way], for example, connected the north and the south through the west side making use of old railway tunnels and linking existing streets; underpasses along the Aurelian walls aimed to speed up the traffic in the central area. The Olympics acquired a clear right-wing connotation through the Christian Democrat city administration, which, together with the Christian-democrat national government, presented themselves under the flag of modernity and efficiency. Rome was no longer the rhetorical, pompous city built by fascism, nor was it the war-torn place of neo-realist cinema; rather, another Rome, one of modernity, of modern events and rituals, comparable to the London of the 1948 Olympics, was offered to the visitors.

But the planners missed the chance offered by the Olympic Games to implement the main master plan's proposals. Huge public investment in infrastructure went to the areas which were out of the plan's remit. For instance, nothing was built on the eastern quadrant. There were many reasons for this choice, including some already established facilities realised during the fascist era, but the fact remains that planners continued to try to orient development towards the east, while public intervention, including that for the new sport facilities, focused in the opposite direction. Together with the failed realisation of the eastern directional axis, such choices aggravated the pressure on the centre, and caused the switch in use from residential to offices in the area surrounding the walls and produced an even more problematic model of public transport. The main infrastructure became the ring road, which the plan had unsuccessfully opposed. When the master plan was finally adopted in 1965, after three years of bureaucratic procedures, it was already out of date in many respects, beginning with its mistaken forecast of a population growth of up to 5 million, something that has never been realised.

All this happened within a framework of tense debate, which saw citizens taking a stance on very different issues, and which was widely reported in the local press. Today we tend to think of the 1950s and the beginning of the 1960s as a time of new splendour in the nation. Despite the number and the extent of social and economic problems, there was an intensity and excitement tied to the process of changing modes of governance, exploring new paths in the arts and humanities, and engaging in brave new challenges, be it the construction of the 'Autostrada' and the new hydropower plants, the increased publication and translation of books, or the renovation of universities and research institutions.[20] General conditions may have been unsatisfactory, but it seemed possible for everybody freely to express advice, critique or opposition. This was certainly true in the artistic domain, but it was equally the case in politics and through it, obviously, in planning: it was not a time of intellectual or operative stagnation at the national level, or in the capital city. Rome's cultural life in the 1950s was by no means stagnant, be it the avant-garde theatre with Carmelo Bene and others, literature with Moravia and Pasolini, or the cinema,[21] which, mainly produced in Rome, interpreted social change with a sensibility that remained long unrivalled, giving the country a long-lasting mark of modern creativity.[22] Along with the birth of the Italian comedy, only later fully understood, the movies by Antonioni, Visconti and Fellini, going beyond the neo-realisud of the post-war time, recounted the uneasiness of the new consumer society. The Roman public debate, in which most intellectuals participated, took advantage of such a lively atmosphere.

Notes to Chapter 6

1. Augusto Graziani (ed.), *L'economia italiana 1945–1985* (Bologna: Il Mulino 1989).
2. Piero Berselli, *Venerati maestri* (Milan: Mondadori, 2006).
3. Marisa Fantin and Laura Fregolent (eds), *Astengo 1. Editoriali di urbanistica dal 1949 al 1976* (Rome: INU, 2010).
4. Giulio Carlo Argan and others, *Profili dell'Italia repubblicana*, ed. by Ottavio Cecchi and Enrico Ghidetti (Rome: Editori Riuniti, 1996).
5. Paola Di Biagi (ed.), *La grande ricostruzione. Il piano Ina-Casa e l'Italia degli anni cinquanta* (Rome: Donzelli, 2010).
6. Italo Insolera, *Roma moderna. Un secolo di storia urbanistica 1870–1970* (Turin: Einaudi, 1992; repr. 2001); Antonio Cederna, *I vandali in casa* (Bari: Laterza, 1956).
7. Mario Sanfilippo, *La costruzione di una capitale. Roma 1945–1991* (Cinisello Balsamo: Silvana-Pizzi, 1994).
8. Insolera, *Roma moderna*.
9. Ibid.
10. Giovanni Berlinguer and Piero Della Seta, *Borgate di Roma* (Rome: Editori Riuniti, 1960; 2nd edn 1976); Giuseppe Cuccia, *Urbanistica edilizia infrastrutture di Roma Capitale 1870–1990* (Rome and Bari: Laterza, 1991); Franco Ferrarotti, *Roma da capitale a periferia* (Rome and Bari: Laterza, 1970); Anne-Marie Seronde-Baboneaux, *Rome, croissance d'une capitale. De l'urbs à la ville* (Paris: Edisud, 1980).
11. Alberto Clementi and Francesco Perego (eds), *La metropoli 'spontanea'. Il caso di Roma* (Bari: Dedalo, 1983).
12. Alice Sotgia, *INA Casa Tuscolano. Biografia di un quartiere romano* (Milan: Franco Angeli, 2010).
13. Ludovico Quaroni, *Immagine di Roma* (Bari: Laterza, 1969).
14. Insolera, *Roma moderna*.
15. Vittorio Vidotto, *Roma contemporanea* (Rome and Bari: Laterza, 2006).
16. Piero Samperi, *Mezzo secolo di urbanistica romana* (Venice: Marsilio, 2008).
17. Piero Rossi Ostilio (with Ilaria Gatti), *Roma. Guida all'architettura moderna 1909–2000* (Rome and Bari: Laterza, 2000); Gianni Accasto, Vanna Fraticelli and Renata Nicolini, *L'architettura di Roma capitale 1870–1970* (Rome: Golem, 1971).
18. Samperi, *Mezzo secolo di urbanistica romana*; Lando Bortolotti, *Roma fuori le mura* (Rome and Bari: Laterza, 1988).
19. Cuccia, *Urbanistica edilizia infrastrutture di Roma Capitale 1870–1990*.

20. Silvio Lanaro, *Storia dell'Italia repubblicana. L'economia, la politica, la cultura, la società dal dopoguerra agli anni '90* (Venice: Marsilio, 2001).
21. Eugenio Scalfari, *La sera andavamo in Via Veneto. Storia di un gruppo dal 'Mondo' alla 'Repubblica'* (Milan: Mondadori, 1986).
22. Giuseppe Brunetta, *Cent'anni di cinema italiano* (Rome and Bari: Laterza, 1991).

CHAPTER 7

❖

A Very Old Neo-Liberalism: The Changing Politics and Policy of Urban Informality in the Roman *Borgate*

Alessandro Coppola

Introduction

This chapter aims to examine critically recent evolutions and transformations in the political and policy treatment of informal urban developments in Rome from the perspective of contemporary debates and theories of neo-liberal urban governance. The primary focus is the emergence of new policies and devices — *Consorzi di Autorecupero* — aimed at the self-organisation and mobilisation of property owners in informally built areas of the city which will be studied through an empirically based enquiry into the implementation of such policies and devices. The essay is organised as follows: in the first section, I briefly present the historical terms of the development of urban informality in post 1945 Rome; in the second, I introduce the trajectory of its politicisation and its constitution as a specific policy object; in the third and fourth, I discuss the emergence — within this trajectory — of a new emphasis on ownership and self-organisation; in the fifth, I present the outcome of fieldwork conducted in two Roman *borgate* — Morena and Centrone — focusing on the local *Consorzi*. The conclusion addresses the significance of contemporary debates on urban neo-liberalism and governance in the areas of critical geography, planning and urban studies.

The Development of the Informal Metropolis

Between 1945 and 1975, Rome's population grew by almost 800,000 inhabitants, mostly the result of internal migration from southern and central rural regions.[1] Because of the lack of an extensive industrial sector, migrants were attracted by the expansion of the construction industry and the low-skilled service sectors on one side, and the highly skilled service sector on the other.[2]

The booming housing demand associated with the demographic increase proved to be a challenge for Rome's deeply unbalanced local urban planning and for a housing provision system that, since national unification, had been characterised by the influence of private land interests, the lack of a consistent public inventory of developable land, the over-production of middle- and upper-class housing, and the under-production of working-class housing.[3] Particularly, after the Second World War, specific land and real-estate interests exercised significant influence on the design and implementation of planning decisions through the establishment of strong ties with local political powers dominated by the Christian Democrats (DC). Under the hegemony of this network of interests, defined as *Blocco edilizio*, the city expanded chaotically, primarily in the form of very dense urban neighbourhoods oriented to middle- and upper-class demand.[4]

In this context, much of the housing demand from migrants employed both formally and informally in the low-skilled service sector, and from the lower classes more generally, was largely ignored. The lack of affordable housing in the private market was coupled with a persistent under-production of public housing that was instrumental in maintaining the hegemony of private land and real-estate interests over the planning process.[5] From the 1950s, a consistent component of this demand was directed towards solutions provided by an expanding system of informal and illegal housing provision. Informal settlements of variable size and quality continuously expanded within the city and in its periphery throughout the post-war decades: in 1951, 150,000 people lived in such settlements, a number growing to 400,000 in 1961 and finally peaking at around 800,000 in 1981.[6]

Much of this informal activity led to the creation of the *borgate*, informal settlements developed on privately owned land often located in peripheral areas close to major arterial roads. Most *borgate* followed a similar development pattern in which certain landowners, excluded from development opportunities by urban planning decisions, made their land available through the establishment of a parallel illegal land market. Lower-class migrants and Romans then bought, with or without the mediation of third parties, individual plots of land which they later developed, often in the form of self-designed and self-built single-family homes.[7] Over time, the process increased in scope and sophistication with the involvement of a wider range of mediators and professionals and, from the 1970s, with the appearance of a housing supply oriented to the middle and upper classes.[8]

The informal nature of the *borgate* was obvious in that it encompassed the illegal subdivision and marketisation of land, the building of housing not in compliance with the established city planning regulations and procedures, the resort to labour and design services provided by the inhabitants themselves or accessed on the black market, and the absence of any security of tenure.[9]

From the 1950s, the *borgate* became the arena for the political activism of the left, especially of the Italian Communist Party (PCI). Through a complex and innovative set of urban actors, the most important of which was the *Unione Borgate*, the PCI was able to establish its political and electoral hegemony over these informal settlements.[10] The campaigns promoted by the PCI and its urban organisations framed the issue of urban informality in neo-Marxist theorisations of Rome's peculiarly backward position and function in the larger neo-capitalist development path taken by post-war Italy.[11] In particular, the entrenchment of a spatial dualism of the city between relatively well-equipped, formal residential areas for the middle and upper classes, and an under-resourced, frequently informal lower-class periphery was interpreted as one of the most distinctive outcomes of the fact that the local bourgeoisie depended on the extraction of urban rent rather than on industrial profits, and the political hegemony of the *Blocco edilizio* over city politics.[12] Rooted in this framework, the PCI's urban agenda proposed an assertive state intervention in the ownership and management of urban land and the production of housing for the lower-classes. At the same time, the party also pushed for policies aimed at bringing infrastructure and essential services to informal settlements.[13]

The recognition of voting rights for internal migrants living in the *borgate*, who had been prevented from becoming formal residents of the city by the continuing existence of Fascist legislation, was another of the PCI's goals, one that became law as early as 1961.[14]

Under the pressure of the PCI's campaigning, the city administration, controlled at the time by the Christian Democrats (DC), began to implement policies aimed at the upgrading of the *borgate*. In 1965, the new land-use plan (Piano Regolatore Generale, PRG) acknowledged the existence of informal settlements, while later, in the early 1970s, the administration promoted an initial plan for the extension of sewage and water networks, the construction of new schools, and the building of new public housing complexes.[15]

These policies gained momentum during the following decade when the PCI — thanks in particular to an electoral landslide in the *borgate* — took control of city hall with the goal of 'healing the urban fracture' between the centre and the city's peripheries, still largely illegal.[16] In 1978, the new administration, through a pivotal zoning decision, the so-called *Variante Borgate*, acknowledged the existence of many other informal settlements, and launched ambitious plans for extending infrastructures, public transport, and social services, while allowing new legal, market-rate housing.[17]

In the same period, a new housing plan was launched with the aim of significantly increasing the production of public and social housing, and pursuing, through a more rational and advanced organisation of the construction industry,[18] a more transparent agreement between the city and key players in the real-estate industry. Large modernist public and social housing projects were designed to satisfy the housing needs of low-income demand while limiting the further expansion of informal settlements and improving access to services in the existing ones.[19]

However, these planning decisions and regeneration policies did not solve the central problem of tenure. Despite a first regional legislative attempt in 1980, the legal controversy between the state and the individuals who had built informally had to be resolved by national legislation. In 1985, after a series of failed attempts, and in a heated political climate, parliament passed the so-called *condono edilizio* that introduced an amnesty for people who had built housing for their own use illegally, and granted them the right to become owners.[20] The new legislation required that in order to make their properties completely legal, individuals applying for the *condono* had to pay a fine and a development fee. For its part, the city administration had to implement regeneration plans, the *Piani di recupero*, aimed at realising basic infrastructures and services according to established national planning regulations. With over 400,000 requests, Rome became the city with the largest number of *condono* files to be processed in the country.[21]

From the Right to the City to the Right to Property

Since the 1960s, Italian critical social theorists had explained the rise of informal urban settlements as one of the main socio-spatial products of the 'backward modernity' characterising the process of urban expansion and modernisation of post-war Rome. Both the role of the land and the housing system in the overall urban economy and the distinctive characteristics of both systems were questioned and their characteristics were later deemed typical of the larger 'southern-European housing system'.[22] The development of informality has been one of the most evident epiphenomena of this positioning. As in other southern European cities, the extent of housing informality in Rome has been the product of the large-scale activation of family-based housing strategies by internal migrants who structured their integration in the urban system around real-estate self-promotion and wealth-building in the context of an enduringly weak labour market and welfare state.[23]

The state, in its articulations across different arenas, from national government to city administration, has played a strategic role in consolidating and perpetuating such strategies and, therefore, with respect to their wider implications for the development trajectory of the city of Rome. This role functioned passively, in the form of the lack of action in certain domains — the state did not restrict, in the majority of cases, illegal building activity — and actively through policies which explicitly addressed the issue of the legalisation and upgrading of informal developments.

For instance, in the 1950s and 1960s, the absence of reforms and the very partial implementation of existing legislation in the land and housing provision systems had set the stage for the existence of the informal land and housing markets that have been ostensibly tolerated by key state actors, notably the city administration.[24] By the 1970s and 1980s, the set of policies promoted by the city administration under the mounting influence of the PCI and its urban organisations implied a partial evolution in the role of this key state actor. Through a form of social and spatial redistribution of fiscal resources, these local policies aimed at ensuring wider and better access to those urban rights of social reproduction in the form of 'collective consumption'[25] that had been denied to migrants living in the *borgate*; these included the expansion of networked infrastructures and services on the one side, and the relative decommodification of housing on the other. A result of such policies was the development of a more inclusive, socially legitimate legal framework, which was expected to contain the expansion and the role of the informal sector over time. This new structure was based on and entailed the promotion of precise, explicit policy initiatives pursuing the formalisation and titling of illegal assets — the 1980s *condono* being the most important of these initiatives — through the demand for a minimal *ex-post* contribution towards the costs of urban development and the expenditure of significant public funds.[26]

From this perspective, the planning decisions acknowledging the existence of the *borgate* promoted by the city administration and the *condono* promoted by national government are among the most important *de facto* policy tools deployed by the Italian state to secure its larger goal of widespread access to homeownership.[27] Thanks to the *condono*, the *borgate* have become the areas of the city with the highest incidence of homeownership,[28] triggering a process of massive, albeit unplanned, access to urban rent on behalf of specific groups that had been extremely marginal in the class structure of the city.[29] Through these policies, hundreds of thousands of families have accessed homeownership in the form of the possession of a tangible asset that can be deployed as collateral in any financial transaction. They have entered the real-estate market as suppliers of assets whose values have been steadily and consistently appreciating over time and, in this way, have established flourishing family economies built around the inter-generational transmission of housing or capital created through the commodification of housing.[30]

In this way, the *borgate* dwellers ceased to be 'pariahs' with no stake in the capitalist economy and became homeowners able to privatise and appropriate a part of the value accruing from the socio-spatial redistributive policies of the city administration. Apparently, the *borgate* have ceased to be spaces of exception, a dystopian condition that was also the basis for the successful organisation of the victims of this very condition,[31] and have become 'normalised' and integrated into the 'ordinary city' and its political and economic functioning.

Associating and Mobilising Homeowners: The Development of the *Consorzi di Autorecupero*

The *condono* accomplished a process of change in the locus of urban agency in the *borgate* so that the main constituent of the politics and the policy of informality was no longer made by their residents but by those who owned homes there. The potential for homeowners to develop new social capital within wider regeneration and valorisation processes became a source of interest for policy-makers, and this, in turn, set the stage for the design of innovative planning and urban policies in the 1990s. For instance, a 1995 city ordinance established the principle of the direct mobilisation of owners involved in the *condono edilizio* in the design and construction of infrastructures and services in their area of residence. Based on the second *condono edilizio*, promoted by the centre-right majority led by Silvio Berlusconi in 1994, it allowed property owners to deposit the development fees required to secure the legal ownership of their homes in newly established local associations, the Associazioni Consortili di Recupero Urbano (ACRU, generally referred to as *Consorzi*). These *Consorzi*, which were to be formed on the free initiative of property *owners* in the areas established through previous planning decisions, were given the right to use their budget for the design and implementation of public infrastructures such as roads, sewage and water systems, public parks, and educational and recreational facilities. Although their budgets remained formally part of the city budget, the city government's role was limited to the supervision, assessment and final authorisation of the projects presented by the *Consorzi* themselves.[32]

Subsequent changes in city regulations granted the *Consorzi* the power to collect development fees paid by private developers for new real-estate projects being implemented in the same areas, which would have otherwise been collected in the city budget, and to call for open bids for the design and realisation of those public works they decided to implement.[33] These two changes significantly enlarged the autonomy of the *Consorzi*, granting them powers that generally belonged only to public agencies. All the same, despite their role and responsibilities, the *Consorzi* have a rather slim management structure in the form of a president and a board of directors elected by the members who have the decision-making power for the projects in that area to be realised. For the actual implementation of their programmes, however, they depend on intermediary structures for support in the design and construction of the projects; these structures also manage the lengthy, cumbersome process of filing individual owners' amnesty requests at the *Ufficio Speciale Condono Edilizio*, the office set up by the city government following the *condono*. These intermediary organisations have been created through organisations dominated by the PCI, as in the case of AIC Recupero, and promoted with the support of the Unione Borgate, and by younger coalitions of *Consorzi*, such as the Consorzio Recupero Urbano Città di Roma, in their turn promoted by the Consorzio Periferie Romane, probably the largest of these organisations. The city administration lacks regularly assessed data regarding the number of the *Consorzi* and their activities, but the *Consorzio Periferie Romane* states on its website that it has forty-five member organisations across the city, twelve of which have successfully completed infrastructural programmes in the areas where they operate.[34]

In the following sections, I present two case studies of the *Consorzi* operating in two neighbouring Roman *borgate*, Morena and Centroni. These case studies are based on fieldwork undertaken between spring 2012 and the winter of 2013, consisting of fifteen in-depth interviews with key local and urban actors, participant observation of community events, territorial surveys, and analysis of relevant planning and policy documents.

Case Study: The *Borgate* of Morena and Centroni

The *borgate* of Morena (43,000 inhabitants in 2011) and Centroni are located southeast of the urban core along Via Anagnina, a major arterial road extending beyond the Grande Raccordo Anulare (Gra), the 68 km long ring road surrounding Rome. Both *borgate* developed in the 1950s following a fairly typical pattern where local landowners illegally subdivided their properties in plots ranging from 500 to 1,000 square metres and sold them to migrant families. These families developed them, mainly through self-promotion and self-construction, as single-family homes, but, with the complete absence of basic infrastructure, such as sewage, lighting, paved roads and schools.[35] The city's land plan of 1965, Piano Regolatore Generale, zoned one of the two *borgate*, Morena, as an 'F1' area, the newly established zoning typology for informal developments that were to be legalised. It also set the stage for interventions that would lead to upgrading and future regeneration.

Throughout the 1960s and the early 1970s, informal development continued to spread, invading areas that had been zoned for public parks and agriculture in the 1965 plan. These more recent developments were later included in the PRG and zoned as 'O' areas, the new zoning typology established by a pivotal decision, the so-called *Variante delle Borgate*, promoted by the PCI-controlled city administration in 1978, and implemented from 1983 on. Thanks to the implementation of these successive planning initiatives, from the late 1960s to the 1980s both *borgate* benefited from significant public investment in the development of basic infrastructures, the sewage system, primary schools still in use today, and an enlarged public transport system. From the 1990s, new real-estate investments burgeoned in the two areas. However, as in many other *borgate*, these real-estate developments were implemented in very patchy ways because of the inability of developers to comply with regulations and to fulfil agreements (that often implied the provision of new public amenities in lieu of the payment of development fees) on the one hand, and the inability of the city administration to enforce them on the other.

Today, despite public and private investment, these two *borgate* are still far from achieving the urban living standards prescribed by national and local regulations and are still overly characterised by a highly privatistic and minimalist understanding of urban living. Gated single family homes and small condominiums often equipped with well-kept private gardens and courtyards are insulated from a public realm lacking basic features such as a coherent, safe system of pedestrian paths and public spaces. Mobility is almost exclusively dependent on private cars and traffic is one of the main concerns in the area; recreational opportunities are limited to a few commercial outlets.

While they have often been romanticised as 'villages' of an 'archipelago-city',[36] *borgate* such as Morena and Centroni seldom have the kind of localised social capital and high-quality public space that urban neighbourhoods or villages are said to have. Instead they function as plain 'residential platforms'[37] located at one end of increasingly extended commuting trajectories covered daily by metropolitan inhabitants in their private vehicles.[38]

Consorzi di Autorecupero

The Consorzio di Autorecupero Morena Sud began in 1997 through the initiative of the local Neighbourhood Committee, which was historically linked to the Unione Borgate. Roughly 250 property owners decided to become members of the Consorzio, about 50 per cent of all owners living in the area. According to its President, a long-term resident of the *borgata* and owner of a small construction company, the founders of the Consorzio saw 'the opportunity to use the fees that still had to be paid for their amnesty requests to upgrade infrastructures and services in the area'.[39] Despite the relatively high number of contributors, the sum of individual fees deposited in the budget was limited as the 1985 law *condono* had required only very small fees that could not cover local infrastructural needs. Therefore, the Consorzio's president began to establish ties with real-estate developers active in the area, persuading them to deposit the fees they would otherwise deposit with the city with the Consorzio. This enabled it to increase its initial budget by €450,000.[40]

Regarding the projects planned and implemented, the Consorzio first promoted the idea of investing in the creation of a public park, but, after the emergence of a controversy around property rights for the area where the park was to be located, it proposed a new scheme aimed at rehabilitating the roads and footpaths around the only public transport link in the *borgata*. Despite initial hopes, the Consorzio was only able to begin this project in 2010, thirteen years after its foundation, though it was then completed by 2012.

Based on its founders' membership in the Unione Borgate, the Consorzio Morena Sud chose to contract the intermediary organisation AIC Recupero to carry out all design and procedural duties linked to implementing the projects. Despite the participationist rhetoric deployed at the time of its foundation, the Consorzio had no active participatory members at the time of the research. Board of directors' meetings were rare and were convened to coincide with the meetings of the Morena neighbourhood committee whose leadership overlapped with that of the Consorzio. Both the president and many directors sat on both bodies. The Consorzio's agenda also had clear links with the Neighbourhood Committee's historic platform, that is, following a shared 'minimalist' approach, the Consorzio planned interventions almost entirely directed to the upgrading of the roads and the sewage system with no significant reference to any higher-level public spaces and amenities.

The Consorzio di Autorecupero di Centroni-Villa Senni was founded at the end of the 1990s and at the time of the research it had a membership of over 550 property owners who, unlike those of Morena, had filed their *condono* requests under three different laws, those of 1985, 1994 and 2004. Because of the larger number of members and the consistent fees due under the 1994 and 2004 *condoni*, the Consorzio Centroni was able to raise a total sum of *c*.€4 million, significantly more than Morena. This financial success also derived from the greater ability of the Consorzio's President to collect fees generated by real-estate development initiatives. Since 2000, in the context of the implementation of the *Piano di recupero*, the area had experienced a significant expansion in housing and demographic terms, although some of the fees collected by the Consorzio were generated by real-estate development initiatives located not only within the perimeter of the Consorzio but also elsewhere in the borough.

The role of the Consorzio's President has been the key to achieving this success. An architect who had been involved in several of these real-estate projects, he persuaded developers for whom he worked to deposit their development fees in the Consorzi budget instead of that of the city. At the same time, the Consorzio Centroni showed some degree of solidarity towards the less fortunate neighbouring

Consorzio Morena Sud; for instance, in at least one case, its President had asked a private developer who was willing to deposit his fees in the coffers of the first to deposit them in those of the second, a 'favour' that was apparently later returned by the Consorzio Morena Sud's president. Overall, the greater financial wealth of the Consorzio Centroni has allowed it to implement a larger programme of initiatives: new segments of the sewage system have been built; roads and footpaths have been paved; and recently a new square has been created which, though completed by the time of the research, had not been opened due to persistent bureaucratic problems with the city administration.

In addition to these successful initiatives, the Consorzio still had a significant amount of funding that could be used for other projects. Notable among them was a public park. It had already been designed and presented to the city administration, but approval had been denied for reasons that were not immediately clear, but which illuminate one of the many distortions in the ongoing activity of the Consorzi. At the time of the research, given the stress that austerity measures had imposed on the city budget, the city administration, which, at least formally, controls the Consorzi's budgets, denied approval to certain local projects not on the grounds either of quality or of their pertinence to local needs, but in order to use the funding for other initiatives. In the case of the Consorzio Centroni, the approval was denied so that the funding could be directed to an anti-flooding infrastructure required in a neighbouring *borgata* where significant real-estate development activity was anticipated in the near future. Although the Consorzio resisted the decision, thereby underlining the incoherence and inconsistency of the city administration, the administration was ultimately able to move forward with its decision.

Neighbourhood Committees

In both areas, in the absence of a real participatory base, the Consorzi rely on the existence of Neighbourhood Committees for formulating projects and for managing on a day-to-day basis their relationships with the city and borough administrations. As already mentioned, most neighbourhood committees located in the *borgate* had developed during the 1960s and 1970s often through the support of the PCI and its urban organisations.

Both in Morena and Centroni, as long as the choice of Aic Recupero as the intermediary agency is recognised, the affiliation of the two Consorzi to the Unione Borgate can be explained by these historical links. The leadership of both Consorzi was, at the time of the research, in the hands of two individuals who were members of the PCI until its dissolution in 1991; in the first case and probably in the second, they became members of the Democratic Party (PD), the most recent heir of the PCI.[41]

Neighbourhood committees have evolved over the years, and in both Morena and Centroni they enjoyed a certain degree of formalisation, since they were on the record of the borough register of the neighbourhood committees. They both presented themselves as entities that were 'autonomous from the political parties and open to people of any background', even if, especially in the case of Morena, a pattern of strong involvement of PDs activists was easily traceable. Moreover, they proposed highly localised agendas with very few references to issues beyond the daily life of the two *borgate*.

Regarding Morena, the committee was managed by a board of directors composed of 15 residents, not all of whom were active, who were elected by 200 residents, and a president who was also the Consorzio president. The directors and the president were intent on 'making sure that the voice of the neighbourhood is heard',[42] when important decisions were taken at city and borough levels. This duty was pushed ahead through the establishment and the maintenance of contacts and relationships with the borough and city administrations and with some borough council members (mostly of the PD).

The committee's agenda had been consistent across the years and its platform included requests relating to the continuing lack of infrastructure and services that characterises the area, with a strong focus on physical aspects like roads, footpaths and parks, but with less attention to broader social development. At that time, the committee was increasing its attention to environmental issues, for instance, by organising initiatives promoting bicycles as a sustainable mode of transportation in the *borgata*. But their capacity to mobilise residents had been weak over the years, and their own activists regretted their failure to promote social events, such as neighbourhood parties, and the very scarce participation of residents in public demonstrations and meetings.

In purely quantitative terms, their most successful communication channels were a website and a Facebook page subscribed to by about 550 residents. On these pages, alongside more typical postings such as committees' platforms and news, or information about life opportunities in the neighbourhood, the committee's activists regularly posted information on matters of local interest with a strong focus on planning, urban development and city services. Without a specific page, the very limited information regarding the Consorzio's activities was posted on the Committee's own pages.

In Centroni, the Comitato di quartiere is a more recent development. It was only in 2012, through a new President, that the committee was formally recognised by the borough administration. The board of directors, composed of nine residents, held weekly meetings in the office of the Consorzio president. In Centroni too, the committee's main focus had been to develop ties with municipal and city institutions, alerting them to specific, often very minor, problems in the neighbourhood. Unlike Morena, it did not have an organic public platform, but was nonetheless active in proposing specific projects focusing on infrastructural aspects of development. With the support of the president, the committee dealt with specific problems that arose in the neighbourhood, for instance, a dispute regarding the structural faults in the local primary school building. The Comitato lacked a webpage but had a Facebook group in which about 160 residents participated, the committee posting information about its activities, the residents mostly posting complaints about local issues. According to the committee's president, and based on my own observation, levels of local engagement were extremely low in the Centroni area.

One More Case of an Actually Existing Neo-liberalism: The Vetero-liberalism of the Roman *Borgate*[43]

The case of the Consorzi brings to light another case of 'actually existing neo-liberalism',[44] representing a conflation of different motives and rationales that have all been part of often disconnected strands of neo-liberal urban policy, in both its 'traditional' and 'social investment' variations.[45]

First, the concerns of the Consorzi have moved to property ownership and away from a serious reconsideration of the conceptualisation and practice of urban citizenship linking the exercise of specific rights of voice, particularly the possibility of deciding what public infrastructural projects should be implemented, to the possession of property. This in many ways represents a step backwards in the Marshallian conceptualisation of citizenship towards renewed forms of 'property citizenship' and the creation of local polities explicitly based on ownership.[46]

Second, this reconsideration of citizenship is linked to a process of governance rescaling, one which, in line with the rediscovery of neighbourhoods by neo-liberal urban policies, actively mobilises a new scale to deploy new forms of social organisation.[47] This is, moreover, based on the idea of directly 'responsibilising' in the provision of formerly government designed and provided urban services.[48] This 'responsibilisation' of citizens is associated with the development of an entrepreneurial logic of collective action[49] and a strategic use of contractual forms of public action.[50]

Third, the creation of this new governance scale strategically leverages on the existing one to induce new patterns of uneven geography,[51] thereby contributing to an urban environment in which access to certain basic urban rights depends on the 'market potential' of single areas, and more particularly on the potential development fees that can be generated in them. From a policy framework, taking into account the city as a whole — as in the case of the mentioned 1970/80s socio-spatial redistributive policies promoted by the city administration — the Consorzi embody a shift to a framework based on the valorisation of the growth potential of its individual parts. This being said, it is equally important to emphasise how this 'actually existing neo-liberalism' is deeply embedded in and determined by structural and non-structural characteristics of the local environment.[52]

From this perspective, the two study areas exemplify a situation shared by most *borgate* in Rome: very high homeownership is combined with a persistent lack of 'urbanity', which is evident in the lack of collective infrastructure and related activities and in the fragility of local social capital networks. If the *condono* was successful at turning what once was 'dead capital' into 'living capital',[53] it has been quite unsuccessful in generating those localised networks of social capital that, following neo-liberal accounts, are the by-product of individual accumulation strategies associated with homeownership.[54] At least for the two districts discussed here, the level of mobilisation and participation among individual owners has been insufficient, since only a small portion of them have become members of the Consorzi and even among members participation in the design, implementation and assessment of projects has been very limited, if not entirely absent. Decisions about projects have been entrusted to the Consorzio's presidents and to a few neighbourhood committee activists. Most members seemed to regard their membership as a way to facilitate and simplify the 'condono' transaction with the state rather than as an opportunity to exercise forms of 'local sovereignty' based on individual/family accumulation and investment strategies. In this context, there did not materialise the anticipated risk or expectation of a neighbourhood polity monopolised by individual owners seen as rational agents involved in the subordination of public choices, at least those that can be achieved by the Consorzio, to the valorization of their assets.

This failure seems to be a function of long-term local factors, such as the entrenched individualistic and privatistic culture that has been one of the key components in the birth of the 'informal metropolis',[55] the limited cultural capital of residents living in previously informal areas[56] and the persistent weakness of the institutional and regulatory frameworks in which the activity of Consorzi is embedded.

From this perspective it is important to underscore how, despite all its limitations and in the absence of precise estimates of its quantitative significance, the 1995 city decision that introduced the device of the *consorzi* has unleashed the development of a fairly extended and densely specialised network of property owners, professionals, developers, elected officials and bureaucrats actively engaged in this policy field. This network, which has proved to be increasingly influential on public decisions, developed in part from the evolution of inherited forms of social and political capital, in part from the city- and neighbourhood-level organisations developed from the 1960s, and in part from the formation of new groups and organisations.[57] But, despite the significance of this network, the Consorzi have not been adequately supported by their main actors, who have continued to operate in quite traditional and conservative ways with little serious investment in strategic support, training and evaluation. At the same time, an extremely slow implementation of projects has fuelled disillusionment and retreat among residents and members. In addition, the city administration's non-linear decisions produced what might be called a sort of 'functional heterogenesis' of the Consorzi. As is evident in the case of Centrone, the city administration made an opportunistic use of the Consorzio's budget, treating it as an 'unexpected' niche of public finance in times of acute budgetary difficulty, to be used in a discretionary way so as to implement other development decisions more likely to generate an influx of fiscal resources. The lack of institutional oversight led to other more endogenous forms of degeneration of their original function that, in this case, actually radicalised the neo-liberal character of the Consorzi.

Since the Consorzi were authorised to collect the fees of new development projects, the financial advantages enjoyed by the Consorzio Centroni derived both from the more intense building activity that has characterised the area in recent years and from the ability of its president to establish direct ties with property developers. Without these additional revenues, neither of the Consorzi would have reached the financial capacity to implement initiatives of any significance. This poses the question of the formalisation of the relationship between private developers and the

Consorzi. As we have seen, on the one hand, individual owners did not seem to exercise any strategic leadership in relation to the Consorzi's choices, and, on the other, private developers were more willing and effective at putting pressure on them, thus undermining the declared participatory goals of the institution.

Thus, the practice that sees the Consorzi acquiring fees paid by developers for projects implemented in areas beyond their perimeters illuminates a pattern of increasing privatisation of urban planning regulations and policies where individual actors, in this case the Consorzi, freely move and compete in the 'market' of development fees. At a microscale, this mechanism leads to distorted patterns in the distribution of public resources and the development of social networks based on clientelistic, potentially untransparent exchanges between professionals, developers and political leaders.[58]

In conclusion, what can be considered a neo-liberal project from the point of view of its 'policy morphology' is the result of a far more complex hybridisation of long-standing cultural patterns, inherited social and political capital, and entrenched institutional and regulatory frameworks. In the case of the Consorzi, and wider innovative planning policies implemented in the city of Rome,[59] elements of neo-liberal restructuring of public policy continue to operate in a context characterised by low levels of social organisation, inadequate institutional quality, and the lack of accountability and reliability of laws and regulations.[60] For these reasons I argue that, in the case of the recent evolution of the politics of urban informality in Rome, we can talk of *vetero-liberalism* instead of *neo-liberalism*: a form of rescaled, property-based, competitive urban policy that, even if it presents a shared morphology with mature neo-liberal experimentation, is more entrenched in the inheritance of long-term local historical contingencies than in the integration of local polities into global policy mobilities.[61]

Notes to Chapter 7

1. Luigi De Rosa, *Roma del Duemila* (Rome and Bari: Laterza, 1999).
2. Franco Ferrarotti, *Roma da capitale a periferia* (Rome and Bari: Laterza, 1970).
3. Alberto Violante, *La metropoli spezzata* (Milan: Franco Angeli, 2008).
4. Italo Insolera, *Roma moderna. Un secolo di storia urbanistica 1870–1970* (Turin: Einaudi, 1992; repr. 2001).
5. Ibid.
6. Alessandro Coppola, 'Le borgate romane tra '45 e '89: esclusione sociale, movimenti urbani e poteri locali', in *Tracce di quartieri. Il legame sociale nella città che cambia*, ed. by Marco Cremaschi (Milan: Franco Angeli, 2008), pp. 161–86.
7. Giovanni Berlinguer and Piero Della Seta, *Borgate di Roma*, 2nd edn (Rome: Editori Riuniti, 1976).
8. Alberto Clementi and Francesco Perego (eds), *La metropoli 'spontanea'. Il caso di Roma* (Bari: Dedalo, 1983).
9. Alessandro Coppola, 'Evolutions and Permanences in the Politics and Policy of Informality: Notes on the Case of Rome', *Quaderni di Urbanistica Tre*, 2 (2013), 35–40.
10. Berlinguer and Della Seta, *Borgate di Roma*; Coppola, 'Le borgate romane'.
11. Violante, *La metropoli spezzata*.
12. Ferrarotti, *Roma da capitale a periferia*.
13. Coppola, 'Le borgate romane'.

14. Guido Crainz, *Storia del Miracolo Italiano. Culture, identità, trasformazioni fra anni cinquanta e sessanta* (Rome: Donzelli, 1996).

15. Coppola, 'Le borgate romane'.

16. Francesco Perego (ed.), *L'Urbanistica della sinistra in Campidoglio* (Rome: Edizione delle Autonomie, 1981).

17. Alessandro Coppola, 'Roma, la metropolizzazione parassitaria e i suoi modi informali', in *Fuori raccordo. Abitare l'altra Roma*, ed. By Carlo Cellamare (Rome and Bari: Donzelli, 2017), pp. 209–23.

18. Ella Baffoni and Vezio De Lucia, *La Roma di Petroselli. Il sindaco più amato e il sogno spezzato di una città per tutti* (Rome: Castelvecchi, 2011).

19. Stefano Garano and Piero Salvagni, *Governare una metropoli. Le giunte di sinistra a Roma 1976–1985* (Rome: Editori Riuniti, 1985).

20. Paolo Berdini, *Breve storia dell'abuso edilizio in Italia* (Rome: Donzelli, 2010).

21. Ibid.

22. Judith Allen and others, *Housing and Welfare in Southern Europe* (Oxford: Blackwell, 2004).

23. Ibid.

24. Vezio De Lucia, *Se questa è una città. La condizione urbana nell'Italia contemporanea* (Rome: Donzelli, 2006).

25. Manuel Castells, *La question urbaine* (Paris: François Maspéro, 1972).

26. Liliana Padovani, Thomas Maloutas, Judith Allen, James Barlow, and Jesús Leal, *Housing and Welfare in Southern Europe* (Oxford: Blackwell, 2004).

27. Filippo De Pieri, *Le ragioni di urna ricerca*, in Bruno Bonomo and others (eds), *Storie di case. Abitare l'Italia del boom* (Rome: Donzelli, 2008), pp. xi–xxx.

28. AIC and Unione Borgate, *Periferie di Mezzo. Servizi, innovazioni, sostenibilità: un nuovo sistema urbano* (Rome, 2010).

29. Perego (ed.), *L'urbanistica della sinistra*; Hernando De Soto, *The Other Path: The Invisible Revolution in the Third World* (New York: Harper and Row, 1989).

30. Hernando De Soto, *The Mystery of Capital: Why Capitalism Triumph in the West and Fails Everywhere Else* (London: Black Swan Books, 2000).

31. Violante, *La metropoli spezzata*.

32. Carlo Cellamare, 'Politiche e processi dell'abitare nella città informale/abusiva romana', *Archivio di Studi Urbani e Regionali*, 97–98 (2010), 145–67.

33. Roma Capitale, www.comune.roma.it (2016).

34. Consorzio Recupero Periferie Romane, www.qualità urbana.it (2005).

35. Piero Della Seta and Roberto Della Seta, *I suoli di Roma. Uso e abuso del territorio nei cento anni della capitale*, intr. by Giulio Carlo Argan (Rome: Editori Riuniti, 1988).

36. Fabiola Fratini, *Roma arcipelago di isole urbane. Scenari per Roma del XXI Secolo* (Rome: Gangemi, 2000).

37. Mauro Magatti (ed.), *La città abbandonata* (Bologna: Il Mulino, 2007).

38. Giovanni Caudo and Alessandro Coppola, *Periferie di cosa? Roma e la condizione periferica* (Rome: Carocci, 2006).

39. Author, Interview (2013).

40. Author, Interview (2013).

41. PCI dissolved in 1991 giving birth to a new party that in 2009 founded — with some other smaller centre-left parties — the Democratic Party (PD).

42. Author, Interview (2013).

43. *Vetero*, from the Latin *vetus–veteris*, means old, antique, the opposite of *neo*.

44. Neil Brenner and Nik Theodor, 'Cities and the Geography of Actually Existing Neoliberalism', *Antipode*, 34.3 (2002), pp. 349–79.

45. Jacques Donzelot, 'Il neoliberismo sociale', *Territorio*, 46 (2008), 89–92.

46. Étienne Balibar, *Cittadinanza* (Turin: Bollati Boringhieri, 2012).

47. Ota de Leonardis, 'Una nuova questione sociale? Qualche interrogativo a proposito di territorializzazione delle politiche', *Territorio*, 46 (2008), 93–98.

48. Brenner and Theodor, 'Cities and the Geography'.

49. Massimo Bricocoli, 'Non di solo locale. Riflessioni sulle politiche di quartiere in Italia', *Territorio*, 46 (2008), 109–13.
50. Paolo Perulli, *Il dio contratto. Origine e istituzione della società contemporanea* (Turin: Einaudi, 2012).
51. Neil Robert Smith, *Uneven Development: Nature, Capital, and the Production of Space* (Athens and London: The University of Georgia Press, 1984).
52. Marco Cremaschi, 'Dopo il neoliberismo: quali politiche?', *Territorio*, 46 (2008), 118–22.
53. De Soto, *The Mystery of Capital*.
54. Coppola, 'Le borgate romane'; Richard Ronald, *The Ideology of Home Ownership: Homeowner Societies and the Role of Housing* (London: Palgrave Macmillan, 2008).
55. Perego (ed.), *L'urbanistica della sinistra*.
56. Violante, *La metropoli spezzata*.
57. Coppola, 'Le borgate romane', 'Roma, la metropolizzazione parassitaria'.
58. Carlo Donolo, *Disordine. L'economia criminale e le strategie della sfiducia* (Rome: Donzelli, 2001).
59. Coppola, 'Roma, la metropolizzazione parassitaria',.
60. Cremaschi, 'Dopo il neoliberismo'; Donolo, *Disordine*.
61. Eugene McCann, 'Urban Policy Mobilities and Global Circuits of Knowledge: Toward a Research Agenda, *Annals of the Association of American Geographers*, 101.1 (2011), 107–30.

CHAPTER 8

❖

Regeneration and Social Inclusion between Policy and Practices: The Case of Pigneto

Carlotta Fioretti

Social inclusion, together with the upgrading of the built environment and the development of the local economy, is a key goal for the regeneration of urban areas. Italy, like other European countries, has promoted programmes aimed specifically at enhancing social inclusion, in particular Neighbourhood Contracts (*Contratti di Quartiere*) — Area-Based Initiatives in neighbourhoods affected by multiple deprivation. This chapter explores the use of this programme in the city of Rome, highlighting the peculiarity of the case of the Pigneto area. A characteristic of regeneration in Rome has been that in addition to institutional programmes, bottom-up practices, which sometimes arise independently, sometimes in reaction to official regeneration policies, have been important. By focusing on the case of Pigneto, the chapter seeks to compare the outcomes in terms of social inclusion of institutional policy and of informal practices.

Together with economic development and environmental sustainability, social inclusion is a key goal for regeneration policy. For Robert and Sykes regeneration means:

> Comprehensive and integrated vision and action which leads to the resolution of urban problems and which seeks to bring about a lasting improvement in the economic, physical, social and environmental condition of an area that has been subject to change.[1]

Drawing on that definition, the ultimate objective of regeneration is to reverse the decline of specific urban areas, the major causes of which could be socio-economic transformations (deindustrialisation, unemployment), demographic challenges (ageing population, immigration) and neglect of the built environment (ageing building stock, lack of maintenance). In other words, urban decline is a complex problem where factors pertaining to different domains (social, economic and physical) are interlinked; so, in order to tackle it, a comprehensive approach, which acts jointly on all aspects of the problem, is required. That does not simply mean the coexistence in space and time of different kinds of actions that are functionally connected, but the acknowledgement of the surplus value deriving from the establishment of a nexus between those actions.[2] In Italy, regeneration, understood as a comprehensive and integrated vision began in the 1990s. Before that period, renewal policies were more focused on physical and normative aspects closer to spatial planning (restoration of buildings, realisation of mobility infrastructures, norms for public housing and building sanctions). Tedesco[3] describes accurately the evolution of such policy in Italy and explains how, from the post war-period onwards, it has been possible to talk about reconstruction, reuse, valorisation, rehabilitation or redevelopment. But it was only in the 1990s that a productive season of interventions for the peripheries and large urban areas began, linked to the family of regeneration programmes and plans, which within Italian urban studies are referred to as 'complex' or 'integrated' programmes (*programmi complessi, integrati*).[4]

The most innovative aspect of these programmes is the focus on integration and on citizen participation. Integration is a multifaceted concept, where, in the best cases, besides the already mentioned physical and normative aspects, there is an attention to economic development, environmental sustainability and social cohesion; in other words, there is an attempt to integrate different domains of intervention to achieve holistic regeneration. However, in the majority of cases integration has meant that these programmes were realised through a combination of public and private funding. Integration refers also to the effort of putting together different kinds of actors (public and private institutions, civic sector, local associations), a challenge that is becoming increasingly important with the shift from government to governance which implies the attempt to involve citizens directly in the decision-making process, through public participation. Based on the tradition of advocacy planning[5] and communicative planning,[6] the concept of public participation refers, here, to the possibility of the citizen (as an individual, or a representative of a local community) having an active role in the processes of urban transformation and their outcomes.[7]

The Italian system lacks an overarching national regeneration policy; rather it is made up of a series of programmes, generally funded through competitive bidding procedures,[8] ascribable to two main sources: a first group of initiatives promoted by the national (or in certain cases regional) government,[9] and a second group of programmes promoted by the EU, in particular the European Community Initiative 'URBAN'.[10] The role of the latter programmes has been extremely important for the development of a regeneration policy in Italy in that the EU has had a crucial role in terms of funding, tools and guidelines for the development of both policies and practices.

However, the peculiarity of the Italian context has resulted in distinctive characteristics at the local level, which have influenced the programmes' implementation. European initiatives, following those countries with a long-term history of urban regeneration practice, focused on certain types of neighbourhoods and areas suffering multiple deprivation, such as large social housing estates in the French and Dutch experiences, or low-demand areas in Britain. In Italy, however, the focus has been mainly on 'peripheries', heterogeneous areas where, while there may be a certain percentage of public housing, it is generally scattered rather than being concentrated in large uniform estates. Thus, peripheries have a mixture of housing tenures, including private and low-cost ownership. The profile of the population is diverse, with micro pockets of social exclusion, characterised by multiple deprivation, an ageing population and low turnover. The typical problems of Italian peripheries are: isolation and distance from the centre in physical and functional terms; poor-quality built environment and lack of facilities, infrastructures and services. As regards the public housing stock in particular, another major problem is the widespread lack of repair of properties, caused by serious management difficulties.[11]

Foreign labour immigration is a new issue for Italian peripheries, one that became evident in the late 1990s and early 2000s, and is becoming increasingly important. Today, migrants suffer from housing exclusion in that they rarely access the public housing system, and often live in deprived cheap private rented stock, located in most cases in the peripheries. Being generally more vulnerable, migrants are associated with social exclusion, and their presence raises issues of cultural diversity, such as spatial conflicts between native and immigrant residents about different and sometimes incompatible uses of urban spaces (for example, on the occupation of public spaces by Muslims for prayer because of the lack of designated places for worship).

If these are the particular characteristics of the areas addressed by regeneration, there is also an Italian specificity in terms of the policy system. Unlike other European countries such as France or Britain, Italy does not have a specific national agency for urban regeneration, or a clear national urban agenda. From the early 1990s it began a process of devolution to the Regions of housing, planning and also regeneration policies, which contributed to the progressive weakening of central government. However, the situation has slightly changed in recent years, with the promotion of national urban programmes (Piano Città, PON Metro), the institution of a committee for urban policy inside the national government (Comitato Interministeriale per le Politiche Urbane) and in 2014 a debate aimed at finalising a national urban agenda.[12]

The consequence of this devolution to the Regions has meant more flexibility and experimentation at the local level, although not all local administrations have reacted in the same way to the innovations introduced by national and European programmes of urban regeneration. Sometimes, lacking national directives, local authorities themselves tried to overcome the inadequacy of the administrative machine through pilot projects. One of the best, Participated Periphery (Periferia Partecipata, PP) was introduced by the Rome Council, which tried to introduce innovation from the inside to the way of working of the local authority in the field of planning. This is discussed further below.

Rome's Peripheries: From Renewal to Regeneration

In Rome, the problematic of urban peripheries has been particularly harsh. Since the Second World War, the city has developed in a spontaneous, deregulated way: the lack of affordable housing and appropriate housing policies led to the proliferation of illegal and self-built settlements (*lottizzazioni abusive, borgate, borghetti, baraccamenti*) which grew around the legal *borgate*, which were built during fascism along the consular roads to host people evicted from the clearance of central areas. In the 1980s the so-called 'illegal city' hosted 800,000 inhabitants, representing 28 per cent of the built environment of the city.[13] These areas lacked services such as schools, public transport, gathering spaces and basic infrastructures such as a public sewage system. The result was a dual city with a strong social, functional and physical gap between the city centre and the periphery, the first a rich location of government offices and the major employers of the city, with layers of astonishing architecture in its monuments, the other a place of marginalisation and squalid conditions. Therefore, for years, the Local Authority set the regeneration objectives focusing on basic physical aspects of the environment such as the realisation of much-needed services and infrastructures.[14]

In the 1990s, through the activation of the European Community URBAN programme, an integrated approach to regeneration was introduced in Rome, but the experience was not particularly significant, especially in terms of community participation. In most cases, residents were only involved during the advanced stages of construction works.[15]

The real turn occurred a few years later in the late 1990s. Thanks to a long tradition of dialogue between the public administration and the most active groups of citizens, particularly about environmental issues, the left-wing local government developed a project called Participated Periphery (Periferia Partecipata, PP) based on the concept of community-led planning. The Department for the Periphery, Local Development and Work Policies (Assessorato per le Periferie, lo Sviluppo Locale e il Lavoro) of the Council started up a series of projects and policies to encourage community involvement with the aim of integrating renovation of the built environment, which had been the traditional approach to working in the periphery, with social development.

Among the Department's initiatives is the stabilisation of the activity of the Special Office for Participation and Neighbourhood Workshops (Ufficio Speciale Partecipazione e Laboratori di Quartiere, USPEL), which from 1996 to 2001 set up an experimental series of Municipal Neighbourhood Workshops and training courses on participatory planning for council employees. From 2001 USPEL has been absorbed into the Fourth Operative Unit (U.O. IV) Sustainable and Participated Local Development (Sviluppo Locale Sostenibile e Partecipato), in charge of designing and implementing regeneration programmes for the peripheries mainly through the tool of Neighbourhood Contracts (*Contratti di Quartiere*).

The U.O. IV was not a pilot project like Periferia Partecipata and it became an ordinary organ of the Council. Through this shift, its aims became the transformation of forms of public participation as an official *modus operandi* of the Council.

FIG. 8.1. Localisation of Neighbourhood Contracts in the map of Rome

This involved overcoming the opposition of other groups to these innovative new practices. A successful result was the approval in 2006 of the internal 'Regulation for citizen participation in decision-making in urban rehabilitation' (resolution no. 57, 2006 *Regolamento della partecipazione dei cittadini alle scelte di riqualificazione urbana*). The U.O. IV aimed to act as a bridge between centralised and decentralised local administration structures, recognising boroughs[16] as crucial arenas for participation, and confronting the difficulties arising from the different political majorities existing at the various administrative levels. Finally, it developed the idea of building spaces in the territory itself to establish permanent dialogue with citizens, an idea initially proposed by USPEL through the neighbourhood workshops.

These Neighbourhood Contracts represent the Italian regeneration programmes implemented in Rome that have the strongest focus on social inclusion. The Neighbourhood Contracts are Area-Based Initiatives, inspired by European URBAN Programmes, targeting areas characterised by neglect of buildings and of the built environment, lack of services, social exclusion and serious housing hardship. Their main objective is to trigger processes of regeneration, starting from the public housing stock, through measures of physical rehabilitation, enhancement of local occupation and reduction of social malaise.

Since 1999, nine Neighbourhood Contracts have been successively implemented in Rome, integrating national funding obtained through bidding procedures with

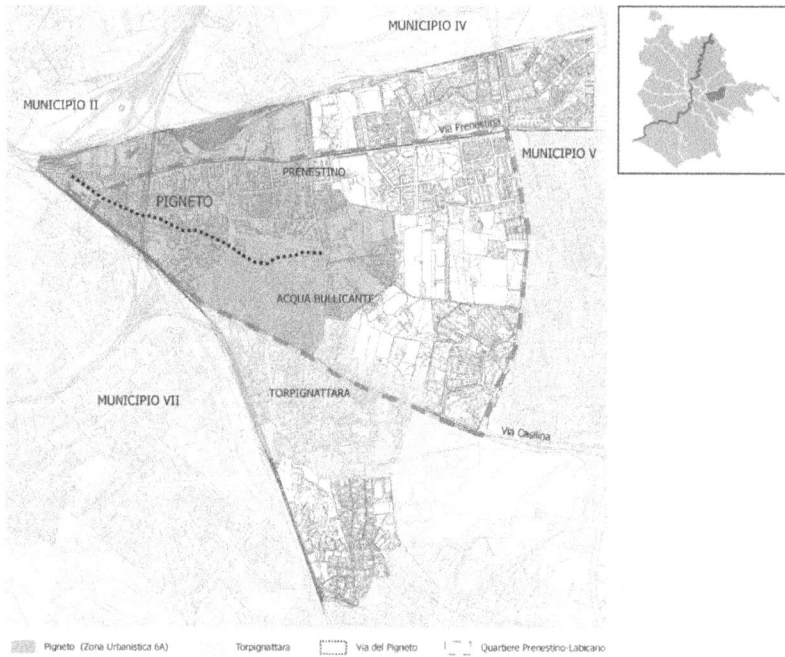

MUNICIPIO IV

MUNICIPIO II

MUNICIPIO V

Via Prenestina

PRENESTINO

PIGNETO

ACQUA BULLICANTE

MUNICIPIO VII

TORPIGNATTARA

Via Casilina

Pigneto (Zona Urbanistica 6A)   Torpignattara   Via del Pigneto   Quartiere Prenestino-Labicano

Fig. 8.2. Pigneto–Prenestino–Torpignattara: a neighbourhood that is three-in-one

regional and local resources (fig. 8.1). The U.O.IV presented seventeen proposals to the national call for Neighbourhood Contracts in 2002. Building on previous experiences, the proposals were prepared through the collaboration between Council and boroughs and with the participation of local residents. Four proposals out of seventeen were funded and realised.

In the following section the case of Pigneto, one of these regeneration programmes, will be analysed.[17] In particular, an attempt will be made to understand through a specific case how urban regeneration has been practised in Rome, especially with the objective of promoting social inclusion. This highlights the extent to which it is possible to talk about holistic regeneration, and those actors who are bringing about the eventual regeneration process.

Pigneto: An Urban Mosaic

Pigneto is a district located in the inner eastern periphery of Rome, in the V Municipio (VI Municipio until 2012). It is a triangular area, squeezed by two major roads of Roman origin, the Prenestina and the Casilina. Via del Pigneto crosses the whole area from west to east, connecting Piazza Caballini to Via dell'Acqua Bullicante.

The area's boundaries are ambiguous, because they include a large territorial unit and a variety of neighbourhoods and subzones within it. Boundaries change according to the perspective, whether it be administrative, historical or that of inhabitants' perceptions. Depending on which of these different definitions is deployed, Pigneto either does or does not include the neighbouring areas of Prenestino and

FIG. 8.3. The heterogeneity of housing types

Torpignattara. The uncertainty of the actual extent of the area has been acknow-ledged since its beginnings, a neighbourhood seen as 'three in one', with the districts of Pigneto, Torpignattara and Acqua Bullicante overlapping with each other.[18]

Historically, Pigneto was a working-class neighbourhood, which spontaneously developed at the beginning of the twentieth century around local industries: the pharmaceutical industry, Serono, located at the beginning of Via del Pigneto; the textile factory, SNIA Viscosa, at Prenestino; the Pantanella mill in Via Casilina; the ATAC (local transport agency) plants at Porta Maggiore. The majority of inhabitants were workers, railwaymen or artisans, many of whom were immigrants from southern Italy attracted by the labour opportunities during fascism and after the war. The characteristics of this area, dense in relational bonds, inspired many of the cinematographers of Italian neo-realism and the neighbourhood was also a setting for Pasolini's work, particularly *Accattone* (1961) and his novel *Ragazzi di vita*, both of which describe the extreme poverty and variety of these zones:

> They must have covered at least three miles, from the Via Boccaleone down through the Via Prenestina to Acqua Bullicante, passing by a field full of shit, a village made up of shacks, an apartment house as big as a mountain, and a weather-beaten factory building. [...][19]
> When, step by step, they had put Porta Furba behind them and had pene-trated deep into a jungle of gardens, roads, wire-mesh fences, villages of hovels,

vacant lots, construction sites, groups of tenements, and ponds, and were almost
up by the Borgata degli Angeli, between Tor Pignattara and Quadraro [...].[20]

From the viewpoint of urban design, the area grew without regulation to such an
extent that Pigneto has been defined as an 'urban mosaic'[21] formed by a heterogeneity
of housing types and of urban morphologies. The *villini* area developed in the 1930s
in the form of a garden city, characterised by low density, high-quality, detached
housing, built for state employees and railway workers, stands alongside self-built
housing, the heritage of the spontaneous *borgate*. These are located in the interstices
of high-density housing, tall apartment buildings (6–8 floors), and are mainly part
of the speculation of the 1960s and 1970s (fig. 8.3).

The lack of a master plan also meant a general lack of public spaces in terms of
accessible green areas, playgrounds, squares etc. Today the few public spaces are
characterised by neglect and lack of maintenance, which contributes to the disrepair
of the poor quality built environment.

Besides the urban morphology, the area presents some critical considerations in
terms of its socio-economic context. The Pigneto area, in 2013 comprising almost
50,000 inhabitants, has the highest population density of Rome with 20,289 residents
per square kilometre, and with a very low service provision in comparison:

Population	Pop density (res/km^2)	Ageing index (>65/<14)	Foreigners (%)
47,680	20,289	202	18

(Source: Roma Statistica (2013).) Demographically, it has an ageing population,
testified by an ageing population index that in 2000 was almost double the city
average. Today the index is 202 (202 elderly for every 100 young people), compared
to the general figure for Rome of 160. This trend is partially counterbalanced by
the growing number of immigrants who tend to be younger (a high percentage of
25–44 years) and have more children. The area is one of the most multi-ethnic in
Rome, with a percentage of foreign residents that has increased from 2 per cent
in 1991 to 18 per cent today, well beyond the city average (12 per cent). The main
nationalities are Bangladeshi, Chinese and Romanian (fig. 8.4).

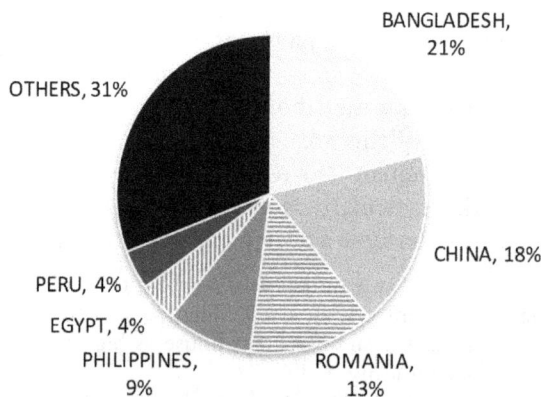

FIG. 8.4. Percentage of first six nationalities in respect of the overall number of
foreign residents (ISTAT 2010).

A further influx of younger people has been provided by the new 'creative class' of students and artists, who began to move into the neighbourhood in the late 1990s, attracted by the romantic heritage of Pasolini, and the cultural connotations of the neighbourhood.[22] The population had been traditionally employed locally in the transport sector and in industry, and although the majority of the factories closed down with the deindustrialisation process of the 1960s and 1970s, historically the neighbourhood showed considerable vitality in commercial enterprises, which made it self-sufficient. During the 1990s there was a significant reduction of local traditional shops following a wider national trend, which saw corner shops hit by the competition of large retailers, and this followed a progressive trajectory of decay and transformation of the neighbourhood. Since 2000, this trend has been counterbalanced by the growth of ethnic businesses, and the reconversion of some commercial premises into pubs, restaurants and other nightlife venues, located in a relatively confined area in the west, closer to the city centre. Rather than being characterised mainly by social deprivation, the neighbourhood is now internally polarised, with some parts badly off and in decline and others better off, and characterised by a differentiation in terms of housing tenures, commercial vitality and the social profile of the population.

Renewal and Regeneration Policies: The Institutional Response

From the 1980s, the local administration decided that the area of Pigneto needed renewal in terms of physical rehabilitation of buildings and provision of new services. This renewal began in the 1990s through new investments mobilised in public–private partnerships and the use of the new planning tools that facilitated them, the 'complex' programmes (*programmi complessi*). *Rinascimento Pigneto*, 'Pigneto Renaissance',[23] was the slogan used during the Veltroni administration (2001–08) to refer to a series of renewal actions undertaken in the 1990s and the beginning of 2000s[24] which made use of the PRIU (Programma di Riqualificazione Urbana) begun in 1995. The synergy between public and private actions (respectively 10 public actions and 9 private actions with a total investment of €23 million) aimed at closing the gap between the different areas of the neighbourhood, by realising specific interventions along Via del Pigneto, which, in crossing the whole neighbourhood, constitutes its backbone. The objective was to overcome the socio-spatial polarisation by refurbishing the most dilapidated areas and promoting new local hubs with a strong functional relationship to Via del Pigneto.

The project, belonging to the first generation of 'complex' programmes, did not have explicit social goals and the anticipated results were purely physical, aimed at the refurbishment of the built environment. However, there was also a commitment to improving the quality of the neighbourhood for the local community, making the closed and fragmented urban fabric more permeable, and creating new services and meeting points in the form of squares, a civic centre and a centre for the elderly.

Besides the PRIU other projects such as the realisation of three stops of the new underground Metro C line, and initiatives aimed at transforming the disused factories, in particular, Snia Viscosa and Serono, were also intended to produce a profound transformation of the neighbourhood. The idea was to give a social and cultural function to Snia Viscosa, using it as a park, a social centre and a space for the University La Sapienza. The social centre Ex-Snia was born in 1995 from the squatting of part of the disused factory, and since 1997 part of the area has been transformed into a public park. The University La Sapienza campus has not yet been realised. In the last twenty years, different attempts at privatisation of the area have been put forward, but they were always opposed by local committees. Serono, however, would be converted into a hotel and conference centre, but with the relation with the neighbourhood preserved, through the renewal of the closed pedestrian street and the use of a part of the factory for collective purposes. The hotel was realised and opened in 2010. The public spaces inside the complex were opened in 2011 while the refurbishment of the pedestrian area of Via del Pigneto was accomplished in May 2015.

The major criticism of this ambitious set of initiatives is that, although private interventions were completed quite rapidly, the public ones have been in progress for years, with some either never realised or, when realised, disregarding the expectations of the inhabitants.

At the beginning of the 2000s, thanks to the funding made available by the Region of Lazio, another important programme was implemented, a Neighbourhood Contract, carried out by the Fourth Operative Unit of the Council (U.O. IV) 'Sustainable and Participatory Local Development'. This Neighbourhood Contract was in line with the objectives of the PRIU, but it was more advanced in terms of integration in all its multifaceted meanings. Besides the integration between public and private actors, the Neighbourhood Contract promoted the participation of citizens in the design process and aimed to integrate different policy sectors to promote objectives of physical rehabilitation (€1,332,458 for environmental/physical interventions) together with economic development (€444,153) and social inclusion (€444,153).

The participatory process was organised on the basis of a preliminary programme realised by the U.O. IV after an informal meeting with some major local stakeholders. It lasted four months and it included public assemblies and operative workshops managed with the tools of 'visioning' and 'action planning'.[25] The U.O. IV directly invited specific local organisations, the Borough (Municipio VI), associations, unions, neighbourhood committees, entrepreneurs' representatives and the self-organised social centre located in SNIA Viscosa. This process was located in a socio-cultural context with a strong history of activism, thanks to the presence of organised groups that over time had carried on many campaigns for raising the conditions of the area.[26] The groups grew from a left-wing tradition since the neighbourhood was working class, had been particularly active in the antifascist struggle and had been a scene of clashes during the Resistance, as testified in movies such as *Roma città aperta* (Rossellini, 1945).

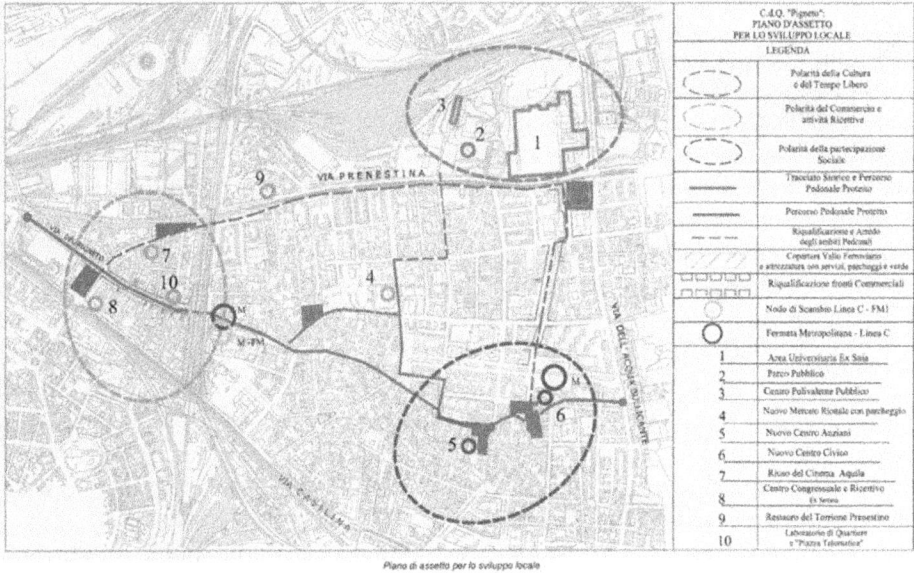

Piano di assetto per lo sviluppo locale

FIG. 8.5. Strategic plan of local development for Pigneto.
Source: Comune di Roma, Municipio Roma VI, Regione Lazio. 2002.
Programma Integrato di Recupero Urbano 'Contratto di Quartiere' Pigneto,
Programma Definitivo (Roma: Comune di Roma).

The participation process resulted in a 'strategic plan' (fig. 8.5) organised around three hubs, each with a specific focus: commercial development for the first area of Via del Pigneto already characterised by a certain vitality, culture and leisure for the area around the SNIA Viscosa factory, social cohesion and participation for the Torpignattara–Acqua Bullicante district. The strategic plan included a wide range of interventions scheduled for the short, medium or long term, some funded inside the Neighbourhood Contract itself (integrating Regional and Council resources), others funded by other actors, public and private. The plan included long-term actions, not immediately practicable, as they did not have funds allocated for them. Nonetheless, the overall regeneration process in Pigneto seemed promising because the area-based approach allowed the local authority to concentrate a certain amount of resources over the years in the same area. Furthermore, the Council seemed to recognise the spontaneous market-led processes of transformation. The strong strategic framework, built in a consensual manner with the inhabitants, was taking up the challenge of accompanying those changes, and reducing the negative external factors deriving from pressure on trade and rent through the establishment of a strong public infrastructure.

Social Inclusion beyond the Rhetoric

The short-term actions specifically funded by the Neighbourhood Contract con-sisted in a set of interventions for urban renewal and for social and economic promotion. They included the renovation of a major street axis (Via Prenestina) and its surroundings, the restoration of a cinema (Nuovo Cinema Aquila, which would become an important cultural hub, but then be closed between 2015 and 2016 due to management issues) and a plan for sustainable mobility, encouraging pedestrian and cycle paths. For the promotion of social inclusion, half of the funds were allocated for the completion of social infrastructures started by the PRIU in 1995 but not completed (in particular the centre for the elderly, the civic centre and the multi-functional centre in the SNIA).

The Neighbourhood Contract also provided for people-focused actions related to immigration, which had been identified as a priority during the participation process. These included a family support project in schools and information seminars for foreigners inside the local job centre. Other funds were employed at a later stage to promote action-research realised by the University Roma Tre, through the Observatory on racism 'Favara', a project whose objective was to analyse the level of inclusion of migrants in the local society, and encourage their participation in the process of transformation of the neighbourhood. The results of their research were published in 2011.[27]

The economic initiatives seemed to become mixed with the social ones through the realisation of a *piazza telematica*, that is, a computerised information-point, to be located in the public area of the Serono factory, which aimed to function as a local agency of development, promoting the local economy, cultural life and public participation.

In general terms, the programme was more innovative in its premises than in its actual implementation. Its multi-dimensional action was weak, with the major part of the funding deployed in physical refurbishment, but what seems more important is that spatial planning was leading social promotion and economic development. The Neighbourhood Contract was in line with this typically Italian way of understanding social action where the focus is on places, in this instance through the realisation of physical spaces (the *piazza telematica*) as containers for social activities and triggers for social inclusion processes, rather than a focus on the people and processes that could eventually activate these spaces.

The plan did also include a few people-focused projects, for instance those related to immigration, but they did not produce any significant results, because they were based on short-term aims, and there was a lack of integration between the departments of the Council, which should have provided continuity. This lack of real inter-sectorial integration prevented the tackling of complex issues in a coordinated way, within different policy sectors. Immigration, for example, was considered only from the social point-of-view. The programme did not promote migrant entrepreneurship in the framework of economic development, despite the flourishing of ethnic firms in the area, which contrasted with the progressive closure of local shops. The confused project of the *piazza telematica* was never realised.

The emphasis on local participation, a significant innovation in the programme, also revealed critical weaknesses; in particular, it largely involved representatives of organised groups, which constituted a real limit in reaching a wider range of citizens, especially those from the most marginal groups and those who usually tend not to participate.[28] This was especially the case for migrants, who were not part of structured groups, and who were contacted only through their 'political' representatives in the local political parties. The action-research conducted by the University of Roma Tre discovered other migrants' networks, but it was too late, because the process of participatory planning did not continue in the implementation phase of the programme.

The other major limit of the initiative was that none of the innovations introduced in the initial design of the programme were retained in subsequent phases. For instance, with regard to the idea of establishing a permanent workshop (*laboratorio di quartiere*) for citizens' participation within the *piazza telematica*, the private partner had refurbished the Serono complex quite rapidly, but after several years, the spaces destined for collective use still remained empty, so from 2008 the Pigneto Neighbourhood Committee has informally occupied them for their weekly meetings. Today in these spaces, instead of the *piazza telematica*, there is the local library, but the aim of maintaining a dialogue between local residents and institutions seems to have been lost. The long delay in the realisation of public amenities, attributed to the lack of dialogue and information, strongly compromised the success of the programme and led to progressive disappointment with the project among those who initially had enthusiastically participated in its design.

The Reaction of Local Committees and its Unpredictable Outcome

In general, public action in Pigneto has been weak. The regeneration programmes, despite their integrated nature and innovative objectives, suffered from the typical deficiencies of all Italian complex programmes: priority accorded to physical rehabilitation, short-term goals, one-off (not mainstream) funding. The public–private partnership mechanism seemed to be unbalanced, with exaggerated leanings towards private interests, in part because of the nature of the neighbourhood and the fragmentation of the properties, in part because of a lack of any long-term strategy and commitment from the public sector. A lot seemed to be delegated to the will and the power of other actors: private, third sector, neighbourhood committees.

However, even if it did not create new networks the Neighbourhood Contract, with its emphasis on participation, did help to reinforce some already existing social networks and local bonds, in particular around the presence of Neighbourhood Committees. Although the participation process lacked continuity, the involvement of civil society in itself made citizens more demanding,[29] and more attentive to the effective enforcement of the commitments signed in the 'Contract'. The local forces, mobilised around Neighbourhood Committees, used the Contract to protest, and to encourage the Council to fulfil the promises made. This led to a rupture in the relation between Council and citizens ratified through the public participation process. However, it was not a complete failure, because this antagonism led to positive gains; in particular, it succeeded (where the Neighbourhood Contract had failed) in including migrants as active agents in the improvement of their living environment.

In the last fifteen years some specific areas of Pigneto have attracted a new population (students, artists), which led to a progressive 'trendification' of the area, with the opening of a considerable number of pubs and leisure venues in the pedestrian zone of Via del Pigneto. Whether this constitutes gentrification or not,[30] it is clear that the neighbourhood has experienced a rise in real-estate values, with the consequent risk of expulsion of its most vulnerable inhabitants. Migrants participated in this process by fuelling the private rentals sector, with the consequent capital accumulation in the hands of housing owners, but they also frequently constituted one of the groups hardest hit by population displacement. The first issue that saw the joint action of local organisations and immigrants was precisely this risk of gentrification, an issue that residents always considered crucial and criticised regeneration programmes for not being responsive to.

The Neighbourhood Contract focused on macro transformation, for example in the case of the Serono Factory, which became a luxury hotel, but it insisted on the private investor also providing public spaces and facilities for the wider community. These mitigation measures were insufficient, in particular because the Neighbourhood Contract did not support the promotion of public and affordable housing for the less privileged although this is one of the major goals of this type of regeneration programme. In 2010 and 2012, two different groups of Senegalese who had lived for years in rented accommodation in two different buildings suffering from physical decay, received eviction notices. On both occasions, the Neighbourhood Committees and the network of local associations mobilised in support of the Senegalese through demonstrations, legal counselling and self-refurbishment actions that shared the same aim of the defence of the area from speculation and the preservation of affordable homes for disadvantaged groups.

A second issue raised by the local associations concerned 'denied public spaces', that is, potential resources that are not viable either because they are neglected, or still under construction (some for years) or designated for public use but never realised. These groups organised several initiatives aimed at denouncing the transformation agreed by the Public Administration since the 2000s, which had supported private interests at the expense of shared public ones, so further impoverishing the area. They included the production of dossiers mapping all the 'denied spaces' and explaining how the public institutions had failed to realise their own promises. Public demonstrations, such as the one in 2010, 'Our territory is not a monopoly',[31] drew further attention to these failures.

If many of the initiatives were purely aimed at protesting, others were more productive and encompassed the vitalisation of available spaces through cultural initiatives. For example, in the case of the activities organised in Piazza Perestrello, a square refurbished by a private company which, in exchange, was given the concession for building a private parking lot under it, the works remained suspended for nearly seven years, thus removing a key gathering space for the community. After pressure from the citizens, finally, the square was refurbished and opened to the public in 2011, but the project that was to have included public facilities such as playgrounds and a market place was quite disappointing, looking more

FIG. 8.6. Piazza Perestrello during a neighbourhood festival.

like a concrete plain. For this reason, since its opening, the local committees have organised yearly neighbourhood festivals, with performances by different local actors, and the realisation of temporary street furniture to make the square more viable and lively (fig. 8.6). This was just one of the actions undertaken, but it is particularly worthy of notice because it was one of the occasions when the migrants' associations consistently joined the initiative. In particular, the Bangladeshis and Chinese contributed to the event, through the involvement of their associations, schools and local shops. They believed in the importance of working together with all local organisations for common struggles linked to issues of daily living such as providing the neighbourhood with social spaces and services for *all* families rather than concentrating only on those related to the specific needs of immigrants.

Although these festivals began on a voluntary base, in recent years they have involved institutional partners, in a sort of bottom–up process.[32]

Conclusions

Urban regeneration in Italy, and more particularly in Rome, arrived quite late in comparison with other European countries, and it has been characterised by two major elements of discontinuity with the previous urban policy tradition. The first innovative aspect is the promotion of multi-dimensional actions, which, in the case of deprived and peripheral neighbourhoods paid specific attention to social inclusion. The second innovation regarded participatory processes. The case of Pigneto helps to deconstruct the rhetoric behind Italian regeneration, highlighting not only the limits experienced in practice, but also the specific opportunities that can arise in local environments.

Neighbourhood Contract was the Italian regeneration programme most attentive to social aspects. The initiative activated in Pigneto was particularly innovative in its initial phase, through a strong process of citizen participation. However, despite its premises, the programme was ultimately weak in its implementation, especially for the promotion of social inclusion, the provision of public infrastructures for the local community and the integration of migrants. A reason behind these limits was the lack of a long-term strategy by the Rome Council.

U.O. IV attempted to establish participatory planning and community development as the usual way of working of the Administration, creating permanent spaces of dialogue with citizens in the peripheries. However, those practices ended in 2008 with the change of the Mayor and the Council. In Pigneto, the regeneration programme delays meant an increase in antagonism in the groups involved in the participation process.

Another aspect characterising regeneration policy in Rome in general and Pigneto in particular was the weak role of the local administration, which strongly delegated to other stakeholders, private and third sector groups, and organised civil society in the form of the neighbourhood committees. This happened in a place with a strong cultural and political heritage. Such a legacy was passed on to the present-day local society, creating a neighbourhood dense in social bonds and social capital, as demonstrated by the activism of its neighbourhood committees in the local political arena. Regeneration policies in Pigneto occurred at a juncture characterised by a particular political harmony between the Council, the Borough and the local committees, all three left wing. While the Council acknowledged this potential, it was not always able to take full advantage of it.

The necessity of considering non-institutional actors in regeneration practices is recognised, but it seems more difficult to put into practice, particularly when the challenge is to empower a community where there are already powerful actors. The Council relied too much on existing local networks in the phase of participation, and this constituted a limit to the process itself, which could not involve less structured politicised actors, such as migrants, whose active involvement only occurred later, within the initiatives promoted in response to the failures of the regeneration programmes. Although local associations have always been sensitive to the immigration issue, episodes like the counter-action to the eviction of the Senegalese and the activities in Piazza Perestrello marked a turning point in the attitude towards immigrants. In the beginning, local associations had a 'charity' approach, translated mainly into caring and support for vulnerable migrants, but in the demonstrations and activities for the defence and revitalisation of the neighbourhood, 'native' and immigrant inhabitants were involved side by side in the same struggles to challenge gentrification and revitalise public spaces, so in this case it is possible to talk about actual integration.

However, these bottom-up processes are not exempt from risks in as much as immigrants groups seem to take a subordinate role in actions initially promoted by committees that are exclusively Italian. The Italians set the priorities in claims to the institutions, so that the encounters with the Local Authority and immigrant demands then pass through them. Furthermore, neighbourhood committees often have a clear political connotation, which is unrepresentative of the extremely fragmented composition of the entire neighbourhood.

The risk, in general, is that local associations use immigrants' causes in political campaigns (both supporting them and more frequently opposing them), as seems to have happened in Rome in November 2014 when several local committees demonstrated against immigration, the decay of peripheries, and the mayor, Ignazio Marino.[33] In a varied neighbourhood such as Pigneto, the political manipulation of immigration risks fuelling internal conflicts. At this historical juncture, the economic crises worsen tensions, in particular in areas that seem to be far from the attention of the public. Now, more than ever, the Local Administration needs to prioritise the regeneration of peripheries, learning from mistakes, but also capitalising on positive experiences.

In conclusion, this overview of the regeneration policy in Rome and more specifically in Pigneto can help to identify some valuable general elements as recommendations for a regeneration agenda in Italy that is attentive to social inclusion. The case of Rome suggests, first, the importance of working at the level of processes as a priority; this means investing not only in the realisation of works, but even more importantly in institutional learning and institutional capacity-building. Only a strong Local Administration, internally coordinated, with a clear long-term strategy and skilled internal personnel can face the challenge of integrated urban policy, citizen participation and local governance, three key ingredients for successful regeneration.

This also seems to be a prerequisite for implementing a good balance between hard and soft policies, that is physical/spatial and social/less concrete interventions. Too often the priority in Italy has been only the first, with the belief that the creation of containers for social activities will automatically lead to social inclusion. However, as the case of Pigneto exemplifies, this has been demonstrated as false. Attention must also be paid to contents as well as containers. The focus on soft actions means a commitment to long-term strategies, that is, again, attention to processes, to the realisation of the regeneration policy from the design to its implementation.

Institutional learning means building on previous experience to avoid reinventing the wheel or repeating the same errors. In the case of Rome, the experience of U.O. IV should be a starting point for shaping mechanisms of integrated policy implementation. Secondly, the Local Authority must learn from practices of citizen; in this specific case, the approach to migrants' inclusion is particularly interesting. An updated approach to regeneration should take into account the phenomenon of immigration that strongly characterises Italian peripheries today. Immigrants should not be considered exclusively as a social problem to be solved but as a potential resource together with other citizens in regeneration processes, but this can happen only if immigrants are recognised as part of the local society and given the means to participate in it. The importance of immigration indicates that the aim of regeneration should be less the unrealistic ideal of a cohesive local society, and more one of managing conflicts and building an inclusive plural society.

Notes to Chapter 8

1. *Urban Regeneration: A Handbook*, ed. by Peter Roberts and Hugh Sykes (London: Sage, 2000), p. 17.

2. Liliana Padovani, 'L'innovazione nei programmi d'intervento integrati: prospettive e problemi come emergono dalle esperienze italiane in atto', in *L'azione integrata nelle politiche di rigenerazione urbana*, Conference Proceedings Daest, Iuav, Venezia 2–4 Dicembre (1999). That means that instead of having separate policy (economic, social, spatial) tackling respectively the economic, social and spatial problems of a neighbourhood, there is an integrated action aimed at tackling a single complex problem, recognising the importance to work on the interconnections between the different aspects of the problem.

3. Carla Tedesco, 'Italia. Senso, strumenti ed esiti dell'area-based approach ai problemi urbani', in *Politiche urbane e progetti locali in Francia, Gran Bretagna e Italia*, ed. by Paola Briata, Massimo Bricocoli, and Carla Tedesco (Rome: Carocci, 2009), pp. 101–33.

4. Paolo Avarello and Manuela Ricci, eds, *Dai programmi complessi alle politiche integrate di sviluppo urbano* (Rome: Inuedizioni, 2000).

5. Paul Davidoff, 'Advocacy and Pluralism in Planning', *Journal of the American Institute of Planners*, 31.4 (1965), 331–38.

6. Patsy Healey, 'Planning through Debate: The Communicative Turn in Planning Theory', *The Town Planning Review*, 63.2 (1992), 143–62.

7. For a collection of cases of participation in Italian planning see Giancarlo Paba and Camilla Perrone, eds, *Cittadinanza attiva. Il coinvolgimento degli abitanti nella costruzione della città* (Florence: Alinea, 2002); Marianella Sclavi, *Avventure Urbane. Progettare la città con gli abitanti* (Milan: Elèuthera, 2002); Andrea De Eccher, Elena Marchigiani, and Alessandra Marin, eds, *Riqualificare la città con gli abitanti* (Monfalcone: Edicom Edizioni, 2005).

8. National or regional government asks local authorities and organisations to bid for funds rather than allocating them according to objective need. Similar procedures were used also in English regeneration programmes such as the Single Regeneration Budget.

9. Initiatives such as Programmi Integrati ('PrInt', in English 'Integrated Programmes'), Programmi di Riqualificazione Urbana ('PRIU', Programmes of Urban Rehabilitation), Programmi di Recupero Urbano ('PRU', Programmes of Urban Refurbishment), Programmi di Riqualificazione Urbana e di Sviluppo Sostenibile del Territorio ('PRUSST', Programmes of Urban Rehabilitation and Sustainable Development); Contratti di Quartiere ('CDQ', Neighbourhood Contracts), Piano Città (City Plan). Among them, the Neighbourhood Contracts are probably the most innovative programmes at the National level, with major attention on social inclusion aspects, and experimentation in community participation.

10. Urban Pilot Projects, Urban, Urban II, but also programmes funded through the EU structural funds 2000–2006 and 2007–13 such as 'PIUSS', Piano Integrato di Sviluppo Urbano Sostenibile (Integrated Plan of Sustainable Urban Development).

11. Judith Allen and others, *Housing and Welfare in Southern Europe* (London: Blackwell, 2004).

12. Antonio Calafati (ed.) *Città, tra sviluppo e declino. Un'agenda urbana per l'Italia* (Rome: Donzelli, 2015).

13. Bruno Bonomo, *Il Quartiere Delle Valli. Costruire Roma nel secondo dopoguerra* (Milan: Franco Angeli, 2007).

14. Marco Cremaschi, 'Riqualificazione e rigenerazione urbana a Roma', <http://cremaschi.dipsu.it/politiche-della-casa-e-dellabitare/riqualificazione-e-rigenerazione-urbana-a-roma-2/> (2009) [accessed 15 November 2014].

15. Giuseppe Panebianco, *La città muove le torri, L'esperienza del Programma Urban a Roma* (Rome, 2002).

16. Rome Council is divided into fifteen administrative districts called *Municipi*, which have management and financial autonomy.

17. The empirical material employed in this paper has been developed mainly during my doctoral research titled 'Shared or Divided Cities: Places, Negotiations and Policies of Urban Immigration. The Case of Torpignattara, Rome', achieved in 2011 at Roma Tre University. The research employed a mix-method, with extensive field work, in-depth interviews to key informants, informal interviews to inhabitants, data analysis. The case study has been updated in 2014, adding information acquired during the research project 'Small Council and Social Cohesion'.

18. Stefania Ficacci, *Tor Pignattara. Fascismo e resistenza di un quartiere*, (Milan: Franco Angeli, 2007).

19. Pier Paolo Pasolini, *The Ragazzi* (Manchester: Carcanet, 1986), p. 120. Original quote in Italian: 'Si dovevano esser fatti almeno quattro chilometri, venendo da via Boccaleone, per la Prenestina, all'Acqua Bullicante, da una prateria piena di merda, a un villaggetto di catapecchie, da un palazzone grande come un monte a una fabbrichetta arruzzonita' (Pierpaolo Pasolini, *Ragazzi di vita* (Torino: Einaudi,1972), p. 111).

20. Pasolini, *The Ragazzi*, p. 138. Here is the Italian: 'Quando ch'ebbero lasciato alle spalle, passa passo, Porta Furba e si furono bene internati in mezzo a una Shangai di orticelli, strade, reti metalliche, villaggetti di tuguri, spiazzi, cantieri, gruppi di palazzoni, marane, e quasi erano arrivati alla Borgata degli Angeli, che si trova tra Tor Pignattara e il Quadraro.' (Pasolini, *Ragazzi di vita*, p. 129)

21. Carmelo G. Severino, *Roma mosaico urbano. Il Pigneto fuori Porta Maggiore* (Rome: Gangemi, 2005).

22. Sandra Annunziata, 'The Desire of Ethnically Diverse Neighbourhood in Rome. The Case of Pigneto: An Example of Integrated Planning Approach', in *The Ethnically Diverse City*, ed. by Frank Eckardt and John Eade (Berlin: Berliner Wissenschaftsverlag, 2011), pp. 601–23; Sandra Annunziata, 'A Comparative Urbanism of Two Gentrifying Neighbourhoods: Focusing on What Was Lost in Translation between New York City and Rome', Talk given at the Urban Salon, 19 January, UCL London (2015).

23. With a probably wanted assonance with the famous 'urban renaissance' of Sir Richard Rogers.

24. Comune di Roma, *Rinascimento Pigneto* (Rome: Comune di Roma, 2004).

25. Visioning and Action Planning are two techniques for participatory planning. The first one is used to support a group of stakeholders in developing a shared vision for the future, the second one is used to individuate problems and needs of a specific district.

26. Giovanni Allegretti, *Inchieste locali, Comune di Roma*, URBACT — rete 'Partecipando' (Rome: Urbact, 2004).

27. Francesco Pompeo, ed., *Pigneto-Banglatown. Migrazioni e conflitti di cittadinanza in una periferia storica romana* (Rome: Meti, 2011).

28. Allegretti, *Inchieste locali*, pp. 35–43.

29. Ibid.

30. See for example Annunziata, 'The Desire of Ethnically Diverse Neighbourhood in Rome' and A Comparative Urbanism of Two Gentrifying Neighbourhoods'.

31. Comitato di Quartiere Pigneto-Prenestino, 'Rinascimento Pigneto: le promesse tradite', *La Pigna*, http://www.lapigna.info/index.php/territorio/38-articolo/102-rinascimento-pigneto-le-promesse-tradite [accessed 15 November 2014].

32. In 2014 local stakeholders constituted an Association called *Alice in Marranellaland* with the aim of promoting the quality and accessibility of the public spaces, the multi-ethnic nature of the neighbourhood, the social and cultural capital, through the realisation of the neighbourhood festival and correlated events: <http://www.romamultietnica.it/l-intercultura-a-roma/festival/item/14956-alice-nel-paese-della-marranella.html> [accessed 22 March 2018].

33. Giulia Cerasi and Luca Monaco, 'La marcia delle periferie dietro al Tricolore: "basta Marino, no all'immigrazione"', *La Repubblica*, 15 Novembre 2014: <http://roma.repubblica.it/cronaca/2014/11/15/news/la_marcia_delle_periferie_dietro_al_tricolore_basta_marino-100612243/> (2014) [accessed 15 November 2014].

CHAPTER 9

❖

Redefining Italian Spaces:
Piazza Vittorio and Migratory Aesthetics

Federica Mazzara

Whoever wants to see the Italy of 2020 or 2050 should go to Piazza Vittorio. There, it's possible to run across a Chinese girl who speaks in Roman dialect, or a Bengali infant dressed in the local football team's jersey.[1]

Piazza Vittorio: A Multicultural Laboratory

This article analyses the extent to which recent immigration into Italy has produced new cultural representations, and the way they can help us understand the everyday practices that are currently transforming and redefining Italian urban spaces.

The particular space I investigate in this article is Piazza Vittorio Emanuele II — generally referred to simply as Piazza Vittorio — in Rome, a square and a surrounding neighbourhood which has witnessed significant and often contested physical and cultural changes in the past decades, worthy of further exploration. These changes are especially connected to the settlement in and around the square of an ethnically hybrid group of people, immigrants from many different countries, who have gradually affected its urban and cultural landscape.

Starting from Certeau's suggestion that 'ordinary practitioners of the city [...] are walkers, *Wandersmänner*, whose bodies follow the thicks and thins of an urban "text" they write without being able to read it',[2] this chapter will follow the migrants as particular kinds of 'walkers' in the city of Rome, walking in a specific place that they re-write and represent through social, aesthetic and cultural acts.

The presence of immigrants has, in fact, contributed to making Piazza Vittorio, and its new practices of urban living, less obscure and more 'readable', through a series of migratory aesthetic performances and everyday expressions that this article presents and analyses. I borrow the term 'migratory aesthetics' here from Mieke Bal. According to Bal, 'migratory, in this sense, is the fact that migrants (as subjects) and migration (as an act to perform as well as a state to be or live in) are part of any society today, and that their presence is an incontestable source of cultural transformation'.[3] Aesthetics becomes migratory when such practices (artistic, literary, filmic, architectural and urban) take place in a space made up of people whose lives and performative identities are fused by mobility.

The central suggestion of this article is, then, that within the cultural and physical area of Piazza Vittorio, it is possible to trace an 'alternative cartography of social space',[4] where migrants become subjects of agency who use mass media and aesthetic forms — such as literature, cinema, music and performance art — in order to demand cultural and social visibility together with a political voice. Seen from this perspective, Piazza Vittorio is a place of potential cultural transformations giving expression to a migratory aesthetics that produces a new urban text, and consequently a new way of looking at immigration as a cultural source.

Being located next to the Stazione Termini, the main railway station in Rome, Piazza Vittorio has always been a place of passage and a point of aggregation, especially after the establishment of the market in 1902.[5] Its location in the centre of metropolitan passages has contributed to the popular perception that the square is not a safe place to be; what is, of course, important to underline here is that it did not become unsafe, if unsafe at all, because of the presence of immigrants. As a continuing place of passage Piazza Vittorio is a vulnerable urban space, transitory and opaque; it seems consistently foreign, unintelligible, and its layers of shifting languages, shop fronts, inhabitants, and passing visitors render it a somewhat unreadable or chattering cityscape.

As all the multi-ethnic quarters, Piazza Vittorio and the Esquilino present many contradictions and are often given as examples of social and cultural tensions in Italy. On the one hand, Piazza Vittorio has today become a kind of emblem of tolerance and solidarity. Demonstrations in Rome in favour of immigration and integration are usually organised in the square, while local associations (the Apollo 11 cultural association, which I discuss below, and the Piazza Vittorio Cricket Club), websites (*Esquilinotizie*, *Roma Multietnica*) and performances (the end of Ramadan, the Chinese and the Bangladeshi New Year, Tai Chi exercises) contribute to promoting the new multi-ethnic reality of the square — and of the entire city — as a positive aspect of social and cultural evolution, rather than something to be sceptical about, to fear or to reject. On the other hand, the square is also the favourite location of counter-voices that promote the idea that immigration is the real cause of the social and economic crisis in Italy. In the specific case of Piazza Vittorio, immigrants have been indicated as the people to blame for a perceived 'degeneration' and 'degradation' of the square and for the loss of its 'Italian character'. As a counterbalance to the gradual multiculturalism of the area, political and social actions have been promoted by 'neighbourhood organisations' (often supported by right-wing associations) declaring their intention of 'cleaning up' the area.[6]

One place is especially active in this regard: the Fascist social centre Casa Pound, located near Piazza Vittorio in Via Napoleone III. It promotes a xenophobic agenda that often finds its favourite location in Piazza Vittorio.[7] It especially uses the square as a showcase by posting on the walls of the surrounding buildings unauthorised placards that promote a feeling of distrust and fear and encourage violent acts.

In this context of social and political tension, Piazza Vittorio functions as a frame through and in which citizens project, display and perform their different cultural personalities, or, in other words, the square is used as a contested shop window, which, according to Rachel Bowlby's definition, can be variously a source of pleasure, surprise, dreaming absorption, curiosity, desire, disturbance, and more, in all sorts of combinations.[8]

Many of the places near Piazza Vittorio that are somehow affected by immigration are indeed the sources of diverging feelings. The market, the gardens, the shops and the other urban topoi of this area are objects of observation both from sceptics — who reject the idea that Piazza Vittorio, and Italian society in general, is moving towards a multicultural dimension — and from interested observers who look at the square as a multicultural laboratory, an inspirational source of promising intercultural expressions.

Literary Voices from the Square

A first example of cultural expression sparked by Piazza Vittorio comes from literature. In 2006 the Algerian-Italian writer Amara Lakhous wrote and published a highly successful novel that took inspiration from the Piazza. He had personally experienced its new multicultural reassessment when he moved, as a refugee, to Rome in 1995. The novel, entitled *Scontro di civiltà per un ascensore a Piazza Vittorio* (Clash of Civilizations over an Elevator in Piazza Vittorio) has been translated into several languages, and is now in its fourteenth impression in Italy. A film adaptation was released in 2010, contributing to making this book an outstanding literary 'case' in Italy. One reason for its success is Lakhous's ability to talk about the contradictions that Italians display about immigration from the 'privileged' position of a migrant himself, who is well acquainted with the Italian language, culture and urban spatiality and through a strategic use of humour that is able to strike Italian readers on delicate issues such as immigration, integration and racism.

The novel tells the story of a murder committed in a building near Piazza Vittorio, in which both locals and immigrants live. The murder is merely a pretext for introducing the reader to an extraordinarily varied group of figures who are being questioned by the police about the prime suspect, Ahmed (better known as Amedeo), who mysteriously disappeared after the murder took place. Through these witness statements the reader learns what each of the characters thinks about the square and its multicultural urban life. The Italian characters are presented as dangerously prejudiced: the Neapolitan concierge, Benedetta Esposito, thinks that the immigrants are the real reason for all crimes in Italy, and those living in her building in particular are responsible for the neglect of the elevator, a space she protects; Elisabetta Fabiani believes that the ones responsible for her missing little dog are the Chinese living in Piazza Vittorio, since she has been told that the Chinese eat dogs. Prejudices and stereotypes are expressed by these characters through a narrative discourse that subtly satirises them, deconstructing their limited ethnic categories.

The most interesting aspect of the novel, for the purpose of this essay, is the fact that the city of Rome, and in particular Piazza Vittorio and its neighbourhood, may be considered a central protagonist itself, a complex and contested character. The city in this novel, as Parati has observed, 'reveals itself as a fluid entity composed of spaces to which migrants want to assign new meanings'.[9] The fluidity of the square guides the human characters, especially the immigrants, in search of their personal and intimate spatial dimensions. The migrants (and not exclusively in ethnic or political terms) are the real residents and users of the Piazza (in the novel as in real life). They move around the gardens, the market, the station and other places nearby: the Iranian Parviz likes to feed pigeons in the nearby square of Santa Maria Maggiore in order to recall nostalgically his family back in Iran and to forget his present state of exclusion and non-belonging in the host country; in her limited spare time the Peruvian Maria Cristina Gonzáles, who is being exploited in her job as carer for an old lady, walks to the Stazione Termini — a place of passages, of departures and arrivals, of endings and beginnings — to meet her compatriots. All these places become for the migrants 'spaces of memory', within the larger space of the city of Rome and of the Italian country, where they are mostly trapped in a prison of solitude and marginalisation.

The migrant figures are embodiments of Certeau's pedestrians, for whom walking 'is to lack a place. It is the indefinite process of being absent and in search of a proper [place]'.[10] The result is a city seen as 'an immense social experience of lacking a place broken up into countless tiny deportations (displacements and walks), compensated for by the relationships and intersections of these exoduses that intertwine and create an urban fabric'.[11] These tiny deportations and displacements are daily practices in Piazza Vittorio and in Lakhous's novel, where people have created and continuously weave their own intercultural urban fabric, finding a 'cure to homesickness' as stated by Lakhous in relation to his personal experience of the square:

> Piazza Vittorio, with its fountains, its market, and its gardens, cured me of my homesickness. During my early days as an exile, I would wake every night with the same agonizing nightmare: I saw myself walking barefoot, desperate, without a destination, in the midst of an interminable desert, in search of a drop of water. I was thirsty. Sometimes, in the middle of the night, I would step outside to confront my fears and to quench my thirst at the fountains of Piazza Vittorio. The water running from those fountains calmed me, but I was not only in need of water: I thirsted for freedom, youth, love, beauty, and above all, life. After a few weeks, the nightmare receded.[12]

Piazza Vittorio, in Lakhous's narrative, is a space 'inflected by otherness'[13] and as such it is subjected to acts of appropriation, redefinition and transgression by migrants whose 'walks' perform and construct a new urban language. An interesting example of a space in the novel that testifies to the possibility for a social mobility is the elevator of the building where most of the characters live. This space is the object of constant negotiation and compromise in the novel, not simply between different inhabitants but between different cultures. Benedetta Esposito, in particular, projects onto the elevator her own world-view, by deciding who is allowed to access it and who is not — typically, the immigrants. As Graziella Parati observes:

> Benedetta sees the elevator as an entrance into a culture and a community that she has to monitor as she attempts to control the space other people can appropriate. As an outsider, she defines her level of belonging by her ability to exclude others from gaining access to movement: to the vertical motion, that is, of the elevator, symbolizing mobility, even social mobility.[14]

Performing as the guardian of the elevator, as the one with the power to control its social use, Benedetta can express her sense of 'integration' and superiority, despite being an immigrant herself from the South of Italy, an 'internal other'[15] and therefore both a similar and a different kind of immigrant to Parviz, Maria Cristina and Iqbal.

The elevator is also the space around which we encounter all the novel's characters, who project their fears and hopes into its transitory yet heavily regulated social space. The Italian professor from the north of Italy considers the elevator to be the epitome of discipline and order, and use of it should be restricted to 'civilised' people. Parviz likes the elevator because while he is there he can meditate. Its movement up and down reflects his own life, which has been full of shifts, turns and breakdowns: 'Now you're up, now you are down. I was up... in Paradise... in Shiraz, living happily with my wife and children, and now I'm down... in Hell, suffering from homesickness'.[16] By contrast, Amedeo/Ahmed avoids using the elevator because of a claustrophobic feeling that brings him back to his past in Algeria, where he lost his fiancée, Bàgia, killed by fundamentalists. The elevator represents for him a space of death — 'it reminds me of a tomb', he says[17] — and 'a metaphor of memory'.[18] The equation of memory and death is, in fact, ubiquitous in the novel, where all the immigrant characters struggle with a sense of homesickness that they try to overcome by filling the 'empty' urban spaces they inhabit with their own stories, cultural practices and memories.

Amedeo, in particular, is the immigrant character who knows the city of Rome better than the locals. Sandro Dandini, the owner of the Bar in Piazza Vittorio, says that Amedeo

> knows the history of Rome and its streets better than I do, in fact better than Riccardo Nardi, who is so proud of his origins, which go back to the ancient Romans. Riccardo drives a taxi and has been going up and down the streets of Rome every day for twenty years.[19]

Amedeo's ability to wander around the centre and the periphery of Rome and the knowledge he has of the Italian language and Italian culture have assigned to him the 'privilege' of being considered a native; nobody believes that Amedeo is in fact Ahmed, and nobody believes he murdered the Gladiator.

Amedeo controls the city by walking, and this has allowed him to perform a new, non-migrant, identity, relieving him of suspicion. His knowledge of the Italian urban cartography has saved him from a dimension of marginality and exclusion, while his identity is still trapped in a past of sorrow and a sense of guilt. As Parati has observed, the city for Amedeo/Ahmed is divided along two lines: 'the horizontal explorations that turn him into a *flâneur*, a cosmopolitan mediator between cultures, and the vertical, repetitive up and down, of a metaphorical elevator that traps him into that process of remembering that he needs to escape'.[20]

Amedeo, together with the other immigrants, contributes to making the place of Piazza Vittorio a space, or a 'practiced place' in Certeau's words,[21] by their act of walking and therefore by their act of writing an alternative urban text that subverts the order imposed by socio-cultural conventions. In this new cartography the logic and geometry of history imposed by locals collapses and a new hybrid language is inscribed transforming a contested place of transit into a liveable migratory space.

Piazza Vittorio, together with its micro-spaces, mirrors, in Lakhous's novel, the fluid identities of migrants who aim at creating their own alternative non-linear trajectories, while natives, as Parati argues, tend to obstruct this project by acts of repression and control of spaces they think are rightfully their own. Lakhous is able to read the new urban fabric of Piazza Vittorio as affected by immigration, offering a perspective where migrants create their own 'poetics of space'. As if following a Bachelardian intuition, Lakhous realises that any spatial aesthetics has its own temporal history that is inscribed by the dwellers through intimate acts of recollection, imagination and daydreaming. Amedeo/Ahmed, Parviz, Maria Cristina and even Benedetta find within Piazza Vittorio, and in its nearby spaces, an intimate dimension, a shelter from their sense of displacement.

Another interesting literary case related to Piazza Vittorio that I want to consider is a short story, also written in Italian, by the Brazilian writer Claudiléia Lemes Dias, who, after spending most of her life in Brazil, migrated to Rome in the 1990s. The story is called 'Livia e il drago' (Livia and the Dragon) and is included in a collection, *Storie di extracomunitaria follia*, 2009 (Tales of Immigrant Madness), about migrants living in Rome, told through a tangle of literary realism and striking metaphors that at times create a surreal atmosphere. In this book, Rome is again the protagonist together with a host of immigrant figures who face the challenge of integrating in a city sometimes charming, sometimes impenetrable and illegible.

'Livia e il drago' tells the story of a strange encounter between an old lady who lives in Piazza Vittorio and a Chinese dragon, who is hanging around the square waiting for the beginning of the Chinese New Year celebration, where it is expected to perform. In the Chinese New Year celebration in Piazza Vittorio the dance of the dragon is the biggest attraction. In the story, the dragon enters Livia's apartment from the window, and engages her in a bizarre conversation. Livia is not exactly a tolerant and welcoming person when it comes to immigrants in Piazza Vittorio. The description the reader is given of the market from her point of view is exemplary of her prejudiced attitude towards the new arrangement of the square:

> It was not easy to face the market of Piazza Vittorio for a person like her. She was yanked around by that mixture of nationalities, between vegetables and spices of unknown taste and that psychedelic matching of fruits of captivating colours; it was like doing a physiotherapy session in Hell.[22]

Until the late 1990s, the market represented the real soul of the square, especially the local food stands. As Lesley Caldwell notes, 'by 1980 its 470 stalls had invaded everything forming a double ring of seven hundred metres round the garden which, enveloped in market rubble, was home to a population of down-and-outs'.[23] Within a larger project of gentrification, which involved the whole Esquilino district, the market was moved inside a building (a former military compound) located just one block away in Via Principe Amedeo, and is now called the Nuovo Mercato Esquilino (New Esquilino Market). The new market is remarkable especially for the variety of products on offer, not merely local, not even simply Italian. In the Esquilino market you can find many foreign food products sold by the 'new' Italians, which mirror the new spirit of the area, in a combination of colours and smells that almost respond to an aesthetic need. Like many other places around Piazza Vittorio, the market is at the centre of public discussion. There are those who think that in its new location the market has lost its initial and traditional atmosphere of a place where one could find seasonal 'local' products, and those who think that it is the best compromise between different ethnicities and food traditions, while testifying to the present multicultural life of the city. Immigrants have undoubtedly contributed to making the market and the nearby square a more complex place, where everything is continuously changed and enlivened by the merging of different cultural realities. The market, like the square, has become the expository window for intercultural performances, an intimate space where the 'new' local communities are given the chance to display a piece of their cultural memory, of their identity in a place where they have no voice or space in which to express it.

In Lemes Dias's short story the market represents for Livia the epitome of chaos and displacement. She feels rejected in a space that she was used to seeing as familiar and reassuring, a place she felt she owned, according to social conventions. More precisely, Livia is seized by a sense of the uncanny; she suddenly finds herself estranged at home; she projects onto the square the 'presences of diverse absences',[24] but as a deported walker herself she participates, against her will, in the re-inscription of the new urban text of Piazza Vittorio.

What is most irritating for Livia about the process of change in the area where she grew up is what many people in Rome today refer to as 'the Chinese invasion':

> Walking around the neighbourhood where she was born and had grown up, Livia couldn't accept seeing signs written almost exclusively in Chinese. The herbalist, the fishmonger and the wine bar she used to go to till just a few years before had left the space to clothes shops, identical to each other, with items made in the same way and cheap.[25]

Livia's fictional interpretation of the Chinese presence in Piazza Vittorio mirrors a common and more general feeling of the locals who perceive the Chinese, more than anything else, as commercial invaders of the area.[26] Since the late 1990s shops owned by the Chinese immigrants have spread into almost all the streets converging on the square, replacing a greater variety of older shops that provided important services to the people living nearby. Without apparently any logical planning, the owners have given these shops a new look and function responding more to an international business rationale than to the real needs of the inhabitants of Piazza Vittorio. The Chinese, in other words, have reshaped these commercial spaces according to specific aesthetic requirements of window shopping: the shops do all look alike, the walls are all made of white panels, from which some cloth items hang, and the windows are marked by Chinese writings that appear as incomprehensible signs to non-Mandarin-speaking people. This unreadable and impenetrable reality of Chinese culture in the urban practice of the Roman square is transformed, in the story by Lemes Dias, into an example of migratory aesthetics through the use of a typical character of Chinese folk culture: the dragon.

The dragon of the story when asked by Livia what it thinks about the demonstration against the Chinese shopkeepers in Piazza Vittorio, which she is going to join that same day, gives a wise and straightforward explanation:

> 'I think it's you who sell off the shops'.
> 'Ah! So now it's our fault?' Livia, got angry, looking scathingly at him.
> 'It's not a matter of fault! It's a matter of buying and selling. Why don't we protest together against the exploitation of workers, both Chinese and Italian? That's the real problem!'[27]

The dragon challenges the reasons why so many Chinese migrants are allowed to take possession of the many shops in and around Piazza Vittorio, while Livia and the other Italians are blinded by xenophobic rage and hostility, since as natives 'they need to apply a strategy of scapegoating in order to explain any urban problem'.[28]

But most importantly, the dragon is the symbol of another face of the Chinese presence in Piazza Vittorio: the performative dimension that finds in the gardens of the square its elective space. The Chinese New Year's Eve party in the gardens of the square is a significant urban and cultural event, one of the most impressive examples of the rehabilitation of the gardens that took place after the arrival of immigrants in the area. At the end of the story the dragon hovers above Piazza Vittorio to join its compatriots and celebrate the New Year, with a performance aimed at thanking the ancestors for all the good things received in the past year.

The dislocation of the Chinese traditional performance into the gardens of Piazza Vittorio establishes a migratory aesthetics of temporal and spatial exile, where the Chinese perform acts of memory and nostalgia activated by the past and projected onto the 'new' cartography of Piazza Vittorio. Through acts of what Toni Morrison calls 'rememory',[29] the Chinese immigrants claim a cultural visibility that contrasts with the one imposed by Livia and the locals like her, who limit their view of the Chinese immigrants to a narrow and obscure issue of mere transfer of human capital.

The Musical and Filmic Project of the 'Orchestra of Piazza Vittorio'

The last example of a migratory aesthetics practice[30] revolving around Piazza Vittorio that I want to explore is a project involving at least two forms of artistic media: film and music. I am referring to the 'Orchestra of Piazza Vittorio' founded in 2006 by Agostino Ferrente and Mario Tronco, both Piazza Vittorio dwellers. They decided to create a multicultural orchestra involving musicians from different countries living in the Esquilino district. They ended up finding more than thirty musicians, not necessarily from Piazza Vittorio but more or less from Rome, who were able to play at least fifteen different culturally specific instruments. Behind the orchestra there was another bigger project that unfortunately still remains a dream. With the aim of saving the famous old Apollo Theatre, located in Via Giolitti, which was about to be turned into a bingo hall, Tronco and Ferrente formed an Association, the so-called Associazione Apollo 11, composed of local artists as well as the local residents devoted to the multicultural character of the Esquilino quarter. The Association promotes cultural events and is still working to become a more active cultural centre. The main purpose is to involve the immigrants of the neighbourhood both as audience and as producers of cultural events. Because of the lack of interest of the local authorities — they gave the Association permission to open and use the theatre, but did not offer any funding — the Apollo theatre is still a ruin, and will most likely remain so for the Association and for the Esquilino district. The Apollo 11 has, in the meantime, used the basement of a school close to Piazza Vittorio that has become 'Il Piccolo Apollo', from which the Association continues to organise cultural events, and where the orchestra has rehearsed for many years. The orchestra itself represents the first important and successfully realised project of the Association. While it was taking shape, Agostino Ferrente was documenting everything with the help of a video camera. A documentary film called *L'Orchestra di Piazza Vittorio* was the result.

In Ferrente's docu-musical, we gradually learn about the considerable difficulties involved in getting different musical traditions to work together, as well as in overcoming the troubles facing anybody trying to deal with visas and work permits in a country run on scepticism and resistance towards immigration, especially in those years when the rumours about Piazza Vittorio's decay, due to immigration, were at their peak. Each musician brought to the orchestra his or her own instrument and personal background of popular music, creating a fusion of cultures and traditions, old and new sounds, unknown instruments and voices from around the world, though not without difficulty.

The musical performances enacted by the immigrant characters in the documentary are all moments of nostalgic recollection; all the people involved in this project are immigrants who used to be musicians in their own country, but who had to give up once they arrived in Italy. Here they became anonymous immigrants with no time, no space, and no right to voice their cultural belongings and expressions. Mario Tronco is a musician himself and his project gave them the opportunity to 'talk back' by performing as artists. In so doing, these people have gained a visibility that is not usually accorded to immigrants in Italy. They did this by playing specific musical instruments that mirror each specific culture and by mixing different musical genres.[31] This makes the orchestra a dynamic multicultural laboratory in itself, where different religions, languages and customs meet in the name of music, a cultural expression that in this case is the object of compromise and rearrangement. As people migrate, music and song are among the cultural productions that travel with them 'contributing to the construction of memory and identity as well as bearing witness to change and transculturation'.[32]

An interesting aspect that the documentary is able to show is the difficulty that the orchestra has been encountering with the legal aspect of this multicultural project. Making the presence of immigrants legal in Italy, and in Europe in general, is always a complex and long process that involves much negotiation and patience and is not always successful. Millions of immigrants still live in hiding in Italy, against their will. These bureaucratic obstacles are common when it comes to immigration in Italy affecting the freedom these subjects have to express themselves as citizens, as persons and as cultural contributors.

The Orchestra of Piazza Vittorio functions as an ideal global community, where intercultural clashes find their way into a combination of unusual rhythms and combinations of notes. The result is a new experience for everyone — for the audience, of course, but first and foremost for the musicians involved, who share their talents by discovering new ways of playing and of performing musical narratives.

Piazza Vittorio, from which the Orchestra takes its name, is once again the expository window through which the artists involved project their personal experiences as musicians and as dwellers of a space that is being remapped. The orchestra and the film become pretexts for aestheticising the experience of migration, and emphasise their impact on the urban fabric of the Piazza. An early sequence of the film shows the two Italian artists, Mario Tronco and Agostino Ferrente, driving a Vespa around the Equilino district, and in particular around Piazza Vittorio, in search of immigrant musicians. They drive, walk and explore the area tracing not ordinary tracks, entering the shops of immigrants not as ordinary consumers, but as writers of an alternative text who aim at redefining a chaotic urban chatter as a cultural and aesthetic space for exploring and empowering multiculturalism.

Two scenes, in particular, show the aesthetic impact that migrants have on this space: an out-take scene presented as an extra in the DVD of the film shows a Chinese couple elegantly dancing an Argentinian tango in the garden of the square. This scene suggests a hybrid encounter that finds in the square its ideal stage, its 'contact zone'. This migratory performance aims at relocating identities in transit in a space that witnesses acts of agency, which also become a political act of urban appropriation. The same thing takes place in the opening scene of Ferrente's docu-musical, where one of the Indian musicians dressed in traditional garments performs a folk song while an Indian woman dances. Also in this case the garden of Piazza Vittorio becomes the stage for a live cultural performance remapping that space through an intercultural and nostalgic act played as if in a street theatre. In these two scenes, migrants invite the viewer to participate in an artistic transformation of the urban space where everyone can potentially become a 'displaced walker'.

Conclusion

The migratory aesthetic practices analysed in this chapter, from Lakhous's and Lemes Dias's literary examples to the musical and filmic project of the Orchestra of Piazza Vittorio, show how, rather than simply offering an unreadable, foreign and prosaic otherness, immigration in Italy today provides cultural representations that contribute to the mapping of the fleeting cartography of transitory spaces, such as Piazza Vittorio in Rome.

The aesthetic element of these cultural acts, their ability to make a transitory urban space legible, allows for an alternative discourse around immigration to be opposed to the most dominant political, economic and social discourses that tend to treat immigrants as an unauthorised presence in Italy or consider their identities to be somehow subservient to their migrant roles. The immigrants' ability to express a migratory aesthetics in relation to a specific urban space empowers their presence in that place and makes them visible. The result is a web of alternative tracks and traces that redefine the Italian space projecting it into a rich intercultural dimension.

Notes to Chapter 9

1. Amara Lakhous, 'Piazza Vittorio: A Cure for Homesickness', *Review: Literature and Arts of the Americas*, 42.1 (2009), 134–37 (p. 136).
2. Michel De Certeau, *The Practice of Everyday Life* (Berkeley and Los Angeles: University of California Press, 1984), p. 93.
3. Mieke Bal, 'Lost in Space, Lost in the Library', in *Essays in Migratory Aesthetics: Cultural Practices between Migration and Art-Making*, ed. by Sam Durrant and Catherine M. Lord (Amsterdam and New York: Rodopi, 2007), pp. 21–35 (p. 24).
4. Rocío G. Davis, Dorothea Fischer-Hornung and Johanna C. Kardux, 'Introduction', in *Aesthetic Practices and Politics in Media, Music, and Art: Performing Migration*, ed. by Rocío G. Davis, Dorothea Fischer-Hornung, and Johanna C. Kardux (London: Routledge, 2010), pp. 1–14 (p. 4).
5. Piazza Vittorio, located in the Esquilino quarter, is surrounded by arched buildings and is the only square in Rome built in the Piedmontese style — its construction dates from the period when the capital of the Kingdom of Italy, originally centred in Turin, was moved to Rome in 1870. These elegant buildings containing luxurious apartments were originally destined for bureaucrats and public servants. The structure of the square is quite unusual; its huge rectangular space is mostly occupied by a gated garden, in which are the ruins of Villa Palombara (1680), and in particular its main entrance, the Porta Magica [Magic Gate], on which are inscribed alchemical formulas in Hebrew and Latin. The Villa was destroyed when the land on which it stood was sold for the development of Rome's new main railway station in nearby Piazza di Termini in the 1860s. The garden also hosts a compound of ruins dating from ancient Roman times, the remains of a fountain known as the Trofei di Mario [Trophies of Marius]. Until a few years ago, Piazza Vittorio was known in particular for being the site of Rome's largest inner-city market, around the garden, which channelled and fed the urban and social life of the square. After the market was moved to an indoor space not far away, the square re-acquired its original nineteenth-century elegance.
6. Cf. Paolo Favero, 'Italians, the "Good People": Reflections on National Self-Representation in Contemporary Italian Debates on Xenophobia and War', *Outlines: Critical Practice Studies*, 2 (2010), 138–53.
7. In this regard, it is important to highlight how in Italy the exposure of Fascist items or Fascist iconography has recently become part of a 'normative' discourse. As part of a process of revisionism, these acts represent an attempt to rewrite contemporary Italian and European history, by relativizing the horrors of Nazism and of the final solution, decriminalising Fascism and its intelligentsia, delegitimising the Resistance movement and demonising Communism (see Angelo Del Boca (ed.), *La storia negata: il revisionismo e il suo uso politico* (Vicenza: Neri Pozza, 2009), p. 9). These voices were especially in line with the 2006 election of a self-declared Fascist mayor, Gianni Alemanno, who promoted his political programme by stressing the intention of removing from Rome, with strict measures, all those who have violated the law and who are not Italian citizens. In so doing, 'Mr Alemanno's victory marks the arrival in the Italian capital of the politics of paranoia that have already triumphed in much of the rest of the country' (Peter Popham, 'Neo-Fascist sweeps in as Rome's Mayor', *The Independent*, 29 April 2008: http://www.

independent.co.uk/news/world/europe/neofascist-sweeps-in-as-romes-mayor-817128.html [last accessed February 2016]). As a consequence, the ban on immigration has become part of a rhetoric that is influencing the consciousness and the gestures of Italians in Rome (and beyond), who feel legitimised to express their fear, anger and rejection of the other by a behaviour that in a democratic country should be criminalised as Fascist, violent and racist. This process of rewriting history eventually led to the removal of the black chapters of Fascism from the public discourse in order to rehabilitate it as an acceptable and harmless phenomenon. This misleading belief is today the agent of several violent acts still embedded in a discourse of manipulation of the past and its memory, protected, as noted by Paolo Favero, 'by the idea that after all, all such things are innocuous given that "we", the Italians, are, "*brava gente*"' (Favero, 'Italians, the "Good People"', p. 145). This is the social, cultural and political context in which Casa Pound and other Fascist organisations operate, and Piazza Vittorio has become the preferred space of their interventions.

8. Rachel Bowlby, *Carried Away: The Invention of Modern Shopping* (London: Faber and Faber, 2000), p. 50.

9. Graziella Parati, 'Where Do Migrants Live? Amara Lakhous's *Clash of Civilizations over an Elevator in Piazza Vittorio*', *Annali d'italianistica. Capital City: Rome 1870–2010*, 28 (2010), 431–44.

10. De Certeau, *The Practice of Everyday Life*, p. 103.

11. Ibid.

12. Lakhous, 'Piazza Vittorio', p. 135.

13. Parati, 'Where Do Migrants Live?', p. 432.

14. Ibid., pp. 436–37.

15. Ibid., p. 435.

16. Amara Lakhous, *Clash of Civilizations over an Elevator in Piazza Vittorio* (New York: Europa Editions, 2008), pp. 16–17.

17. Ibid., p. 42.

18. Parati, 'Where Do Migrants Live?', p. 437.

19. Lakhous, *Clash of Civilizations*, p. 95.

20. Parati, 'Where Do Migrants Live?', p. 442. Amedeo/Ahmed reserves for another space the expression of his most intimate sorrow. It is in the bathroom of his flat in Piazza Vittorio that he feels free to abandon himself to beastly 'wailings' (*ululati*), his secret confessions, his calls for justice.

21. De Certeau, *The Practice of Everyday Life*, p. 117.

22. Claudiléia Lemes Dias, 'Livia e il drago', in *Storie di extracomunitaria follia* (Napoli: Mangrovie, 2010), pp. 67–84 (p. 69). The translations of Lemes Dias's short story into English are mine.

23. Lesley Caldwell, 'Piazza Vittorio: Cinematic Notes on the Evolution of a Piazza', in *Rome: Continuing Encounters between Past and Present*, ed. by Dorigen Sophie Caldwell and Lesley Caldwell (Aldershot: Ashgate, 2011), pp. 189–206 (p. 193).

24. De Certeau, *The Practice of Everyday Life*, p. 108.

25. Lemes Dias, 'Livia e il drago', p. 68.

26. Tracy Wilkinson, 'When in Rome, Use Chopsticks', *Los Angeles Times*, 14 April 2004: http://articles.latimes.com/2004/apr/14/world/fg-ciaomein14 [last accessed February 2016].

27. Lemes Dias, 'Livia e il drago', p. 79.

28. Parati, 'Where Do Migrants Live?', p. 441.

29. Toni Morrison, *Beloved* (London: Vintage, 2007 [1987]), p. 43.

30. There are several other migratory everyday life practices that find in the square of Piazza Vittorio — and in particular inside its gated garden — their ideal location. Among them is the performance of Tai Chi exercises every day at dawn. A Chinese Tai Chi teacher and his students arrive in the garden of the square and start their martial arts exercises; behind them a small group of people, Italians and immigrants, gather and follow their slow motions as if on a stage. The result is a social act that adds a new urban and cultural layer in the palimpsest of the square. The garden and the Piazza around become 'contact zones', social spaces where 'cultures meet, clash, and grapple with each other, often in contexts of highly asymmetrical relations of power' (Mary Louise Pratt, 'Arts of the Contact Zone', *Profession* (1991), 33–40 (p. 33)). As in

Lakhous's and Lemes Dias's texts, here migrants become deliberately the agents of new power relations, projecting the memorised and imaginary representation of their home culture onto a place they remap through acts of 'public' performances that involve an intercultural contact, a contamination between subjects, practices and spaces. It is by acts of memory that migrants are tied to these places that become the depository of a new text they are in the process of narrating. Another public performative act taking place in the garden of Piazza Vittorio has been brought forward by the Piazza Vittorio Cricket Club, an association spontaneously formed by the young dwellers of the Piazza, all Italian-born and mainly from migrant families. They started using the garden of the square for playing amateur matches with improvised equipment, and now they have formed an ambitious team that has already taken part in some official cricket competitions. Interestingly, the association defined itself as 'the association without permission', to stress the independent and unrecognised initiative, and consequently the lack of interest on the part of the official Italian institutions. As in the case of Tai Chi in the garden, the Cricket Club aims at inscribing an alternative public and social discourse in the space of Piazza Vittorio, where migrants and people of non-Italian origin have the chance to enact their own cultural practices, projecting nostalgia in a space that is not simply Italian or national any more.

31. The musicians involved are from India, Senegal, Tunisia, Morocco, USA, Ecuador, Argentina, Hungary and Italy, and the instruments played include, among others, the *tabla* (Indian percussion), *oud* (North African guitar), *kora* (harp used in West Africa) and *conga* (Cuban drums). [o]

32. Davis, Fischer-Hornung, and Kardux, 'Introduction', p. 8.

❖

CHAPTER 10

Negotiating the Present:
Rome, Fabric and Memory

Lesley Caldwell

Introduction

The enduring image of Rome, as the piling-up of past upon present so beautifully evoked by Freud in *Civilisation and its Discontents*[1] as a model for the mind, draws attention to Rome's history as a city where the juxtaposition of different pasts that is the fate of any modern city is particularly notable.

Carlo Aymonino[2] distinguished Rome from other European cities on the grounds that, despite substantial growth and change, continuity was maintained via the series of monuments and buildings that remained integral to its urban structure. Imperial Rome, the nuclei of the medieval city, and the monumental and street planning of the baroque produced three radically different urban landscapes, but until very recently the city lacked a recognisable contemporary landscape in that the rapid development after its establishment as the capital of a united Italy retained the baroque structure without significant transformation. It failed, as occurred elsewhere, to produce a modern structure that engulfed the ancient city. And yet the very extended area which now comprises Greater Rome forms part of an everyday experience of old and new which, while not necessarily organising a way of encountering the world at any completely conscious level, certainly contributes to how people locate themselves in their own particular personal worlds.

In *The Architecture of the City* Aldo Rossi suggests the past is always being experienced in the present in what he calls 'permanences', an idea taken from Poête and Lavedan.[3] What Poête calls 'persistences' are revealed both through monuments and through a city's basic layout and plans. Rossi's own typology of 'permanences' builds upon this in making monuments and housing the central components of the city, contributing to its everyday life and to the structures around which it coheres — homes, shops, bars, transport, businesses, sport and recreation facilities.

In this essay I gesture at Rome's complex modernity through a description of a specific location, surrounded by the remains of antiquity, and lying on the edges of central Rome. The area, known as San Saba fuori le mura, combines the everyday life of a settled population with some foreign visitors, but it is less under siege as

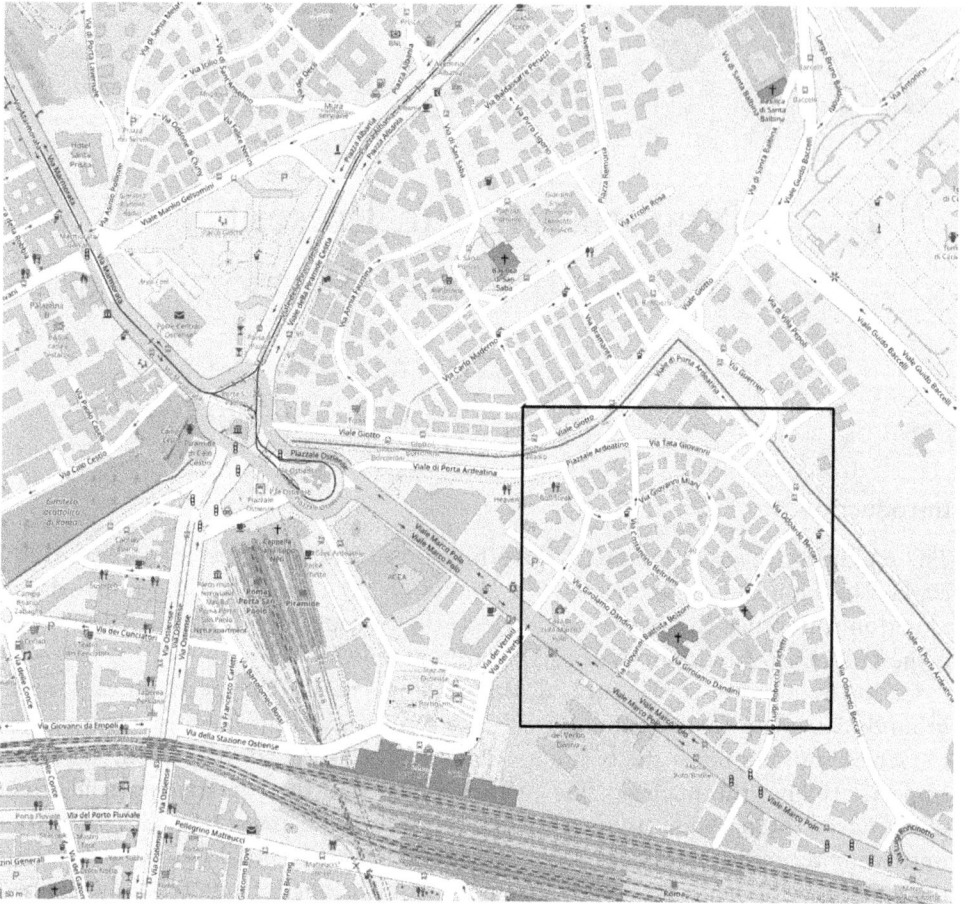

FIG. 10.1. Approximate location of San Saba fuori le mura (Source: Open StreetMap)

tourist destination and heritage city than the city centre, thus largely escaping the considerable damage such a description may embody for those who live there.

In this area, we see a Rome of successive histories and their traces, which are to be discerned most immediately in the monuments of antiquity, and then, less visibly, through the occupied city of the Second World War and the continuing practices of its memorialisation, and most recently together with the contemporary visible presence of the results of global upheavals in the shape of itinerant populations. All of these events belonging to different periods and histories contribute to shaping the lives of its residents, less in any consciously articulated way than as background presence, in much the way Benjamin[4] describes the masses as perceiving architecture, that is, in a state of distraction rather than contemplation. In extending this claim, he argues for habit as an important dimension of perception. Habit and absent-mindedness as central to the perception of architecture and to a sense of the city more generally support Rossi's argument that both ancient and papal Rome are part of the modern city, and, given the extent of the area encompassed by the Mura

Aureliane, the city's ancient walls, not only of the historic centre but well beyond. This is the case even before the vast sprawl of the periphery is considered.

Contemporary discussion of the city has emphasised the routinisation of everyday life and its failure to surprise, shock, excite, or impress, underscored by the tendency to a universalising sameness. Such a perspective draws attention to Rome's similarities with other large cities but diminishes the specificity of the habitus of its citizens. To focus on the local, however, and what its spaces may offer of the experience of a city, challenges the idea of sameness through an attention to the shaping of lived experience by means of the particularity given by history and the built environment, and their impact.

An urban sensibility which pursues the experience of the modern city through an attention to detail, to how apparently marginal structures provide narratives of everyday living,[5] takes up Michel De Certeau's discussion of 'the ways users operate'[6] by challenging ideas of their passivity and non-involvement in their local surroundings. In the introduction to *The Practice of Everyday Life*,[7] he argues that research procedures in the human sciences have insufficiently attended to the way the consumer's act of making or using can be understood as active and creative. Like Freud, in *The Psychopathology of Everyday Life*,[8] he is interested in those procedures that demonstrate 'the intelligibility of present reality', and in how personhood and subjectivity are arrived at and maintained. Although the everyday and everyday life have a long intellectual history from Lukács and Heidegger to Goffman and Habermas,[9] they requires a precise focus or location if they are avoid a generalising ambiguity. In claiming the sphere of the everyday for practices of resistance and subversion, and insisting upon it as the foundation of complex lives, De Certeau makes the parameters of everyday living the creative arena of ordinary people in ordinary situations. These emphases provide a guiding thread in the mapping exercise that follows.

The psychoanalyst Donald Winnicott was equally concerned with creativity as part of the ordinary experience of living, and his popularising book, *Home Is where We Start From*,[10] together with two of his papers from *Playing and Reality*,[11] 'The Place Where I Live' and 'The Location of Cultural Experience', are all concerned with where, whatever their surroundings, someone lives internally. He argues for the centrality of place, materially and psychologically, both in the organisation of the self, and in the self in relation with others, living and dead, known and unknown, as this is negotiated and consolidated through the continuity of lives maintained over time. Through the structures of everyday life, internal and external realities bring the actual world into relation with the inner organisation of the self, and contribute to the distinctiveness of the lives of its inhabitants. If creativity is an essential constitutive aspect of the everyday,[12] its being lived out and experienced in a particular location provides a further dimension to consider.

The Psychopathology of Everyday Life records Freud's passionate curiosity about the everyday through an investigation of Vienna and the Viennese. While it forms part of an intellectual defence of his developing work and his conviction of its importance to a scientific account of the mind, the predictability of the random

FIG. 10.2. The Aurelian walls at Largo Chiarini. (All photographs are by the author.)

desires and impulses of the normal mind that he charts through routines and habitual practices that look distinctly unscientific does offer a convincing argument for the locatedness of these same impulses and practices in everyday experiences shaped by internal and external frameworks and encounters. Freud relishes a particularly Viennese locatedness and its familiarity as the foundation for a more systematic way of looking at his world.

San Saba fuori le mura is a quarter to the immediate south of the city centre. In this account I draw attention to some of the distinguishing features of its built environment, and to the historical processes that have contributed, directly and indirectly, to its inhabitants' ongoing lives there. I emphasise the remains of the past, especially the presence of the city walls, the area's development as a living quarter as part of Fascist ambitions to develop Rome in the direction of the sea, the historical memory of the trauma of Nazi occupation and the local battles of the Second World War focused in this area, their memorialisation in annual commemorations, and in the urban references in the presence of plaques and the naming of significant spaces and streets. Finally, I record the contemporary presence of substantial numbers of the homeless and of migrants around its borders. Above and beyond the sites, events, or battles which offer some of the ways of defining this area, it is the way those same factors continue to impinge on the present that marks its distinctiveness and specificity.

When narrowly and geographically defined, San Saba fuori le mura is relatively anonymous, but when its area is widened even a little, it becomes part of a zone

FIG. 10.3. San Saba housing.

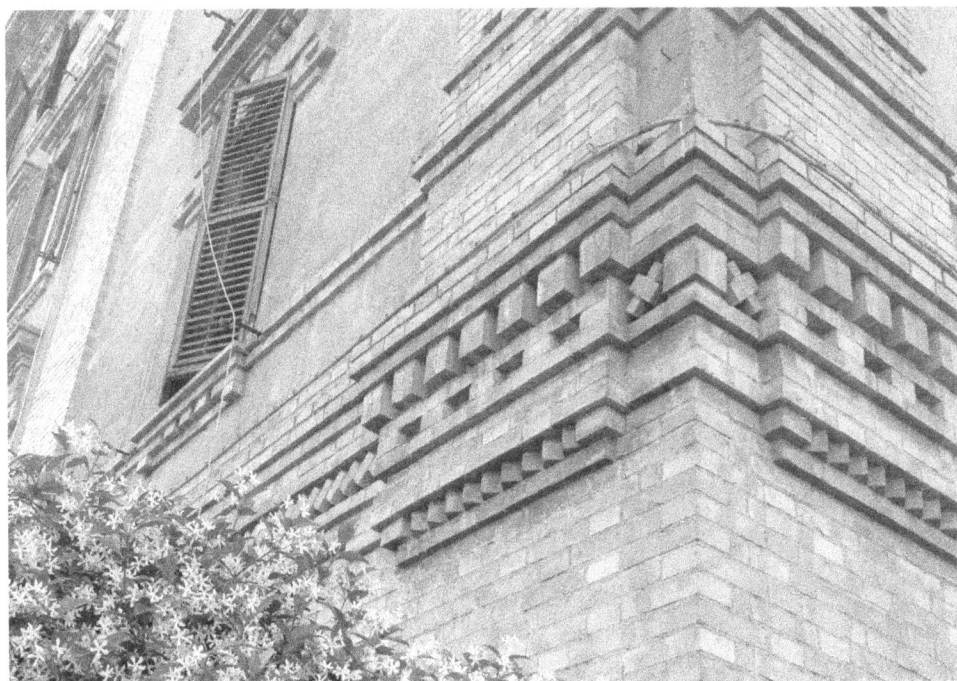

FIG. 10.4. Detail of brick work.

Fig. 10.5. Bastione del Sangallo.

of historical and archaeological importance. Even in its narrowest delineation it is dominated by the presence of the Aurelian Walls. Constructed between 270 and 273, they have a substantial continuity in this part of Rome, and though no longer a boundary marking the edges of the city, or conferring the notion of Roman citizen to those living within them, they remain a massive presence, a signifier of ancient Rome, and its later renewal, with all that that carries in the history of the west. From the beginning they were frequently breached or added to in one way or another, extended beyond their original height of 25 feet, or given the addition of towers,[13] and many of these incursions can still be discerned in their materials and their shape. Built of concrete faced with brick and 12 feet thick, the walls contain a sentinel's passage 13 feet from the ground, which is consistently higher inside than out and the gates, of single or double archways according to importance, have flanking towers.[14] The section adjoining San Saba fuori le mura, which leads out of town, the Bastione of Sangallo, itself the result of earlier war, is imposing and well maintained and, unlike the original walls, it presents an inclined surface. Dating from 1538 and the destruction following the Sack of Rome, it was part of the subsequent town planning and reconstruction undertaken by the Farnese Pope, Paul III, whose arms still appear in marble against the brick.

To arrive from San Saba fuori le mura to San Saba itself involves crossing through the New Porta Ardeatina, a modern road through the walls, opened in 1938/39 for Hitler's visit to Rome.

It takes its name from the ancient church of San Saba and although it has been consistently built upon in successive decades and now includes some of the most desirable Roman real estate beyond the immediate city centre, the central area has

FIG. 10.6. A typical palazzo in the Via Ambrogio Contarini

retained its distinctiveness as a well-designed, early twentieth century district of contained geometric elegance, precision, and order, initially built for workers to a plan by Pirani. The mixed housing stock includes apartment blocks of four or five stories, and little villas (*villini*) of two and three stories with small front gardens. Its architectural interest lies particularly in its use of materials, the style of its brickwork providing a reference to the Roman and the medieval brickwork close by, and in this mixture of small-scale housing types with gardens and internal courtyards. Its streets are named after architects, painters, and sculptors: Piazza Bernini, Via Bramante, Viale Giotto.

San Saba fuori le mura refers to a lozenge-shaped area of housing and local amenities whose clearest boundaries are the Aurelian walls to the east, Piazzale Porta San Paolo to the north, Viale Marco Polo to the west, and the Via Cristoforo Colombo to the south. It is a quiet residential area lying between significant traffic hubs on three sides.

In the massive reorganisation and destruction following the selection of Rome

FIG. 10.7. Tata San Giovanni.

as capital in 1870, 'outside the walls' indicated those areas just beyond the officially regulated provision designated in the *piani regolatori*, which, as unregulated zones, offered sites for a potential free-for-all in terms of building. The major housing development and the roads of San Saba fuori le mura date from the period after the 1931 town plan, and are linked with Rome's Fascist past. It is a hilly area of modest housing blocks, for the most part between four and eight storeys, with some of the original developments augmented in later decades with extra, mostly illegal storeys, and where more recent apartment blocks have filled in the spaces left around the original housing. They are pleasant, undistinguished buildings that could be found in many parts of Rome. There is a mixed community that is still predominantly 'Roman'.

On both the internal and external sides of the walls there is an area of green space alongside the roads which follow the walls, Via Porta Ardeatina outside and Viale Giotto inside, each leading up from Piazzale Porta San Paolo and the Pyramid of Cestius towards other monuments of the ancient world, the Porta San Sebastiano and the Baths of Caracalla. More recently, the placing of plaques invokes histories of war, conflict, death, and commemoration (see below).

Via Ambrogio Contarini, Via Giovanni Miani, and Via Costantini Beltrami are the major streets comprising the spine of this hilly terrain, all of whose streets are named after explorers, navigators, and adventurers, including Chiarini, Marco Polo, and Cristoforo Colombo, the latter two being major roads. The Cristoforo Colombo was initiated in 1937 as one of Mussolini's favoured projects, the Via del Mare, which was to link Piazza Venezia with the sea by way of the Passeggiata archeologica, an inheritance of the town plan of 1909, which then had to be destroyed to enable it. It is bounded to the east by Viale Marco Polo, registered in 1945 February, but under construction earlier, which constituted another early initiative in the push towards the sea, towards what, some years earlier at Tre Fontane, about 5 km from Porta San Paolo, had been chosen as the site for EUR.

The area's centre is the seedy Largo Chiarini, which sits between the apartment blocks and the walls. It contains a very popular bar, the Bar Brunori, whose ageing owners are devotees of the rock music of their youth. An uncomfortable, disorderly arrangement of tables, each with its own plastic pot of plastic greenery, takes second place to the coffee, and to stocks of music, posters of Jimi Hendrix, shelves of vinyl and CDs. The hub of a very diverse community life, it is always surrounded by cars, backed up in rows. It forms part of a straggle of badly maintained shops — pet grooming, grubby hardware, a never-open jewellery shop, a never-patronised hairdresser and beautician. Beyond the raised entrance to a complex of apartment blocks, the next palazzo down the hill now houses a municipal office block. Opposite is a former orphanage, Tata Giovanna, still church property, which contains the local football field. Opposite the bar there is a scruffy park and a children's playground.

From early in the morning till late at night Largo Chiarini and the roads abutting the walls comprise a working zone for prostitutes of different kinds, successive groups catering to different tastes replacing each other as the night advances. The group of women who congregate throughout the day are unglamorous, working women of mixed ethnic origins, predominantly Eastern European and South East Asian, contemporary versions of the friends of *Mamma Roma*. One, a thin, pierced Goth in her late forties, lives in the area and has a teenage son with learning difficulties. The man who begs several days a week outside the bar, a graduate with a family at home in Nigeria, divides his time between this bar and a bigger one in the nearby Via Ostiense, his 'work' bringing him to this inner-city zone, far from where he himself lives. When he first began to beg here some four or five years ago, he spoke of going to France or Germany, of finding work, of the shame and humiliation of standing outside greeting passers-by every day. He no longer appears to entertain these ambitions, has become increasingly hopeless and worn down, and is still looking for steady work beyond begging. He too is a part of local life.

The More Extended Area

This modest urban development is set in an area of walls and city gates, railway lines, and roads that lead into the Piazzale of Porta San Paolo. But to follow the walls out of town is to encounter the succession of gates of the ancient Roman city that puncture the walls' eastern sweep towards the beginning of the Via Appia Antica and further on to the basilica of Saint John Lateran. Beyond Largo Chiarini

FIG. 10.8. Piazzale dei Partigiani.

along the via Ardeatina and the Bastion of Sangallo, the Casa del Jazz *appears* on the right. The former Villa Osio, built in the 1930s by the BNL, was owned by the Banda della Magliana before its takeover by the Comune when Veltroni was mayor.

At the junction with the Cristoforo Colombo, and its relentless flood of traffic, the Porta Ardeatina leads left down towards the Baths of Caracalla before circling the Caelian hill and rising to Saint John Lateran. At the following gate, the Porta San Sebastiano (the Porta Appia), there is the entrance to the museum inside the walls. Breaking away from the circularity of the walls and continuing south along Via Ardeatina into what remains of the Roman *campagna*, there are the Fosse Ardeatine and their stirring memorial (1950).

To follow the walls in the opposite direction left into the city centre is to encounter a much less well-defined presence. From Largo Chiarini, the walls border the Via Porta Ardeatina on the outer side as they continue down into the Piazzale Porta San Paolo. This section has recently been a target of regeneration and tidying with central government money allocated for the 2016 Jubilee. As part of an earlier local government regeneration initiative however, dating from 2002, a kind of extended open museum, Il Parco Lineare Integrato, was planned to be constructed along the walls throughout the city. Conceived primarily with the aims of restoration and preservation of the walls and their integration into their surroundings, the area around Porta Metronia, several gates further east, provides the best example of this regeneration. In the section that includes San Saba it extends internally from

Fig. 10.9. Porticos Station

the 1938 gate along Via Guerrieri, the street leading from San Saba fuori le mura to the junction with viale Giotto, the edge of the original San Saba development. The strip of land skirting the lower internal face of the walls was restored under the Alemanno administration, to become, briefly, a pristine additional green space with benches and modern fountains.

Despite the initial tidying and upgrading and the political capital that derived from it, the rhetorical claims for a municipal park never quite delivered and, in the following years it has returned to a slightly unkempt, minor wilderness of grasses, the benches usually occupied by one or two waiting prostitutes. A local petition to move them on and stop them sitting on the benches has come to nothing.

FIG. 10.10. Grilles to be closed at night.

Beyond Viale Marco Polo, farther away to the west, the border is formed by the railway line and two stations, Ostia Lido (built in 1923) fronting onto Piazzale San Paolo, and Stazione Ostiense at Piazzale dei Partigiani (1938) servicing various regional trains, including that to the airport. The metro stop, Piramide, also dates from the years of Fascist expansion so that the area offers some of the city's most iconic modern buildings in these stations, and also includes Adalberto Libera's winning entry in the competition for new post offices (1934), which lies just beyond on the northern side of the Porta San Paolo in Via Marmorata.

FIG. 10.11. A high rise block: four palazzi between
Viale Marco Polo and Piazzale dei Partigiani.

Porta San Paolo and the Fosse Ardeatine

The large space of Piazzale Porta San Paolo is entered by eight roads, Via Marmorata, the Ostiense itself, Viale Marco Polo, Via Ardeatina, Via Cave Ardeatina, Viale
Giotto, Via Piramide Cestio, and Via Boario, four of them main traffic arteries
dating from different eras. To hear this roll-call of streets and roads is to invoke both
an ancient past and a more recent history of war, of battles fought against Germans
and Fascists, and most recently, a contested history of that earlier period of events
whose interpretation is now being constantly questioned, its ceremonies interrupted
and disputed, memories challenged and revised. Its use as thoroughfare and meeting
place is constant, but at the anniversaries of these events, the Piazzale becomes a
space of commemoration, of official gatherings for the witnessing and registering
of past events of continuing significance for the city of Rome: the war, fascism, the
local resistance, and the massacre itself. This public space gathers together roles and
a function within a social public identity that is simultaneously historical and local,
defined by more or less accessible spaces, symbolically reverberating with recent
trauma, bloodshed, violence, and war.

FIG. 10.12. A column indicates the street name.

The German occupation of Rome lasted nine months, from 8 September 1943 to 4 July 1944; the deportation of the Jews, one of Rome's oldest communities, began on 16 October 1943. During the occupation, the partisans acted against the Germans and the Fascists in various districts, the most famous attack being that of Via Rasella (23 March 1944) in the city centre, with thirty-three casualties. The German retaliation followed the next day when 335 men were rounded up, taken to the quarries [Caves] of the Ardeatine and shot at what are now known as the Fosse [graves] Ardeatine. This trauma was made infinitely worse for the local population by German indecision about the announcement of the deaths and the disposal of the bodies.

The central significance of the area under discussion as a place of memorialisation of the Second World War, of occupation, and of street battles against Fascists and Germans, and its nearness to and association with the Fosse Ardeatine, 'the only European metropolitan massacre', as Sandro Portelli has described it, brings it into focus as a major centre of a recent history of trauma, indicated in its street names:

Fig. 10.13. Street name plaque honouring the Romans killed in 1943

Via di Porta Ardeatina, Via Cave Ardeatine, Piazzale dei Partigiani, Parco della Resistenza.

The Fosse Ardeatine is the symbolic maelstrom in which the space of the city and a century of its stories come together, so that to speak about it is to speak of the whole history of Rome in the twentieth century. This history of this rebel city that was never tamed, as the old Communist song proclaims, a city so different from the clichés and stereotypes, a city that resisted the Nazis actively and passively, intensely and diffusely, and for this paid a terrible price.[15]

The memorial located at the site itself several kilometres from the Piazzale of Porta San Paolo was projected in the immediate post-war period, assigned to the architects Mario Fiorentino and Giuseppe Perugini in 1947 and completed in 1952.

While the Fosse themselves represent one of the most tragic and moving sites of the city; they are also one of the most actively contested in the city's memory, because the massacre by the Germans is connected with the GAP action the day before in Via Rasella. This history and the relation of the partisan attack to the German massacre of 335 Romans is recorded, re-presented and fought over bitterly through the language of victims and perpetrators, of where ultimate responsibility resides. This emerges not only in their annual memorialisation, but in how those anniversaries have been deployed in the appropriation of Rome's recent past, and its current use in present disputes between left and right.

The anniversaries in March and April are displays of the performative activities that Connerton[16] sees as fundamental to the continuation of any cultural memory. They are embedded in the tension between history and the everyday, past and present, the casual layering of one epoch upon another, and, equally significantly, one population upon another, that is the experience of daily life in Rome. These practices continue to have an impact in this urban area, whose former activities as a site of war they celebrate and record, annually recreating it, especially the Piazzale, as a site of multiple cultural meanings that brings together what Connerton calls 'recollection and recollected knowledge of the past' with 'practices of a non-inscribed kind'. These performative activities are a basis for the transmission of cultural memories through the involvement of persons and bodies in particular surroundings and contexts,[17] but they are activities which have become increasingly contested as the history of Italian resistance has become more widely known and its complexities more researched.

In this area, like many areas of many cities, the density of historical association and of former devastation contributes to a multi-layered encounter where the original defensive function of the walls has been long superseded by the crumbling through which they have become picturesque ruins, whose monumentality nonetheless continues to signify the past of antiquity. Both the ceremonies and the plaques recording battles and losses juxtapose different pasts, which assert a common thread of Romanness, and a Rome defended against various enemy others.

The walls remain a symbolic barrier which, while literally confining nothing, draws attention to the former existence of the ancient walled city, and to the always simultaneously existent, non-walled city alongside it. That city is still marked by inclusion and exclusion, an inside and an outside, whose signs, property, class, green space, money, access to goods and services signify 'belonging' of various kinds. This area, itself increasingly gentrified, is part of a slightly down-at-heel Rome and a privileged Rome of private villas and expensive apartments.

Recent Divisions

An equally contested history of the present used to gather on the corner of Viale Marco Polo and Via Ardeatina, opposite the walls in the apex of a triangle formed with them and the Piazzale Porta San Paolo, an area now directly opposite the terminus of the number 3 tram. This little bit of wasteland, an unkempt space, was the meeting place for a group of Ukrainian migrants who would gather in twos and threes at all hours on the two benches. At the weekend their numbers would swell and there were picnics and minor market exchanges in the dust, but, under the increasingly restrictive practices of successive Communal administrations, the benches have disappeared and with them the socialising; grass and weeds cover the area.

From the opposite corner of Viale Marco Polo, a thin finger of land extends south out of town. Heavily built upon with four large three-sided high-rise blocks, the headquarters of the electricity company, ACEA, and its large brutalist fountain, it is bordered to the west by the Via Cave Ardeatina which in its turn is lined on its western side by a straggle of market stalls of the cheapest kind, largely staffed by Asians. Descending, it leads to the metro stop, Piramide, a distinguished building by Piacentini, dating from 1921–24, and ascending it arrives in Piazzale dei Partigiani, whose name immediately evokes that same powerfully invested era of modern warfare, resistance and the street battles fought here and throughout Rome in the 1940s.

Piazzale dei Partigiani remains another significant transport hub, including a major bus terminus that has been subject to significant change and upgrading in the past three years following the reduction in the number of bus routes in operation. Along its squalid perimeters are visible a villa and its gardens, the high-rise blocks and the latticed metal grids of the underpasses that lead to the railway station and the metro line B, which are now all blocked off to prevent their use by the homeless. The station itself, built in 1938 for Hitler's visit to Rome, was in disrepair, as were the mosaics of the same period under its porticos, which almost run into the supermarket located at one end. Over several years the mosaics have been restored, the travertine cleaned, and the lines of the building have become more obvious with the removal of the many buses whose routes have been cut because of the economic crisis. Some incidental planting in their stead seems to augur the beginnings of regeneration in this large piazza, which in the summer is hot, dry, dirty and dusty, in the winter deserted, cold and unwelcoming. Formerly, in all seasons, the homeless of Rome gathered at night under the station's porticos and in the sections of the underground passages, not at that time blocked off. The *squadra mobile* passed quite often to move them on, but also finally to let them be. In the last years new gates have been attached to close off the area at night and to restrict yet another public space from use by the homeless.

The first moves in this direction in Rome began in the late 1980s with the enclosing of monuments, now all fenced in, then of parks, the porches of churches, and now the porticos of the railway station.

The outcasts of today as represented by the refugees and migrants who picnicked in the grass, or huddled together under the porticos in winter, link a wartime Rome of deprivation, massacres and horror with a contemporary Rome of the homeless and of those scraping a living in whatever way they can, a different everyday tragedy, but a tragedy nonetheless. If, as Paul Connerton has argued, material objects have less significance in perpetuating memory than embodied acts, rituals and the normative social behaviours which endorse the idea of society as comprised of shared meanings that people construct and recognise, without necessarily being aware of it, then the disappearance of these small signs of sociality among the current dispossessed reveals the much wider crisis in the contemporary displacement of more significant numbers of people than at any time since the Second World War.

To gather in all the potentially traumatogenic events is to summarise a complex history that would include two world wars and the establishment of Fascism, and specific traumatic events within each of these extended periods: the war itself, the deportation of Jews, the occupation, and the Fosse Ardeatine massacre. The post-war history from 1945 to the present would have to take account of the uprisings, revolts and terrorism of the 1970s and 1980s, on the one hand, and on the other, the results of this history in terms of the city's fabric: a succession of activities of demolition, and rebuilding, in the 1870–1900 period, in the *sventramenti* of the regime, in the wartime bombing and its effects in the 1940s, and then post-war building projects and its effects on the landscape. It would include the results of war in the form of homelessness, starvation and poverty in the immediate post-war period, and similar conditions and their effects for particular groups in the present day.

If trauma and the traumatic have become very over-used words, the enlarging of their range still gathers together something of the connotations of disaster, injury and stress. But trauma, at the point of subjective experience, is a 'failure' of the psychic system, the psychological consequence of an individual's failure to process a revelation that threatens the very existence of the ego. It is the psychic, not only the external, event that can interfere, in an unbearable way, with the individual's understanding of the world, a challenge to the core of the self. The event belongs to reality, but for it to acquire meaning for someone, it has to be perceived and assessed. Approaching psychological trauma as a phenomenon reflecting the struggle of the human psyche to protect itself from chaos when faced with a knowledge that threatens its ability to function assists in explaining the specificity of individual responses to any event, as these depend less on the event itself than on the subject's self and his/her ability to revise a former way of approaching the world. This is serious and difficult work, often without much hope of effecting any real change in the intensely individual consequences and implications for the persons concerned.

In contemporary Rome, the older traumatic events of war and loss exist alongside new dislocations, displacement and individual difficulty. In the descriptive parameters I have outlined here the majority of this zone's citizens live the ordinary lives of settled citizens as they negotiate everyday existence, but they also encounter the signs of both earlier and current disruption and conflict.

In this descriptive mapping exercise, a plotting of a specific local terrain and the constantly interweaving aspects of history and memory to be found there, all these aspects, tangible and intangible, form part of everyday life, and may be understood as contributing to the emotional realities of those who live there, work there, or pass through as itinerant populations. The physical fabric of place, the shape and dimensions of its external surroundings, and the public recording of events through formal practices and informal habits, all play a part in the establishment of the characteristics of this area and its inhabitants, in their relations with self and others, through the ordinary living that is a source of the continuing creativity that maintains the aliveness of a city.

A study of a specific local area centred on history and location raises the question of how its unity and coherence are maintained, but also how its boundaries are to be drawn imaginatively. In this sense imaginative boundaries reorganise the experience of any specific area and how it comes to be understood. What is there to be looked at and remembered provides the framing conditions for understanding any specific area; through them, the quality of life of that area is given by its inhabitants and their interaction with their surroundings. How any community is maintained and stays alive derives from the interpersonal networks that establish affective ties and bonds, but the impact of the built environment, the sense of history and the past, produced through daily visual encounters not only with people, but with landscape and buildings, offers a further dimension for how life is lived in any urban space.

Notes to Chapter 10

1. Sigmund Freud, 'Civilisation and its Discontents' [1930], in *Standard Edition*, ed. by James Strachey et al, 24 volumes (London: Hogarth Press and the Institute of Psychoanalysis, 1953–74), XXI, 59–145.

2. Carlo Aymonino, *Il significato della città* (Milan: Marsilio, 1975).

3. Aldo Rossi, *The Architecture of the City* (Cambridge, MA, and London: MIT Press, 1984), p. 59.

4. Walter Benjamin, *The Work of Art in the Age of Mechanical Reproduction* [1936] (London: Penguin Random House, 2015), pp. 211–44.

5. Michael Keith, 'Walter Benjamin, Urban Studies, and the Narratives of City Life', in *A Companion to the City*, ed. by Gary Bridge and Sophie Watson (Oxford: Blackwell 2000), pp. 401–29.

6. Michel de Certeau, *The Practice of Everyday Life* (Berkeley and Los Angeles: University of California Press, 1984), p. xv; Michel de Certeau, 'Psychoanalysis and its History', in *Heterologies: Discourses on the Other* (Manchester: Manchester University Press, 1986), pp. 3–16.

7. De Certeau, *The Practice of Everyday Life*, pp. xii–xiv.

8. Sigmund Freud, *The Psychopathology of Everyday Life*, *Standard Edition*, VI (London: Hogarth Press and the Institute of Psychoanalysis, 1901).

9. Rita Felski, 'The Invention of Everyday Life', *New Formations*, 39 (1999), 15–31.

10. Donald W. Winnicott, *Home Is Where We Start From* Harmondsworth: Penguin, 1986).

11. Donald W. Winnicott, *Playing and Reality* (London: Tavistock Publications, 1971; republished Routledge, 1991).

12. Donald W. Winnicott, 'Creativity and its Origins', in *Playing and Reality*, pp. 87–114.

13. Samuel Ball Platner, completed and revised by Thomas Ashby, *A Topographical Dictionary of Rome* (Oxford and New York: Oxford University Press, 1926), p. 350. See also Marco Cavietti, 'Between Rome's Walls: Notes on the Role and Reception of the Aurelian Walls', in *Rome: Postmodern Narratives of a Cityscape*, ed. by Dominic Holdaway and Filippo Trentin (London: Pickering & Chatto, 2013), pp. 19–38.

14. Platner, *A Topographical Dictionary of Rome*, p. 350. See also Cavietti, 'Between Rome's Walls'.

15. Alessandro Portelli, *The Order Has Been Carried Out* (New York and Basingstoke: Palgrave Macmillan, 2003), p. 9. See also *Città di parole* (Rome: Donzelli, 2006).

16. Paul Connerton, *How Societies Remember* (Cambridge: Cambridge University Press, 1989).

17. Ibid., p. 4.

BIBLIOGRAPHY

❖

ACCADEMIA DI SAN LUCA, *I disegni di architettura dell'Archivio storico dell'Accademia di San Luca*, ed. by Paolo Marconi, Angela Cipriani and Enrico Valeriani (Rome: De Luca, 1974)

ACCASTO, GIANNI, VANNA FRATICELLI, and RENATA NICOLINI, *L'architettura di Roma capitale 1870–1970* (Rome: Golem, 1971)

ACCROCCA, ELIO FILIPPO, *Portonaccio* (Milan: All'insegna del pesce d'oro, 1949)

AGNEW, JOHN A., *Rome* (Chichester and New York: Wiley & Sons, 1995)

AIC E UNIONE BORGATE, *Periferie di Mezzo. Servizi, innovazioni, sostenibilità: un nuovo sistema urbano* (Rome 2010)

ALLEGRETTI, GIOVANNI, *Inchieste locali, Comune di Roma*, URBACT — rete "Partecipando", Urbact (2004)

ALLEN, JOHN, *Topologies of Power: Beyond Territory and Networks* (New York: Routledge, 2016)

ALLEN, JUDITH, and OTHERS, *Housing and Welfare in Southern Europe* (Oxford: Blackwell, 2004)

ALSAYYAD, NEZAR, 'The End of Tradition or the Tradition of Endings?', in *The End of Tradition?*, ed. by Nezar AlSayyad (London and New York: Routledge, 2004), pp. 1–29

ANGELI, DIEGO, 'I problemi edilizi di Roma', *Nuova antologia. Rivista di lettere, scienze e arti*, 204 (1905)

ANNUNZIATA, SANDRA, 'The Desire of Ethnically Diverse Neighbourhood in Rome. The Case of Pigneto: an Example of Integrated Planning Approach', in *The Ethnically Diverse City*, ed. by Frank Eckardt and John Eade (Berlin: Berliner Wissenschaftsverlag, 2011), pp. 601–23Aymonino, Carlo, *Il significato della città* (Milan: Marsilio, 1975)

ANTONELLO, Pierpaolo, *Contro il materialismo: Le 'due culture' in Italia* (Turin: Aragno, 2012)

——, and ALAN O'LEARY (eds), *Imagining Terrorism: The Rhetoric and Representation of Political Violence in Italy, 1969–2006* (London: Legenda, 2009)

ARDY, SILVIO, *Proposta di creazione di un Istituto Italiano di Urbanesimo e di Alti Studi Municipali, Congresso Internazionale dell'Urbanesimo (Torino 28 maggio 1926), IV Tema*, (Vercelli: S.A.V.I.T. Società Anonima Vercellese Industria Tipografica, 1926)

ARGAN, GIULIO CARLO, *Un'idea di Roma. Intervista di Mino Monicelli* (Rome: Editori Riuniti Interventi, 1979)

——, and OTHERS, *Profili dell'Italia repubblicana*, ed. by Ottavio Cecchi and Enrico Ghidetti (Rome: Editori Riuniti, 1996)

ARMINIO, FRANCO, *Terracarne: Viaggio nei paesi invisibili e nei paesi giganti del Sud Italia* (Milan: Mondadori, 2011)

ASHBY, THOMAS, and GUSTAVO GIOVANNONI, 'Resoconto morale per l'anno MCMX', *Associazione Artistica fra i Cultori di Architettura di Roma. Annuario* (1910–11)

AVARELLO, PAOLO, and MANUELA RICCI. EDS, *Dai programmi complessi alle politiche integrate di sviluppo urbano* (Rome: Inuedizioni, 2000).

AYMONIMO, CARLO, *Progettare Roma Capitale* (Rome and Bari: Laterza, 1990)

BAFFONI, ELLA, and VEZIO DE LUCIA, *La Roma di Petroselli. Il sindaco più amato e il sogno spezzato di una città per tutti* (Rome: Castelvecchi, 2011)

BAL, MIEKE, 'Lost in Space, Lost in the Library', in *Essays in Migratory Aesthetics: Cultural Practices between Migration and Art-Making*, ed. by Sam Durrant and Catherine M. Lord (Amsterdam and New York: Rodopi, 2007), pp. 21–35

BALIBAR, ÉTIENNE, *Cittadinanza* (Turin: Bollati Boringhieri, 2012)

BARBIERI, DARIO, *Per la grande Roma. Formazione e sviluppo delle grandi città moderne* (Milan and Rome: Società Editrice D'Arte Illustrata, 1927)

——, 'Risanamento e diradamento', *La casa*, 17 (August–September 1937), 7–9

——, 'The Urban Problem of Modern Rome', *The Town Planning Review*, 10.3 (September 1923)

BARTOCCINI, FIORELLA, 'Roma di fine secolo. Realtà e interpretazioni', in *Il decadentismo e Roma*, ed. by Fiorella Bartoccini and others (Rome: Istituto di Studi Romani, 1980), pp. 18–22

BARTOLINI, FRANCESCO, *Roma. Dall'unità a oggi* (Rome: Carocci, 2008)

BENEVOLO, LEONARDO, *Roma dal 1870 al 1990* (Bari and Rome: Laterza, 1992)

BENJAMIN, WALTER, *Gesammelte Schriften*, ed. by Helia Tiedemann-Bartels, 7 vols (Frankfurt am Main: Suhrkamp, 1972–89)

——, 'Goethe's *Elective Affinities*', in *Selected Writings*, I, 297–360

——, 'Goethes Wahlverwandtschaften', in *Gesammelte Schriften*, I, 123–201

——, 'Meine Reise in Italien Pfingsten 1912', in *Gesammelte Schriften*, VI, 252–92.

——, *The Origin of German Tragic Drama*, trans. by John Osborne (London: Verso, 1977)

——, 'The Return of the *flâneur*', in *Selected Writings*, II, 262–67

——, *Selected Writings*, ed. by Michael W. Jennings with Marcus Bullock, Howard Eiland, and Gary Smith, 4 vols (Cambridge, MA: Harvard University Press, 1996)

——, 'Theses on the Philosophy of History' [1940], in *Illuminations*, trans. by Harry Zohn (New York: Schocken, 1968), pp. 255–66

——, 'Über den Begriff der Geschichte', in *Gesammelte Schriften*, I.2, 691–704

——, *Ursprung des Deutschen Trauerspiels* [1928] (Berlin: Hofenberg, 2016)

——, 'Die Wiederkehr des Flaneurs', in *Gesammelte Schriften*, III, 194–99

——, and ASJA LACIS, 'Naples', in *Selected Writings*, I, 414–21

——, 'Neapel', in *Gesammelte Schriften*, IV.I, 307–16

BERDINI, PAOLO, *Breve storia dell'abuso edilizio in Italia* (Rome: Donzelli, 2010)

BERLINGUER, GIOVANNI, and PIERO DELLA SETA, *Borgate di Roma* (Rome: Editori Riuniti, 1960; 2nd edn 1976)

BERSELLI, PIERO, *Venerati maestri* (Milan: Mondadori, 2006)

BERTA, BARBARA, *La formazione della figura professionale dell'architetto. Roma 1890–1925* (PhD Thesis, Università degli Studi di Roma Tre, 2008)

BLOCH, ERNST, 'Italien und die Porosität', in *Verfremdungen II. Geographica* (Frankfurt am Main: Suhrkamp, 1964), pp. 155–63

BO, CARLO, *Letteratura come vita* (Milan: Rizzoli, 1994)

BOCQUET, DENIS, *Rome ville technique (1870–1925): une modernisation conflictuelle de l'espace urbain* (Rome: École française de Rome, 2007)

BONOMO, BRUNO, *Il Quartiere Delle Valli. Costruire Roma nel secondo dopoguerra* (Milan: Franco Angeli, 2007)

BONSAVER, GUIDO, *Censorship and Literature in Fascist Italy* (Toronto: University of Toronto Press, 2007)

BORTOLOTTI, LANDO, *Roma fuori le mura* (Rome and Bari: Laterza, 1988).

BOWLBY, RACHEL, *Carried Away: The Invention of Modern Shopping* (London: Faber & Faber, 2000)

BOYLE, NICHOLAS, 'Goethe in Paestum: A Higher-Critical Look at the *Italienische Reise*', *Oxford German Studies*, 20–21 (1991–92), 18–31

BRENNER, NEIL, *New State Spaces: Urban Governance and the Rescaling of Statehood* (Oxford: Oxford University Press, 2004)

——, and NIK THEODORE, 'Cities and the Geography of Actually Existing Neoliberalism', *Antipode*, 34.3 (2002)

BRICOCOLI, MASSIMO, 'Non di solo locale. Riflessioni sulle politiche di quartiere in Italia', *Territorio*, 46 (2008), 109–13

BRUNETTA, GIUSEPPE, *Cent'anni di cinema italiano* (Rome and Bari: Laterza, 1991)

BUCK-MORSS, SUSAN, *Dreamworld and Catastrophe: The Passing of Mass Utopia in East and West* (Cambridge, MA, and London: MIT Press, 2000)

BULS, CHARLES, 'City Aesthetics', *Municipal Affairs*, 3 (1899), 732–41

——, *L'esthétique de Rome*, extract from *Revue de l'Université de Bruxelles* (March 1903)

CAFFARELLI, GIUSEPPE, 'Urbanistica Romana', *Atti del I° Congresso Nazionale di Studi Romani*, II (1929)

CALABI, DONATELLA, 'The Genesis and Special Characteristics of Town-Planning Instruments in Italy, 1880–1914', in *The Rise of Modern Urban Planning 1800–1904*, ed. by Anthony Sutcliffe (London: Mansell, 1980), pp. 55–70

——, 'Italian Town Planning and the Idea of the City in the Early Twentieth Century', *Planning Perspectives*, 3.2 (1988), 127–40

——, *Storia dell'urbanistica europea. Questioni, strumenti, casi esemplari* (Milan: Bruno Mondadori, 2004)

CALAFATI, ANTONIO (ed.), *Città, tra sviluppo e declino. Un'agenda urbana per l'Italia* (Rome: Donzelli, 2015)

CALDWELL, LESLEY, 'Piazza Vittorio: Cinematic Notes on the Evolution of a Piazza', in *Rome: Continuing Encounters between Past and Present*, ed. by Dorigen Sophie Caldwell and Lesley Caldwell (Aldershot: Ashgate, 2011), pp. 189–206

——, 'The Ultimate Public Space: Filming on the Campidoglio', in *Beyond the Piazza: Public and Private Spaces in Modern Italian Culture*, ed. by S. Storchi, Moving texts/Testi mobili, IV (Brussels and New York: Peter Lang, 2013), pp. 167–80

CALZA BINI, ALBERTO, 'L'architetto nella vita moderna', *Annuario della R. Scuola Superiore di Architettura di Firenze* (1932–33)

——, 'Resoconto del Biennio', *Associazione artistica fra i cultori di architettura di Roma. Annuario* (1925–28)

——, 'Tutela e inquadramento statale degli artisti', *Rapporti dell'architettura con le arti figurative*, Convegno di Arti (Rome: Reale Accademia d'Italia, 1936)

CARACCIOLO, ALBERTO, *Roma capitale. Dal Risorgimento alla crisi dello Stato liberale*, 3rd edn (Rome: Editori Riuniti, 1984)

CARBONE STELLA RICHTER, CARMEN, 'Roma 1870–1883: Una capitale senza piano regolatore', *Rivista di urbanistica* (1993)

CASSETTI, ROBERTO, 'Il ruolo delle "funzioni centrali" nella costruzione di un nuovo ordine urbano della città contemporanea', in *Roma contemporanea, storia e progetto*, ed. by Roberto Cassetti and Giovanni Spagnesi (Rome: Gangemi, 2006), pp. 67–107

CASTELLS, MANUEL, *La question urbaine* (Paris: François Maspéro, 1972)

CATTANEO, CARLO, *La città considerata come principio ideale delle istorie italiane* (Florence: Vallecchi, 1931)

CAUDO, GIOVANNI and ALESSANDRO COPPOLA, *Periferie di cosa? Roma e la condizione periferica* (Rome: Carocci, 2006)

——, 'Roma prossima/Future Rome', in *Roma 20–25. Nuovi cicli di vita della metropoli/New Life Cycles for the Metropolis*, ed. by Pippo Ciorra, Francesco Garofalo and Piero Ostilio Rossi (MAXII, Museo nazionale delle arti del XXI secolo-Rome: Quodlibet, 2015), pp. 18–31

CAVIETTI, MARCO, 'Between Rome's Walls: Notes on the Role and Reception of the Aurelian Walls', in *Rome: Postmodern Narratives of a Cityscape*, ed. by Dominic Holdaway and Filippo Trentin (London: Pickering & Chatto, 2013), pp. 19–38

CEDERNA, ANTONIO, *Mirabilia urbis. Cronache romane 1957–1965* (Turin: Einaudi, 1965)

——, *I vandali in casa* (Bari: Laterza, 1956)

CELLAMARE, CARLO, 'Politiche e processi dell'abitare nella città informale/abusiva romana', *Archivio di Studi Urbani e Regionali*, 97–98 (2010), 145–67

CERASI, GIULIA, and LUCA MONACO, 'La marcia delle periferie dietro al Tricolore: "Basta Marino, no all'immigrazione"', *La Repubblica*, 15 Novembre 2014: <http://roma.repubblica.it/cronaca/2014/11/15/news/la_marcia_delle_periferie_dietro_al_tricolore_basta_marino-100612243/> (2014) [accessed 15/11/2014]

CHABOD, FEDERICO, *Italian Foreign Policy: The Statecraft of the Founders*, trans. by William McCuaig (Princeton: Princeton University Press, 1996)

CHAKRABARTY, DIPESH, *Provincializing Europe: Postcolonial Thought and Historical Difference* (Princeton: Princeton University Press, 2000)

CHIODI, CESARE, 'Per la istituzione di una scuola d'urbanismo', in *Scritti sulla città e il territorio 1913–1969*, ed. by Renzo Riboldazzi (Milan: Unicopli, 2006)

CIACCI, LEONARDO, 'The Rome of Mussolini: An Entrenched Stereotype in Film', in *Spaces in European Cinema*, ed. by Myrto Konstantarakos (Exeter: Intellect Books, 2000), pp. 93–100

CIORRA PIPPO, 'Citta, musei, architetture/City, Museums, Architectures', in *Nuovi cicli di vita della metropoli/New Life Cycles for the Metropolis*, pp. 32–43

CIUCCI, GIORGIO, *Gli architetti e il fascismo. Architettura e città 1922–1944* (Turin: Einaudi, 1989)

——, 'Il dibattito sull'architettura e le città fasciste', in *Storia dell'arte italiana. Parte seconda. Dal Medioevo al Novecento*, ed. by Federico Zeri, 15 vols (Turin: Einaudi, 1982), III, 266–78

——, 'L'urbanista negli anni '30: un tecnico per l'organizzazione del consenso', in *Il razionalismo e l'architettura in Italia durante il fascismo*, ed. by Silvia Danesi and Luciano Patetta (Venice: La Biennale di Venezia, 1976)

CLARK, TIMOTHY JAMES, *Farewell to an Idea: Episodes from a History of Modernism* (New Haven: Yale University Press, 1999)

CLEMENTI, ALBERTO, and FRANCESCO PEREGO (eds), *La metropoli 'spontanea'. Il caso di Roma* (Bari: Dedalo, 1983)

CLEMENTI, FILIPPO, *Roma accattona?!* (Rome: Enrico Voghera, 1902)

COLLINS, GEORGE R., and CHRISTIANE C. COLLINS, *Camillo Sitte and the Birth of Modern City Planning* (New York: Random House, 1965)

COMITATO DI QUARTIERE PIGNETO-PRENESTINO, 'Il nostro territorio non è il monopoli', *La Pigna*, 2010: www.lapigna.info/index.php/territorio/38-articolo/127-il-nostro-territorio-non-e-il-monopoli- [accessed 15/11/2014]

——, 'Rinascimento Pigneto: le promesse tradite', *La Pigna*, 2008: <http://www.lapigna.info/index.php/territorio/38-articolo/102-rinascimento-pigneto-le-promesse-tradite> [accessed 15/11/2014]

COMUNE DI ROMA, *Rinascimento Pigneto* (Rome: Comune di Roma, 2004)

CONNELLY, MATTHEW, *Fatal Misconception: The Struggle to Control World Population* (Cambridge, MA, and London: Harvard University Press, 2009)

CONNERTON, PAUL, *How Societies Remember* (Cambridge: Cambridge University Press, 1989)

COPPOLA, ALESSANDRO, 'Le borgate romane tra '45 e '89: esclusione sociale, movimenti urbani e poteri locali', in *Tracce di quartieri. Il legame sociale nella città che cambia*, ed. by Marco Cremaschi (Milan: Franco Angeli, 2008), pp. 161–86

——, 'Evolutions and Permanences in the Politics and Policy of Informality: Notes on the Case of Rome', *Quaderni di Urbanistica Tre*, 2 (2013), 35–40

——, 'Roma, la metropolizzazione parassitaria e i suoi modi informali', in *Fuori raccordo. Abitare l'altra Roma*, ed. By Carlo Cellamare (Rome and Bari: Donzelli, 2017), pp. 209–23

CRAINZ, GUIDO, *Storia del Miracolo Italiano. Culture, identità, trasaformazioni fra anni cinquanta e sessanta* (Rome: Donzelli, 1996)

CREMASCHI, MARCO, 'Dopo il neoliberismo: quali politiche?', *Territorio*, 46 (2008), 118–22.

——, 'Riqualificazione e rigenerazione urbana a Roma', 17 October 2009: <http://cremaschi.dipsu.it/politiche-della-casa-e-dellabitare/riqualificazione-e-rigenerazione-urbana-a-roma-2/> [accessed 15 November 2014]

CUCCIA, GIUSEPPE, *Urbanistica edilizia infrastrutture di Roma Capitale 1870–1990* (Rome and Bari: Laterza, 1991)

DANOWSKI, DÉBORAH, and EDUARDO VIVEIROS DE CASTRO, *The Ends of the World*, trans. by Rodrigo Nunes (Cambridge: Polity, 2017)

DAVIDOFF, PAUL, 'Advocacy and Pluralism in Planning', *Journal of the American Institute of Planners*, 31.4 (1965), 331–38

DAVIS, ROCÍO, DOROTHEA FISCHER-HORNUNG, and JOHANNA C. KARDUX, 'Introduction', in *Aesthetic Practices and Politics in Media, Music, and Art: Performing Migration*, ed. by Rocío Davis, Dorothea Fischer-Hornung, and Johanna C. Kardux, Routledge Research in Cultural and Media Studies (London: Routledge, 2010), pp. 1–14

DE ANGELIS D'OSSAT, GUGLIELMO, *Gustavo Giovannoni, storico e critico dell'architettura* (Rome: Istituto di Studi Romani, 1949)

DE CERTEAU, MICHEL, *The Practice of Everyday Life* (Berkeley and Los Angeles: University of California Press, 1984)——, 'Psychoanalysis and its History', in *Heterologies: Discourses on the Other* (Manchester: Manchester University Press, 1986)

DE ECCHER, ANDREA, ELENA MARCHIGIANI, and ALESSANDRA MARIN, eds, *Riqualificare la città con gli abitanti* (Monfalcone: Edicom, 2005)

DE LEONARDIS, OTA, 'Una nuova questione sociale? Qualche interrogativo a proposito di territorializzazione delle politiche', *Territorio*, 46 (2008), 93–98

DEL BOCA, ANGELO, ed., *La storia negata: il revisionismo e il suo uso politico* (Vicenza: Neri Pozza, 2009)

DELEUZE, GILLES, *Cinema 1: The Movement-Image*, trans. by Hugh Tomlinson and Robert Galeta (Minneapolis: University of Minnesota Press, 2003)

——, *Cinema 2: The Time-Image*, trans. by Hugh Tomlinson and Robert Galeta (Minneapolis: University of Minnesota Press, 1997)

DELLA SETA, PIERO, and ROBERTO DELLA SETA, *I suoli di Roma. Uso e abuso del territorio nei cento anni della capitale*, intr. by Giulio Carlo Argan (Rome: Editori Riuniti, 1988)

DELLI SANTI, DOMENICO, 'L'Opera del Governo Fascista per Roma', *Capitolium*, 12 (March 1928)

DE LUCIA, VEZIO, *Se questa è una città. La condizione urbana nell'Italia contemporanea* (Rome: Donzelli, 2006)

DE PIERI, FILIPPO, *Le ragioni di urna ricerca*, in *Storie di case. Abitare l'Italia del boom*, ed. by Filippo De Pieri and others (Rome: Donzelli, 2008)

DE ROSA, LUIGI (ed.), *Roma del Duemila* (Rome and Bari: Laterza, 1999)

DE' ROSSIGNOLI, EMILIO, *H come Milano* (Milan: Longanesi, 1965)

DE SOTO, HERNANDO, *The Mystery of Capital: Why Capitalism Triumphs in the West and Fails Everywhere Else* (London: Black Swan Books, 2000)

——, *The Other Path: The Invisible Revolution in the Third World* (New York: Harper and Row, 1989)

DIAS, CLAUDILÉIA LEMES, 'Livia e il drago', in *Storie di extracomunitaria follia* (Rome: Mangrovie, 2010)

DI BIAGI, PAOLA (ed.), *La grande ricostruzione. Il piano Ina-Casa e l'Italia degli anni cinquanta* (Rome: Donzelli, 2010)

DONNARUMMA, RAFFAELE, 'Tracciato del modernismo italiano', in *Sul modernismo italiano*, ed. by Romano Luperini and Massimiliano Tortora (Naples: Liguori, 2012), pp. 13–38

DONOLO, CARLO, *Disordine. L'economia criminale e le strategie della sfiducia* (Rome: Donzelli, 2001)

DONZELOT, JACQUES, 'Il neoliberismo sociale', *Territorio*, 46 (2008), 89–92

EDELMAN, LEE, *No Future: Queer Theory and the Death Drive* (Durham, NC and London: Duke University Press, 2004)

ELDEN, STUART, *Terror and Territory: The Spatial Extent of Sovereignty* (Minneapolis: University of Minnesota Press, 2009)

'Elenco dei soci promotori', *Associazione Artistica fra i Cultori di Architettura di Roma. Annuario*, 1 (1891)

ERNESTI, GIULIO, 'La formazione dell'urbanistica in Italia (1900–1950): intersezioni di discipline, conflitti. Fra utopia e realtà', in *La costruzione dell'utopia. Architetti e urbanisti nell'Italia fascista*, ed. by Giulio Ernesti (Rome: Lavoro, 1988), pp. 163–73

FANTIN, MARISA, and LAURA FREGOLENT (eds), *Astengo 1. Editoriali di urbanistica dal 1949 al 1976* (Rome: INU, 2010)

FAVERO, PAOLO, 'Italians, the "Good People": Reflections on National Self-Representation in Contemporary Italian Debates on Xenophobia and War', *Outlines: Critical Practice Studies*, 2 (2010), 138–53Felski, Rita, 'The Invention of Everyday Life', *New Formations*, 39 (1999), 15–31

FERRAROTTI, FRANCO, *Roma da capitale a periferia* (Rome and Bari: Laterza, 1970)

FEYDEAU, ERNEST, *Alger* (Paris: Lévy, 1862)

FICACCI, STEFANIA, *Tor Pignattara. Fascismo e resistenza di un quartiere* (Milan: Franco Angeli, 2007)

FLAUBERT, GUSTAVE, *Correspondance (1854–1861)* (Paris: Conard, 1927)

——, *Salammbô* (Paris: Charpentier, 1881)

FLORA, FRANCESCO, *La poesia ermetica* (Bari: Laterza, 1936)

FORGACS, DAVID, and STEPHEN GUNDLE, *Mass Culture and Italian Society from Fascism to the Cold War* (Bloomington: Indiana University Press, 2007)

FRANCHETTI PARDO, VITTORIO (ed.), *La facoltà di architettura dell'Università "La Sapienza" dalle origini al duemila. Discipline, docenti, studenti* (Rome: Gangemi, 2001)

FRATINI, FABIOLA, *Roma arcipelago di isole urbane. Scenari per Roma del XXI Secolo* (Rome: Gangemi, 2000)

FREEMAN, ELIZABETH, *Time Binds: Queer Temporalities, Queer Histories* (Durham, NC and London: Duke University Press, 2010)Freud, Sigmund, 'Civilisation and its Discontents', in *Standard Edition* (London: Hogarth Press and the Institute of Psychoanalysis, 1930), XXI, 59–145

——, 'The Psychopathology of Everyday Life', in *Standard Edition VI* (London: Hogarth Press and the Institute of Psychoanalysis, 1901)

FUSTEL DE COULANGES, NUMA DENIS, *La Cité antique. Étude sur le culte, le droit, les institutions de la Grèce et de Rome* (Paris: Durand, 1864)

GALASSI, FILIPPO, 'La conferenza del Sig. Charles Buls', *Associazione Artistica fra i Cultori di Architettura di Roma. Annuario* (1902), 9–14

GARANO, STEFANO, and PIERO SALVAGNI, *Governare una metropoli. Le giunte di sinistra a Roma 1976–1985* (Rome: Editori Riuniti, 1985)

GARDINI, NICOLA, 'Das Homosexuelle in Soldati', *Studi novecenteschi*, 35.73 (2007), 195–208

GATTESCHI, GIUSEPPE, *Restauri della Roma Imperiale nel 310 d.C.*, 6 vols (Rome: Comitato di Azione Patriottica fra il personale postale-telegrafico-telefonico, 1924)

GEDDES, PATRICK, 'Two Steps in Civics: "Cities and Town Planning Exhibition" and the "International Congress of Cities" ', *The Town Planning Review*, 2 (1913), 78–94

GHIDINELLI, STEFANO, 'Nota al testo', in Soldati, *Lo smeraldo*, pp. xxxv–xli

GHOSH, AMITAV, *The Great Derangement: Climate Change and the Unthinkable* (Chicago and London: University of Chicago Press, 2016)

GINZBURG, CARLO, 'Perche dobbiamo salvare le soprintendenze', *La Repubblica*, 29 July 2014

GIOVANNONI, GUSTAVO, 'Gli architetti e gli studi dell'architettura in Italia', *Rivista d'Italia. Lettere, scienze ed arte*, 19.1 (1916), 169–76

——, 'Il "diradamento" edilizio dei vecchi centri. Il quartiere della rinascenza in Roma', *Nuova antologia*, 250 (1913), 53–76

——, 'Discorso Commemorativo', *Annuario della Regia Scuola di Architettura di Roma* (1927–28)

——, 'Per le scuole superiori d'architettura', *Architettura e Arti Decorative*, 3 (November 1924)

——, *Questioni di architettura nella storia e nella vita. Edilizia, estetica architettonica, restauri, ambiente dei monumenti* (Rome: Società Editrice d'arte illustrata, 1925)

——, 'Questioni urbanistiche', *L'Ingegnere*, 1 (January 1928)

——, 'Relazione sull'anno accademico 1931–32', *Annuario della Regia Scuola di Architettura di Roma* (1932–33)

——, 'Ricostruzione del vecchio centro o decentramento', *Capitolium*, 4 (July 1925)

——, 'Sistemazioni edilizie della vecchia Roma', *Annuario. Associazione artistica fra i cultori di architettura di Roma* (1916–24)

——, 'Vecchie città ed edilizia nuova', *Nuova antologia*, 249 (1913), 450–65

GIRARDI, FRANCO, GIANFRANCO SPAGNESI and FEDERICO GORIO (eds.), *L'Esquilino e la Piazza Vittorio. Una struttura urbana dell'ottocento* (Rome: Editalia, 1974)

GLYNN, RUTH, *Women, Terrorism, and Trauma in Italian Culture* (London: Palgrave Macmillan, 2013)

GOETHE, JOHANN WOLFGANG VON, *Sämtliche Werke*, ed. by Friedmar Apel, Hendrik Birus, Anne Bohnenkamp, and others, 40 vols (Frankfurt am Main: Deutscher Klassiker Verlag, 1993)

GRIMM, HERMANN, *La distruzione di Roma* (1886), in Luigi Salerno, *Roma communis patria* (Bologna: Cappelli, 1968)

HAMMOND, ANDREW (ed.), *Cold War Literature: Writing the Global Conflict* (London and New York: Routledge, 2006)

HANSEN, MIRIAM, 'The Mass Production of the Senses: Classical Cinema as Vernacular Modernism', *Modernism/modernity*, 6.2 (1999), 59–77.

HARE, AUGUSTUS JOHN CUTHBERT, *Walks in Rome* (London: George Allen, 1893)

HEALEY, PATSY, 'Planning through Debate: The Communicative Turn in Planning Theory', *The Town Planning Review*, 63.2 (1992), 143–62

HELL, JULIA, and ANDREAS SCHÖNLE (eds), *Ruins of Modernity* (Durham, NC and London: Duke University Press, 2010)

HERZFELD, MICHAEL, *Evicted from Eternity: The Restructuring of Modern Rome* (Chicago: University of Chicago Press, 2009)

HORN, EVA, *Zukunft als Katastrophe* (Frankfurt am Main: Fischer, 2014)

IANUZZI, GIULIA, *Distopie, viaggi spaziali, allucinazioni. Fantascienza italiana contemporanea* (Milan: Mimesis, 2015)

——, *Fantascienza italiana: Riviste, autori, dibattiti dagli anni Cinquanta agli anni Settanta* (Milan: Mimesis, 2014)

INSOLERA, ITALO, 'I piani regolatori dal 1880 alla seconda guerra mondiale', *Urbanistica. Rivista trimestrale dell'Istituto Nazionale di Urbanistica*, 28–29 (1959), 6–34

——, *Roma moderna. Un secolo di storia urbanistica 1870–1970* (Turin: Einaudi, 1992; repr. 2001)

——, 'Storia del primo piano regolatore di Roma: 1870–1874', *Urbanistica. Rivista trimestrale dell'Istituto Nazionale di Urbanistica*, 27 (1959), 74–90

IOVINO, SERENELLA, *Ecocriticism and Italy: Ecology, Resistance and Liberation* (London: Bloomsbury, 2016)

JESSOP, BOB, *State Power* (Cambridge: Polity, 2007)

JURAGA, DUBRAVKA, and M. KEITH BOOKER (eds), *Socialist Cultures East and West: A Post-Cold War Reassessment* (Westport, CT, and London: Praeger, 2002)

KEITH, MICHAEL, 'Walter Benjamin, Urban Studies, and the Narratives of City Life', in *A Companion to the City*, ed. by Gary Bridge and Sophie Watson (Oxford: Blackwell 2000), pp. 401–29

LAKHOUS, AMARA, *Clash of Civilizations over an Elevator in Piazza Vittorio* (New York: Europa Editions, 2008)

——, 'Piazza Vittorio: A Cure for Homesickness', *Review: Literature and Arts of the Americas*, 42.1 (2009), 134–37

LANARO, SILVIO, *Storia dell'Italia repubblicana. L'economia, la politica, la cultura, la società dal dopoguerra agli anni '90* (Venice: Marsilio, 2001).

LANCIANI, RODOLFO, 'Notes from Rome', *The Athenaeum*, 3137 (10 December 1887)

LANDI, GIOVANNI CARLO, *Relazione sul progetto della Via Massima* (Rome: Accademia Romana degli Ingegneri, Architetti ed Agronomi, 1875)

LOWE, DAVID, and SIMON SHARP, *Goethe and Palladio: Goethe's Study of the Relationships between Art and Nature, Leading through Architecture to the Discovery of the Metamorphosis of Plants* (Herndon, VA: Lindisfarne Books, 2006)

MAFAI, MARIO, 'Possibilità per un'arte nuova', *Rinascita*, 2 (3 March 1945), 89–91

MAGATTI MAURO (ed.), *La città abbandonata. Dove sono e come cambiano le periferie italiane* (Bologna: Il Mulino, 2007)

MANACORDA, DANIELE, 'Per salvare il nostro patrimonio serve un'alleanza con i cittadini', *La Repubblica*, 1 August 2014: <http://ricerca.repubblica.it/repubblica/archivio/repubblica/2014/08/01/per-salvare-il-nostro-patrimonio-serve-unalleanza-con-i-cittadini36.html>

McCANN, EUGENE, 'Urban Policy Mobilities and Global Circuits of Knowledge: Toward a Research Agenda', *Annals of the Association of American Geographers*, 101.1 (2011), 107–30

MELANDRI, GIOVANNA, 'Introduction', in *Roma 20–25. Nuovi cicli di vita della metropoli/New Life Cycles for the Metropolis*, pp. 10–11

MERLINI, CESARE, 'A Concise History of Nuclear Italy', *The International Spectator*, 23.3 (1988), 135–52

MEROLA, NICOLA, 'La cultura romana del dopoguerra', *Studi romani*, 25.3 (1977), 387–97

MINNUCCI, GAETANO, 'Edilizia cittadina e piani regolatori', *Architettura e Arti Decorative*, IV, 2 (October 1924), 62–90

MORANTE, ELSA, *Pro o contro la bomba atomica e altri scritti* (Milano: Adelphi, 1987)

MORREALE, EMILIANO, *Mario Soldati: Le carriere di un libertino* (Recco and Bologna: Le Mani, 2006)

MORRISON, TONI, *Beloved* (London: Vintage, 2007 [1987])

MORTON, TIMOTHY, *Hyperobjects: Philosophy and Ecology after the End of the World* (Minneapolis: University of Minnesota Press, 2013)

MURA, GIANNI, 'Il cronista del futuro', interview with Mario Soldati, *Epoca*, 19 October 1974

MUSSGNUG, FLORIAN, 'Finire il mondo: per un'analisi del romanzo apocalittico italiano degli anni Settanta', *Contemporanea*, 1 (2003), 19–32

——, 'No New Earth: Apocalyptic Rhetoric in Italian Nuclear-War Literature', in *Beyond Catholicism: Heresy, Mysticism, and Apocalypse in Italian Culture*, ed. by Simon Gilson and Fabrizio De Donno (Basingstoke: Palgrave Macmillan: 2013), pp. 195–216

MUSSOLINI, BENITO, *Opera omnia*, ed. by Edoardo Susmel and Duilio Susmel, 35 vols (Florence: La Fenice, 1964)

NANCY, JEAN-LUC, *After Fukushima: The Equivalence of Catastrophes*, trans. by Charlotte Mandell (New York: Fordham University Press, 2015)

NEGRI, EDGARDO, 'La scuola romana degli architetti e l'opera della associazione artistica fra i cultori di architettura in Roma', *Atti del I° Congresso Nazionale di Studi Romani*, Istituto di Studi Romani, Rome, II (1929)

NEZI, ANTONIO, 'Sistemazioni urbane e questioni edilizie: Padova, il piano regolatore e la zona monumentale', *Emporium*, 387 (1927), 185–94

NICOLOSO, PAOLO, 'Competenze e conflittualità nelle prime proposte sulla figura del tecnico urbanista', *Urbanistica. Rivista trimestrale dell'Istituto Nazionale di Urbanistica*, 86 (March 1987), 38–41

NIXON, ROB, *Slow Violence and the Environmentalism of the Poor* (Cambridge, MA, and London: Harvard University Press, 2011)

'Notiziario', *Roma. Rivista di studi e di vita romana*, 2 (1924)

'Notiziario', *Roma. Rivista di studi e di vita romana*, 4 (1926)

'Notizie varie. Gli urbanisti di Roma', *Architettura e Arti Decorative*, VI, 2 (October 1926)

OJETTI, UGO, 'Il rinnovamento edilizio di Roma. Pro e contro il centro a Piazza Colonna', *Corriere della Sera*, 7 February 1926

OLIVER, KELLY, *Earth and World: Philosophy after the Apollo Missions* (New York: Columbia University Press, 2015)

OSTILIO ROSSI, PIERO (with Ilaria Gatti), *Roma. Guida all'architettura moderna 1909–2000* (Rome and Bari: Laterza, 2000)

PABA, GIANCARLO, and CAMILLA PERRONE, eds, *Cittadinanza attiva. Il coinvolgimento degli abitanti nella costruzione della città* (Florence: Alinea, 2002)

PADOVANI, LILIANA, 'L'innovazione nei programmi d'intervento integrati: prospettive e problemi come emergono dalle esperienze italiane in atto', in *L'azione integrata nelle politiche di rigenerazione urbana*, Conference Proceedings (Daest, Iuav, Venezia 2–4 Dicembre, 1999)

PANEBIANCO, GIUSEPPE, *La città muove le torri. L'esperienza del Programma Urban a Roma* (Rome, 2002)

PARATI, GRAZIELLA, 'Where Do Migrants Live? Amara Lakhous's *Clash of Civilizations over an Elevator in Piazza Vittorio*', *Annali d'italianistica. Capital City: Rome 1870–2010*, 28 (2010), 431–44

PASOLINI, PIER PAOLO, 'È un gioco diabolico *Lo smeraldo* di Soldati', *Il Tempo*, 29 November 1974

——, 'È un gioco diabolico *Lo smeraldo* di Soldati', in *Descrizioni di descrizioni* (Turin: Einaudi, 1979), pp. 417–21

——, *The Ragazzi* (Manchester: Carcanet, 1986)

PAUTASSO, SERGIO, 'Le riviste di poesia del dopoguerra', *Aut aut*, 61–62 (1961), 143–61

PAVIA, ROSARIO, *Le paure dell'urbanistica. Disagio e incertezza nel progetto della città contemporanea* (Rome: Meltemi, 2005)

PEREGO, FRANCESCO (ed.), *L'urbanistica della sinistra in Campidoglio* (Rome: Edizione delle Autonomie, 1981)

PERULLI, PAOLO, *Il dio contratto. Origine e istituzione della società contemporanea* (Turin: Einaudi, 2012)

PETRUCCIANI, MARIO, 'Premesse di una ricerca', *Il presente, poesia e critica*, 4–5 (1952), 1–3

PIACENTINI, MARCELLO, 'Estetica regolatrice nello sviluppo della città', *Rassegna contemporanea*, VI, II, VII (10 April 1913), 31–33

PIACENTINI, PIO, 'Rendiconto morale', *Associazione Artistica fra i Cultori di Architettura di Roma. Annuario*, 7–11 (1897–1901)

'Il piano regolatore del centro di Roma', *Associazione Artistica fra i Cultori di Architettura di Roma. Annuario* (1906–07), 13–18

PICCINATO, LUIGI, 'Cammino dell'urbanistica italiana', *La Tribuna*, 24 April 1937

PISCHEDDA, BRUNO, *La grande sera del mondo. Romanzi apocalittici dell'Italia del benessere* (Turin: Nino Aragno, 2004)

PLATNER, SAMUEL BALL (completed and revised by Thomas Ashby), *A Topographical Dictionary of Rome* (Oxford and New York: Oxford University Press, 1926)

POMPEO, FRANCESCO, ed., *Pigneto-Banglatown. Migrazioni e conflitti di cittadinanza in una periferia storica romana* (Rome: Meti, 2011)

POPHAM, PETER, 'Neo-Fascist sweeps in as Rome's mayor', *The Independent*, 29 April 2008: <http://www.independent.co.uk/news/world/europe/neofascist-sweeps-in-as-romes-mayor-817128.html> [last accessed February 2016]

PORTELLI, ALESSANDRO, *The Order Has Been Carried Out* (New York and Basingstoke: Palgrave Macmillan, 2003)

——, BRUNO BONOMO, ALICE SOTGIA, and ULRIKE VICCARO, *Città di parole* (Rome: Donzelli, 2006)

PRATT, MARY LOUISE, 'Arts of the Contact Zone', *Profession* (1991), 33–40

QUARONI, LUDOVICO, *Immagine di Roma* (Bari: Laterza, 1969)

QUILICI, VIERI, *Roma capitale senza centro* (Rome: Officina Edizioni, 2007)

RANCIÈRE, JACQUES, *The Politics of the Aesthetics*, trans. and intr. by Gabriel Rockhill (London: Bloomsbury, 2006)

'Relazione della Commissione Municipale per lo Studio della Riforma del Piano Regolatore' (July 1924)

'Relazione sul piano regolatore di Roma', *Associazione Artistica fra i Cultori di Architettura di Roma. Annuario* (1908–09), 19–35

'Resoconto morale', *Associazione Artistica fra i Cultori di Architettura di Roma. Annuario*, 1 (1891)

RIBOLDAZZI, RENZO, ' "Armonia e calcolo, necessità e bellezza". Città e progetto urbanistico negli scritti di Cesare Chiodi', in Cesare Chiodi, *Scritti sulla città e il territorio 1913–1969*, ed. by Renzo Riboldazzi (Milan: Unicopli, 2006)

ROBERTS, PETER, and HUGH SYKES, eds, *Urban Regeneration: A Handbook* (London: Sage, 2000)

RODWELL, DENNIS, *Conservation and Sustainability in Historic Cities* (Oxford: Blackwell, 2007)

RONALD, RICHARD, *The Ideology of Home Ownership: Homeowner Societies and the Role of Housing* (London: Palgrave Macmillan, 2008)

ROSSI, PAOLO, *Immagini della scienza* (Rome: Editori Riuniti, 1977)Rossi, Aldo, *The Architecture of the City* (Cambridge, MA, and London: MIT Press, 1984)

ROYO, MANUEL, 'Le temps de l'éternité, Paul Bigot et la representation de Rome antique', *Mélanges de l'école française de Rome*, 104.2 (1992), 585–610

RUSSI, ANTONIO, *Gli anni dell'antialienazione: 1943–1949 (dall'ermetismo al neorealismo)* (Milan: Mursia, 1966)

——, 'Introduzione', *La strada*, 1 (1946), 3–17

——, *Poesia e realtà* (Florence: La Nuova Italia, 1962)

SAMPERI, PIERO, *Mezzo secolo di urbanistica romana* (Venice: Marsilio, 2008)

SANFILIPPO, MARIO, *La costruzione di una capitale. Roma 1945–1991* (Cinisello Balsamo: Silvana-Pizzi, 1994)

SASSEN, SASKIA, *Territory, Authority, Rights: From Medieval to Global Assemblages* (Princeton and Oxford: Princeton University Press, 2006)

SCALFARI, EUGENIO, *La sera andavamo in Via Veneto. Storia di un gruppo dal 'Mondo' alla 'Repubblica'* (Milan: Mondadori, 1986)

SCERBANENCO, GIORGIO, *Il cavallo venduto* (Milan: Rizzoli, 1963)

SCHMITT, CARL, *Der Nomos der Erde im Völkerrecht des Jus Publicum Europaeum* [1950] (Berlin: Duncker & Humblot, 1997).

——, *The Nomos of the Earth in the International Law of Jus Publicum Europaeum*, trans. by G. L. Ulmen (New York: Telos Press, 2006)

SCHOSSBÖCK, JUDITH, *Letzte Menschen: Postapokalyptische Narrative und Identitäten in der neueren Literatur nach 1945* (Bochum: Projektverlag, 2012)

SCLAVI, MARIANELLA, *Avventure Urbane. Progettare la città con gli abitanti* (Milan: Elèuthera, 2002)

SERONDE-BABONEAUX, ANNE-MARIE, *Rome, croissance d'une capitale. De l'urbs à la ville* (Paris: Edisud, 1980)

SEVERINO, CARMELO G., *Roma mosaico urbano: il Pigneto fuori Porta Maggiore* (Rome: Gangemi, 2005)

SHELDON, REBEKAH, *The Child to Come: Life after the Human Catastrophe* (Minneapolis: University of Minnesota Press, 2016)

SICA, PAOLO, *Storia dell'urbanistica. III. Il Novecento* (Rome and Bari: Laterza, 1980)

SMITH, NEIL ROBERT, *Uneven Development: Nature, Capital, and the Production of Space* (Athens, GA and London: The University of Georgia Press, 2010)

SOLDATI, MARIO, *The Emerald*, trans. by William Weaver (New York and London: Harcourt, 1977)

——, *Lo smeraldo*, intr. by Valerio Evangelisti, notes by Stefano Ghidinelli (Milan: Mondadori, 2008)

SOMIGLI, LUCA, and MARIO MORONI, eds, *Italian Modernism: Italian Culture between Decadentism and Avant-Garde* (Toronto, Buffalo, and London: University of Toronto Press, 2004)

SONNE, WOLFGANG, ' "The Entire City Shall Be Planned as a Work of Art": Städtebau als Kunst im frühen modernen Urbanismus 1890–1920', *Zeitschrift für Kunstgeschichte*, 66.2 (2003), 207–36

SORENSEN, ROY A., *Thought Experiments* (Oxford: Oxford University Press, 1992)

SOTGIA, ALICE, *INA Casa Tuscolano. Biografia di un quartiere romano* (Milan: Franco Angeli, 2010)

STAFFORD, FIONA J., *The Last of the Race: The Growth of a Myth from Milton to Darwin* (Oxford: Clarendon Press, 1994)

STEIMATSKY, NOA, *Italian Location: Reinhabiting the Past in Postwar Italian Cinema* (Minneapolis: Minnesota University Press, 2008)

STENGERS, ISABELLE, *In Catastrophic Times: Resisting the Coming Barbarism*, trans. by Andrew Goffey (Lüneburg: Open Humanities Press/Meson Press, 2015)

STEWART, SUSAN, *On Longing: Narratives of the Miniature, the Gigantic, the Souvenir, the Collection* (Durham, NC and London: Duke University Press, 1993)

STÜBBEN, JOSEPH, 'Conferenza del Dott. Ing. J. Stübben di Berlino sull'arte di costruire le città', *Atti del IX Congresso internazionale degli architetti* (Rome, 2–10 October 1911)

SUTCLIFFE, ANTHONY, 'Introduction: The Debate on Nineteenth-Century Planning', in *The Rise of Modern Urban Planning 1800–1904*, ed. by Anthony Sutcliffe (London: Mansell, 1980), pp. 1–10

SYRJÄMAA, TAINA, 'Roman Homes: The Housing Question in "Roma Capitale"', in *The Welfare State: Past, Present and Future*, ed. by Henrik Jensen (Pisa: Edizioni Plus-Pisa University Press, 2002), pp. 111–26

TEDESCO, CARLA, 'Italia. Senso, strumenti ed esiti dell'area-based approach ai problemi urbani', in *Città in periferia. Politiche urbane e progetti locali in Francia, Gran Bretagna e Italia*, ed. by Paola Briata, Massimo Bricocoli and Carla Tedesco (Rome: Carocci, 2009), pp. 101–33

UNGARETTI, GIUSEPPE, *Vita d'un uomo. Tutte le poesie* (Milan: Mondadori, 2003)

VACCA, ROBERTO, *The Coming Dark Age*, trans. by J. S. Whale (Garden City, NY: Doubleday, 1973)

——, *Il medioevo prossimo venturo: la degradazione dei grandi sistemi* (Milan: Mondadori, 1971)

VÉGSÖ, ROLAND, *The Naked Communist: Cold War Modernism and the Politics of Popular Culture* (New York: Fordham University Press, 2013)

VENDLER, HELEN, *Last Looks, Last Books: Stevens, Plath, Lowell, Bishop* (Princeton: Princeton University Press, 2010)

VENTURI, ROBERT, DENIS SCOTT BROWN, and STEVEN IZENOUR, *Learning from Las Vegas*, rev. edn (Cambridge, MA: MIT Press, 1977)

VIDOTTO, VITTORIO, *Roma contemporanea* (Bari and Rome: Laterza, 2006)

VIOLANTE, ALBERTO, *La metropoli spezzata* (Milan: Franco Angeli, 2008)

'La vita dei municipi in Italia', *L'Opinione*, 5 July 1872

WARHOL, ANDY, *The Philosophy of Andy Warhol: From A to B and Back Again* (London and New York: Penguin, 2007)

WILKINSON, TRACY, 'When in Rome, Use Chopsticks', *Los Angeles Times*, 14 April 2004: <http://articles.latimes.com/2004/apr/14/world/fg-ciaomein14> [last accessed February 2016]

WINNICOTT, D. W., *Home Is Where We Start From* (Harmondsworth: Penguin, 1986)

——, *Playing and Reality* (London: Tavistock Publications, 1971; republished Routledge, 1991)

ZABBAN, EDOARDO, 'Napoli e l'Esposizione di igiene', *Nuova Antologia*, 87 (1900)

ZUCCA, GIUSEPPE, 'La tutela di Roma e una nuova coscienza della cittadinanza — Illusione o realtà? — Le vecchie quistioni di Via Condotti e della Fontana dell'Esedra: la crisi', *Rassegna contemporanea*, VI, II, 20 (25 October 1913)

ZUCCONI, GUIDO, *La città contesa. Dagli ingegneri sanitari agli urbanisti (1885–1942)* (Milan: Jaca Book, 1999)

——, 'La cultura igienista nella formazione dell'urbanistica', *Urbanistica. Rivista trimestrale dell'Istituto Nazionale di Urbanistica*, 86 (March 1987), 35–37

——, '"Dal capitello alla città". Il profilo dell'architetto totale', in *Dal capitello alla città*, ed. by Guido Zucconi (Milan: Jaca Book, 1997), pp. 9–70

INDEX

❖

LOCATIONS IN ROME

❖

www.ingramcontent.com/pod-product-compliance
Lightning Source LLC
Chambersburg PA
CBHW080044280326
41935CB00014B/1777

9 781781 887189